CW00972433

Communication
in Personal
Relationships
Across
Cultures

Edited by

William B. Gudykunst
Stella Ting-Toomey
Tsukasa Nishida

Communication in Personal Relationships Across Cultures

SAGE Publications
International Educational and Professional Publisher
Thousand Oaks London New Delhi

Copyright © 1996 by Sage Publications, Inc.

All rights reserved. No part of this book may be reproduced or utilized in any form or by any means, electronic or mechanical, including photocopying, recording, or by any information storage and retrieval system, without permission in writing from the publisher.

For information address:

SAGE Publications, Inc.
2455 Teller Road
Thousand Oaks, California 91320
E-mail: order@sagepub.com

SAGE Publications Ltd.
6 Bonhill Street
London EC2A 4PU
United Kingdom

SAGE Publications India Pvt. Ltd.
M-32 Market
Greater Kailash I
New Delhi 110 048 India

Printed in the United States of America

Library of Congress Cataloging-in-Publication Data

Main entry under title:

Communication in personal relationships across cultures / editors,
    William B. Gudykunst, Stella Ting-Toomey, Tsukasa Nishida.
        p.   cm.
    Includes bibliographical references and index.
    ISBN 0-8039-4671-6 (cloth : acid-free paper). — ISBN
0-8039-4672-4 (pbk. : acid-free paper)
    1. Interpersonal relations. 2. Interpersonal communication.
3. Communication and culture. I. Gudykunst, William B. II. Ting-
Toomey, Stella. III. Nishida, Tsukasa, 1948–   .
HM132.C6249 1996
302.3′4—dc20   96-10000

This book is printed on acid-free paper.

96 97 98 99 10 9 8 7 6 5 4 3 2 1

Production Editor: Astrid Virding
Designer/Typesetter: Christina Hill

Contents

Part III
Emic Perspectives

Part IV
Conclusion

Preface

The study of personal relationships has become an important area of research and theorizing in recent years. Significant advances have been made in the study of personal relationships. There are now two professional associations devoted to the study of personal relationships and each publishes its own journal (i.e., *Journal of Social and Personal Relationships* and *Personal Relationships*). Further, there is an annual (*Advances in the Study of Personal Relationships*) and several book series devoted to the topic.

Most of the research and theorizing on communication in personal relationships conducted to date has taken place in the United States and Western Europe. Although important advances have been made, the research and theorizing on personal relationships tends to have a Western bias; that is, research and theorizing focus on issues that are central to personal relationships in Western cultures. To fully understand communication in personal relationships, it is also necessary to examine how people communicate in personal relationships in non-Western cultures. Our purpose in editing this book was to provide an introduction to the various approaches to studying communication in personal relationships across cultures.

There are two basic approaches to studying communication and culture (see Chapter 1 by Gudykunst & Ting-Toomey for a detailed description of the two approaches). One approach focuses on describing how members of a culture understand their own communication. This method of studying communication and culture is referred to as an *emic* approach. The alternative approach is to compare how a specific aspect of communication occurs across cultures. This method of studying communication and culture is referred to as an *etic* approach.

Etic research often focuses on explaining how communication is similar and different in different types of cultures. To illustrate, there is extensive cross-cultural research explaining how communication varies as a function of individualism-collectivism. Individualism-collectivism is a dimension of cultural variability that focuses on the relative importance of the individual versus the group. In individualistic cultures, the individual takes precedence over the group and in collectivistic cultures, the group takes precedence over the individual.

Both emic and etic research are necessary to understand similarities and differences in communication across cultures. Although there are books in which the authors summarize emic and etic research on interpersonal communication across cultures (e.g., Gudykunst & Ting-Toomey's *Culture and Interpersonal Communication,* Sage, 1988), there are no books that include summaries of communication in personal relationships in specific cultures. This volume was designed to fill this void. As indicated earlier, however, both emic and etic research are necessary to understand communication in personal relationships across cultures. Both approaches, therefore, are included in the present volume.

In the first chapter (Part I), Gudykunst and Ting-Toomey discuss the two approaches to the study of communication in personal relationships across cultures (i.e., emic and etic) in some detail. They also illustrate the major lines of research conducted using the two approaches.

The chapters in Part II are devoted to etic approaches to the study of communication in personal relationships across cultures. In Chapter 2, Gudykunst and Matsumoto examine how Hofstede's dimensions of cultural variability can be used to predict and explain similarities and differences in communication across cultures. In Chapter 3, Hoppe, Snell, and Cocroft examine universal aspects of personal relationships based on Fiske's typology of elementary structures of social life.

The chapters in Part III are devoted to examining communication in specific cultures. We set out to include chapters representing all of the major regions and cultural groups. Unfortunately, several authors were unable to complete their chapters. Even though the chapters included do not represent all cultural groups, they do provide an excellent introduction to communication in personal relationships outside the United States. The authors provide descriptions of communication in personal relationships in China (Chapter 4 by Gao), Japan (Chapter 5 by Nishida), Korea (Chapter 6 by Lim & Choi), Mexico (Chapter 7 by Garcia), Brazil (Chapter 8 by Rector & Neiva), Iran (Chapter 9 by Zandpour & Sadri), Africa (Chapter 10 by Moemeka), and in totalitarian societies (Chapter 11 by Mamali).

The final chapter (Part IV, Chapter 12) is by Ting-Toomey and Chung. In this chapter, the authors provide a summary of the descriptions provided in Part III, examine the major theories that attempt to explain communication across cultures, and provide suggestions for future research on communication in personal relationships across cultures.

William B. Gudykunst, Laguna Beach, CA
Stella Ting-Toomey, Fullerton, CA
Tsukasa Nishida, Shizuoka, Japan

PART

I

INTRODUCTION

CHAPTER

1

Communication in Personal
Relationships Across Cultures:
An Introduction

William B. Gudykunst
Stella Ting-Toomey

Communication and culture reciprocally influence each other. The culture in which individuals are socialized influences the way they communicate, and the way that individuals communicate can change the culture they share over time. Yet most analyses of interpersonal communication ignore this relationship and study communication in a cultural vacuum. Studies of cross-cultural communication, in contrast, examine the influence of culture on communication. Most analyses of communication across cultures compare and contrast communication patterns in various cultures (see Gudykunst & Ting-Toomey, 1988, for a summary of much of this research). There are relatively few analyses of communication within specific cultures. The purpose of this volume is to provide an overview of comparative research on communication across cultures and to examine communication in several cultures very different than the culture in the United States.

In this chapter, we provide an introduction to the approaches used to study communication in personal relationships across cultures. We begin by looking at the nature of culture. Next, we discuss the major approaches to the study of communication and culture.

Culture

There are many definitions of culture (see Kroeber & Kluckhohn, 1952, for examples), but to date no consensus has emerged on one definition. Culture can be seen as including everything that is human made (e.g., Herskovits, 1955) or as a system of shared meanings (e.g., Geertz, 1973), to name only two possible conceptualizations. Culture also has been equated with communication. Hall (1959), for example, believes that "culture is communication and communication is culture" (p. 169). Birdwhistell (1970) takes a slightly different position, suggesting that "culture and communication are terms which represent two different viewpoints or methods of representation of patterned and structured interconnectedness. As 'culture' the focus is on structure, as 'communication' it is on process" (p. 318).

Keesing (1974) isolates two major approaches to defining culture: culture as an adaptive system and culture as an ideational system. Those who see culture as an adaptive tend to see culture as linking people to the ecological systems in which they live. Harris (1968), for example, contends that culture "comes down to behavior patterns associated with particular groups of people, that is, to 'customs' or to people's 'way of life' " (p. 16). Cultural theorists who take this position see cultures as evolving toward equilibrium.

Ideational theories of culture view culture as a cognitive system or a symbolic system. Goodenough (1961), for example, argues that culture "consists of standards for deciding what is . . . for deciding what can be . . . for deciding what one feels about it . . . for deciding what to do about it . . . and for deciding how to go about doing it" (p. 522). Geertz (1966) is one of the major proponents of the culture-as-symbolic-system school of thought. He argues that

the problem of cultural analysis is as much a matter of determining independencies as interconnection, gulfs as well as bridges. The appropriate image, if one must have images, of cultural organization, is neither the spider web nor the pile of sand.

It is rather more the octopus, whose tentacles are in large part separately integrated, neurally quite poorly connected with one another and with what in the octopus passes for a brain, and yet who nonetheless manages to get around and to preserve himself [or herself], for a while anyway, as a viable if somewhat ungainly entity. (pp. 66-67)

Geertz's use of the octopus as a metaphor for culture suggests that cultures are organized and disorganized at the same time.

Keesing (1974) argues that there are problems with both major approaches to culture. Viewing culture as an adaptive system can lead to cognitive reductionism, while viewing culture as a symbolic system can lead to seeing the world of cultural symbols as spuriously uniform. To overcome the problems in both types of definitions, Keesing borrows the distinction between competence and performance from linguistics to explain culture:

Culture, conceived as a system of competence shared in its broad design and deeper principles, and varying between individuals in its specificities, is then not all of what an individual knows and thinks and feels about his [or her] world. It is his [or her] theory of what his [or her] fellows know, believe, and mean, his [or her] theory of the code being followed, the game being played, in the society into which he [or she] was born. . . . It is this theory to which a native actor [or actress] refers in interpreting the unfamiliar or the ambiguous, in interacting with strangers (or supernaturals), and in other settings peripheral to the familiarity of mundane everyday life space; and with which he [or she] creates the stage on which the games of life are played. . . . But note that the actor's [or actress's] "theory" of his [or her] culture, like his [or her] theory of his [or her] language may be in large measure unconscious. Actors [or actresses] follow rules of which they are not consciously aware, and assume a world to be "out there" that they have in fact created with culturally shaped and shaded patterns of mind. We can recognize that not every individual shares precisely the same theory of the cultural code, that not every individual knows all the sectors of the culture . . . even though no one native actor [or actress] knows all the culture, and each has a variant version of the code. Culture in this view is ordered not simply as a collection of symbols fitted together by the analyst but as a system of knowledge, shaped and constrained by the way the human brain acquires, organizes, and processes information and creates "internal models of reality." (p. 89)

Keesing goes on to point out that cultures must be studied within the social and ecological settings in which humans communicate. Rohner (1984) argues that "an individual is a *member* of society . . . individuals *participate* in social systems . . . and *share* cultures" (p. 132).

Keesing (1974) emphasizes that culture is our theory of the "game being played" in our society. He suggests that we generally are not highly aware of the rules of the game being played, but we behave as though there were general agreement on the rules. To illustrate, if we met a stranger from Mars and the Martian asked us to explain the rules of our culture, we probably would not be able to describe many of the rules because we are not highly aware of them. Keesing (1974) argues that we use our theory of the game being played to interpret unfamiliar things we come across. We also use the theory in interacting with the other people we encounter in our society. Keesing also points out that members of a culture do not all share exactly the same view of the culture. No one individual knows all aspects of the culture, and each person has a unique view of the culture. The theories that members of a culture share, however, overlap sufficiently so that they can coordinate their behavior in everyday life.

Approaches to the Study of Culture

There are two basic approaches to the study of cultures: emic and etic. The emic approach focuses on studying cultures from the inside, understanding cultures as the members of the cultures understand them. The etic approach, in contrast, focuses on understanding cultures from the outside by comparing cultures using predetermined characteristics. The distinction between the emic and etic approaches can be traced to Pike's (1966) discussion of phonetics (vocal utterances that are universal) and phonemics (culturally specific vocal utterances). Brislin (1983) argues that in current usage the distinction is employed basically as a metaphor for differences between the culture specific approach (emic, single culture) and cultural general (etic, universal) approaches to research. Berry (1980, pp. 11-12) presents a succinct summary of the distinction (see Table 1.1).

Most sociological and psychological research tends to be etic, whereas most anthropological research tends to be emic. Communication research tends to draw on psychological and anthropological approaches and can be either emic or etic.

When the concepts tested using the etic method are assumed to exist across cultures, they are referred to as imposed etics (Berry, 1969) or pseudo etics (Triandis, Malpass, & Davidson, 1973). Derived etics, in contrast, emerge from empirical data; they are the common features of the concept being studied in the

TABLE 1.1 Examples of Emic and Etic Approaches

Emic Approach	Etic Approach
studies behavior from within the system	studies behavior from a position outside the system
examines only one culture	examines many cultures, comparing them
structure discovered by the analyst	structure created by the analyst
criteria are relative to internal characteristics	criteria are considered absolute or universal

SOURCE: Berry, J. (1980). Introduction to methodology. In H. C. Triandis & J. Berry (Eds.), *Handbook of cross-cultural psychology* (Vol. 2, pp. 1-28). Boston: Allyn & Bacon.

cultures studied. Although the emic and etic approaches are viewed as opposites, they can be integrated. Triandis (1972), for example, recommends that researchers should combine emic and etic data. One way to accomplish this is to elicit attributes of the concepts under study and include aspects that are common across cultures, as well as aspects that are unique to the cultures being studied.

Given this overview of the emic and etic approaches, we briefly review how these approaches are used in the study of communication in personal relationships across cultures. We begin with emic approaches. These approaches are based on anthropological, sociolinguistic, or ethnography of speaking models. Next, we examine etic approaches. These models are based on finding systematic ways that cultures differ and in isolating universal aspects of communication across cultures.

Anthropological Research on Communication: An Emic Approach

Anthropological research typically involves an emic approach to understanding culture. The goal of anthropological research is to describe a culture, or some aspect of a culture, from the perspective of the members of the culture being examined. Most anthropological research examines one culture, but there is research that uses a comparative perspective. Obviously, not all anthropological research focuses on communication. There is, however, extensive anthropological research on communication across cultures. It is impossible to review even the "tip of the iceberg" of anthropological research on communication here; a few illustrative examples, nevertheless, can be provided.[1]

Basso's (1970) research on silence in the Native American subcultures in the United States provides thick descriptions of communication behaviors. To illustrate, he observes that silence in Apache culture is appropriate in the contexts of uncertain and unpredictable social relations. Silence is preferred over talk when the status of the person with whom Apaches are communicating is ambiguous.

Rosaldo's (1973, 1980) research on Ilongot oratory also is useful to understanding cultural differences in communication in personal relationships. She observes that Ilongot oratory employs abundant use of metaphors, flowery expressions, and elaborate rhythms. These styles of speech are used to negotiate relational equality and social harmony. "Plain talk," in contrast, is reserved for power assertion and relational dominance in Ilongot culture.

Hall's (1959, 1966, 1976, 1983) anthropological research is the most frequently cited work in the study of communication across cultures. Hall's (1976) work on low- and high-context communication is particularly important. He defines low-context communication as involving messages in which "the mass of the information [that provides the meaning for the message] is vested in the explicit code" and high-context communication as messages in which "most of the information is either in the physical context or internalized in the person, while very little is in the coded explicit, transmitted part of the message" (p. 79). This schema has been used in emic descriptions of communication in various cultures, as well as in etic comparisons of communication across cultures (see Gudykunst & Matsumoto, Chapter 2 in this volume, for a complete description of low- and high-context communication).

Sociolinguistic Research:
An Emic Approach

Cross-cultural sociolinguistic research is designed to examine the use of language within specific cultures or across cultures. Ochs (1986) argues that most cross-cultural differences in language are "differences in *context* and/or *frequency of occurrence*" (p. 10). She goes on to point out that cross-cultural differences in language usage are a function of "the semantic-pragmatic content covered . . . the number of interlocutors involved . . . the social relationship of the interlocutors . . . the setting . . . the length of the imitative routines . . . and the frequency of occurrence in the experience of young children" (p. 10).

Albert's (1972) study of the cultural patterning of speech in Burundi illustrates sociolinguistic research on language usage. Based on her fieldwork, she notes that members of the Burundi culture use different degrees of formal speech style in accordance with the other person's caste, age, sex, kinship, friendship, contiguous residence, and political-economic ties. Albert points out that "social role and situational prescriptions determine the order of precedence of speakers, relevant conventions of politeness, appropriate formulas and style of speech, including extralinguistic signs and topics of discussion" (p. 86).

Ethnography of Speaking:
An Emic Approach

Research on the ethnography of speaking involves a combination of anthropological and sociolinguistic research. Research on the ethnography of speaking is based on the work of Hymes (1962), Gumperz (1971, 1982), Phillipsen (1975, 1989), and their students. This approach focuses on the distinctive patterns of communication and rules of communication used within specific speech communities (e.g., groups of people who share knowledge of rules for the conduct and interpretation of speech). Of particular importance in the study of the ethnography of speaking is describing culturally shaped ways of speaking (Hymes, 1974).

Katriel (1986) describes *dugri* speech in Israeli Sabra culture. *Dugri* speech (or "straight talk") is used to demonstrate sincerity, assertiveness, naturalness, and solidarity. Katriel contends that *dugri* speech in Hebrew "involves a conscious suspension of face-concerns so as to allow the free expression of the speaker's thoughts, opinions, or preferences that might pose a threat to the addressee" (p. 111). Hebrew speakers use *dugri* speech to demonstrate that they are being true to themselves. Arab speakers, in contrast, use *dugri* speech to demonstrate their concern for honesty by stating information truthfully without concealments and embellishments.

Morris (1981) conducted fieldwork to examine discourse in Puerto Rico. He describes discourse in Puerto Rico as requiring that speakers take great care not to put themselves or others "at risk" and that they must reduce the risk of confrontation in any way possible. Morris points out that this leads to "a systematic blurring of meaning—that is, imprecision and indirectness" in language usage (p. 135). He goes on to point out that the imprecision leads to a "constant problem of interpretation, testing, probing, second-guessing, and investigation, but conducted indirectly" (p. 135).

Dimensions of Cultural Variability:
An Etic Approach

Etic aspects of culture often are examined in terms of dimensions of cultural variability; that is, dimensions on which cultures differ or are similar that can be used to explain differences or similarities in communication behavior across cultures (see Gudykunst & Matsumoto, Chapter 2 in this volume, for details). The major dimension of cultural variability isolated by theorists across cultures is individualism-collectivism (e.g., The Chinese Culture Connection, 1987; Hofstede, 1980; Ito, 1989; Kluckhohn & Strodtbeck, 1961; Triandis, 1995). In individualistic cultures the needs, values, and goals of the individual take precedence over the needs, values, and goals of the group.[2] In collectivistic cultures, the needs, values, and goals of the ingroup take precedence over the needs, values, and goals of the individual (Triandis, 1995).

Other theorists isolate different dimensions of cultural variability. Hofstede (1980), for example, isolates individualism-collectivism and three additional dimensions: uncertainty avoidance, power distance, and masculinity-femininity. Uncertainty avoidance involves the degree to which members of a culture try to avoid uncertainty. In high uncertainty avoidance cultures, uncertainty is viewed as dangerous and members try to avoid it. In low uncertainty avoidance cultures, uncertainty is viewed as a necessary part of life with which members of the culture must deal. Power distance refers to the degree to which inequities in power are viewed as natural and inherent in the individuals in a culture. In high power distance cultures, power inequities are viewed as natural and inherent in the individuals involved. In low power distance cultures, people are assumed to be equal and inequities among individuals are viewed as a function of the roles they fill in particular situations. Masculinity-femininity is a function of the sex roles in a culture. In masculine cultures, there are rigid sex roles for males and females. In feminine cultures, sex roles are fluid and there are not clear expectations for males and females.

Using dimensions of cultural variability as etic concepts allows broad similarities and differences in behaviors to be predicted across cultures. To illustrate, Triandis (1995) argues that the relative focus on the ingroup in individualistic and collectivistic cultures leads to different orientations toward ingroup and outgroup members. Specifically, he suggests that there is a significant difference in the way individuals behave toward ingroup and outgroup members in collectivistic cultures, but the difference is not significant in individualistic cultures. Numerous predictions can be made based on each dimension of cultural variability (see Gudykunst & Matsumoto, Chapter 2 in this volume, for examples).

Although the dimensions of cultural variability are useful in making broad predictions of cultural similarities and differences, each dimension is manifested in a unique way within each culture. Gudykunst and Nishida (1994), for example, point out that to understand collectivism in Japan, emic Japanese concepts (e.g., *wa, enryo*) must be taken into consideration. Some Japanese writers (particularly those in the *Nihonjinron* tradition, who believe that only Japanese can understand Japanese culture), in contrast, argue that Japanese culture is not "collectivistic." To illustrate, Hamaguchi (1980) contends that Japanese culture is "contextualistic." Hamaguchi's discussion of contextualism is similar to most descriptions of collectivism, but it also contains emic aspects of Japanese culture that are not included in general discussions of collectivism. This is to be expected, however, because the way collectivism is manifested in a culture is unique to that culture.

Universal Dimensions of Personal Relationships:
An Etic Approach

Triandis (1977) isolates four dimensions of social relations that appear to be universal.[3] The first dimension is association-dissociation. Associative behaviors include being helpful, supportive, or cooperative, while dissociative behaviors involve fighting or avoiding another person. The second universal dimension is superordination-subordination. Superordinate behaviors include criticizing or giving orders, while subordinate behaviors involve asking for help, agreeing, or obeying. The third dimension is intimacy-formality. Intimate behaviors include self-disclosure, expressing emotions, or touching, while formal behaviors involve sending written invitations to others and similar activities. The final dimension of universal social behavior is overt-covert. Overt behaviors are visible to others, while covert behaviors are not visible to others.

Association-dissociation, superordination-subordination, intimacy-formality, and overt-covert behaviors are universal, but the degree to which they are manifested varies across cultures. Triandis (1984) argues that the association-dissociation dimension is related to Kluckhohn and Strodtbeck's (1961) human nature value orientation. Associative behaviors predominate in cultures in which people assume that human nature is inherently good, and dissociative behaviors predominate in cultures in which people assume that human nature is inherently evil.

The superordination-subordination dimension is similar to Hofstede's (1980) power distance dimension of cultural variability. Triandis (1984) argues that being superordinate and being subordinate are viewed as natural and a function of the characteristics of the people in high power distance cultures. Superordinate and subordinate behaviors are not viewed as natural in low power distance cultures. In low power distance cultures, being superordinate or subordinate is viewed as a function of the roles people play, not of characteristics with which they are born.

Intimacy-formality can be related to the general issue of contact. Triandis (1984) argues that in contact cultures "people touch a lot, they stand much closer to each other, they orient their bodies so they face each other, they look each other in the eye, and they employ greater amplitudes of emotional expression" (p. 324). Noncontact cultures involve the opposite pattern: little touching, standing far apart, little eye contact, and low levels of emotional expression. People in contact cultures tend to express their emotions openly, whereas members of noncontact cultures tend to suppress them.

Triandis (1984) suggests that the overt-covert dimension varies as a function of loose-tight cultural variations. Boldt (1978) defines structural tightness in terms of the role diversity (the number of roles and role relationships) and role relatedness (the nature of the bonds among the roles). The more roles there are and the more tightly they are bonded together, the more structurally tight the social structure is. Triandis contends that there is greater overt behavior in loose cultures than in tight cultures.

Adamopoulos and Bontempo (1986) focus on the universality of three dimensions of interpersonal relations using literary material from different historical periods. They note that affiliation and dominance appear to be universal, without much change over the past 3,000 years. Intimacy, in contrast, also appears universal, but the behaviors that are considered intimate have changed over the years.

Foa and Foa (1974) take a different approach to isolating universal dimensions of behavior. They argue that resources individuals exchange during interaction can be classified into six groups arranged in a circle: love (12 o'clock using the face of a clock to represent the circle), services (2 o'clock), goods (4 o'clock), money (6 o'clock), information (8 o'clock), and status (10 o'clock). These resources vary along two dimensions: (a) particularism—the importance of the individual's (receiver or giver) identity in the exchange (runs vertically up and down the face of the clock, least particularism at 6 o'clock and most at 12 o'clock), and (b) concreteness—the degree to which the resource has face value versus symbolic value (runs horizontally across clock's face, least concreteness at 9 o'clock, most at 3 o'clock).

The closer the resources in Foa and Foa's (1974) framework are to each other, the more similar they are perceived to be and the greater the satisfaction that emerges when resources are exchanged. Foa and Foa's (1974) and Foa et al.'s (1987) research indicates that the resource structure is applicable across cultures.

Fiske (1991) isolates four elementary forms of human relations: communal sharing, equality matching, authority ranking, and market pricing (see Hoppe, Snell, & Cocroft, Chapter 3 in this volume, for details). Communal sharing is "a relationship of equivalence in which people are merged (for the purpose at hand) so that the boundaries of individual selves are indistinct" (p. 13). Equality matching is an equal relationship between people who are distinct from each other and they are peers. Authority ranking is an asymmetrical relationship between two people who are not equals. Market pricing is a relationship mediated by the values of some "market system." The market system, for example, might be based on people's actions, services, or products. Fiske argues that these four models provide the basic "grammars" for social relationships, and they give order to the way individuals think about their social interactions. Fiske's (1993) research supports this claim. The four elementary forms of social behavior are the basis for all other types of relationships, and are universal across cultures.

Fiske (1991) argues that all forms of behavior can be used in any situation in any culture. Members of cultures, however, learn preferences for particular forms of behavior in particular situations. Triandis (1994) contends that people in collectivistic cultures learn to use communal sharing and authority ranking more than equality matching and market pricing. Members of individualistic cultures, in contrast, learn to use equality matching and market pricing more than the other two. Authority ranking also can be seen to vary as a function of power distance (Triandis, 1994). Smith and Bond (1993) argue that market pricing is related to Hofstede's (1980) masculine orientation and equality matching is related to a feminine orientation.

Conclusion

Emic approaches to the study of communication in personal relationships involve describing the meanings people in specific cultures attach to their communication with partners in personal relationships. Etic approaches, in contrast, focus on explaining how communication in personal relationships is similar and different across cultures. Both are viable approaches to the study of communication in personal relationships in and of themselves. A complete understanding of communication in personal relationships, however, requires a combination of both emic and etic approaches. These two approaches are illustrated in the remaining chapters in this volume.

Notes

1. Often it is not possible to tell from the title whether anthropological studies examine communication. We suggest that scholars conducting research in a particular culture become familiar with anthropological research on that culture before beginning the research.

2. We are focusing on the end-points of the dimensions of cultural variability. It may appear that they are dichotomies, but they actually are continuums from low to high.

3. See Lonner (1980) for other approaches to isolating universal structures.

References

Adamopoulos, J., & Bontempo, R. (1986). Diachronic universals in interpersonal structures: Evidence from literary sources. *Journal of Cross-Cultural Psychology, 17,* 169-189.

Albert, E. (1972). Cultural patterning of speech behaviors in Burundi. In J. Gumperz & D. Hymes (Eds.), *Directions in sociolinguistics* (pp. 72-105) New York: Holt, Rinehart & Winston.

Basso, K. (1970). To give up on words: Silence in western Apache culture. *Southern Journal of Anthropology, 26,* 213-230.

Berry, J. (1969). On cross-cultural comparability. *International Journal of Psychology, 4,* 119-128.

Berry, J. (1980). Introduction to methodology. In H. C. Triandis & J. Berry (Eds.), *Handbook of cross-cultural psychology* (Vol. 2, pp. 1-28). Boston: Allyn & Bacon.

Birdwhistell, R. (1970). *Kinesics and context.* New York: Ballentine.

Boldt, E. (1978). Structural tightness and cross-cultural research. *Journal of Cross-Cultural Psychology, 9,* 151-165.

Brislin, R. (1983). Cross-cultural research in psychology. *Annual Review of Psychology, 34,* 363-400.

The Chinese Culture Connection. (1987). Chinese values and the search for culture-free dimensions of culture. *Journal of Cross-Cultural Psychology, 18,* 143-164.

Fiske, A. (1991). *Structures of social life.* New York: Free Press.

Fiske, A. (1993). Social errors in four cultures. *International Journal of Intercultural Relations, 24,* 463-494.

Foa, U., & Foa, E. (1974). *Societal structures of the mind.* Springfield, IL: Charles C Thomas.

Foa, U., Sacedo, L., Tornblom, K., Gardner, M., Glaubman, H., & Teichman, M. (1987). Interrelation of social resources: Evidence of pancultural invariance. *Journal of Cross-Cultural Psychology, 18,* 221-233.

Geertz, C. (1966). *Person, time, and conduct in Bali* (Cult. Rep., Ser. No. 14). New Haven, CT: Yale Southeast Asia Program.

Geertz, C. (1973). *On the interpretation of culture.* New York: Basic Books.

Goodenough, W. (1961). Comment on cultural evolution. *Daedalus, 90,* 521-528.

Gudykunst, W. B., & Nishida, T. (1994). *Bridging Japanese/North American differences.* Thousand Oaks, CA: Sage.

Gudykunst, W. B., & Ting-Toomey, S. (1988). *Culture and interpersonal communication.* Newbury Park, CA: Sage.

Gumperz, J. (1971). *Language in social groups.* Stanford, CA: Stanford University Press.

Gumperz, J. (1982). *Discourse strategies.* New York: Cambridge University Press.

Hall, E. T. (1959). *The silent language.* Garden City, NY: Doubleday.

Hall, E. T. (1966). *The hidden dimension.* Garden City, NY: Doubleday.

Hall, E. T. (1976). *Beyond culture.* Garden City, NY: Doubleday.

Hall, E. T. (1983). *The dance of life.* Garden City, NY: Doubleday.

Hamaguchi, E. (1980). *Nihonjin no rentaiteki jiritsusei: Kanjinshugi to kojinshugi* (Japanese connected autonomy: Contextualism and individualism). *Gendai no Esupuri* (Contemporary Spirit), *160,* 127-143.

Harris, M. (1968). *The rise of cultural theory.* New York: Crowell.

Herskovits, M. (1955). *Cultural anthropology.* New York: Knopf.

Hofstede, G. (1980). *Culture's consequences.* Beverly Hills, CA: Sage.

Hymes, D. (1962). The ethnography of speaking. In T. Gladwin & W. Sturtevant (Eds.), *Anthropology and human behavior* (pp. 13-53). Washington, DC: Anthropology Society of Washington.

Hymes, D. (1974). Ways of speaking. In R. Bauman & J. Sherzer (Eds.), *Explorations in the ethnography of speaking* (pp. 433-451). Cambridge, UK: Cambridge University Press.

Ito, Y. (1989). Socio-cultural backgrounds of Japanese interpersonal communication style. *Civilisations, 39,* 101-137.

Katriel, T. (1986). *Talking straight: Dugri speech in Israeli Sabra culture.* Cambridge, UK: Cambridge University Press.

Keesing, R. (1974). Theories of culture. *Annual Review of Anthropology, 3,* 73-97.

Kluckhohn, F., & Strodtbeck, R. (1961). *Variations in value orientations.* New York: Row, Peterson.

Kroeber, A., & Kluckhohn, C. (1952). *Culture: A critical review of concepts and definitions.* Cambridge, MA: Peabody Museum.

Lonner, W. (1980). The search for psychological universals. In H. Triandis & W. Lambert (Eds.), *Handbook of cross-cultural psychology* (Vol. 1, pp. 143-204). Boston: Allyn & Bacon.

Morris, M. (1981). *Saying and meaning in Puerto Rico.* Elmsford, NY: Pergamon.

Ochs, E. (1986). Introduction. In B. Schieffelin & E. Ochs (Eds.), *Language socialization across cultures* (pp. 1-13) Cambridge, UK: Cambridge University Press.

Phillipsen, G. (1975). Speaking "like a man" in Teamsterville. *Quarterly Journal of Speech, 61,* 13-22.

Phillipsen, G. (1989). Speech and the communal function in four cultures. In S. Ting-Toomey & F. Korzenny (Eds.), *Language, communication, and culture* (pp. 79-92). Newbury Park, CA: Sage.

Pike, K. (1966). *Language in relation to a unified theory of the structure of human behavior.* The Hague, the Netherlands: Mouton.

Rohner, R. (1984). Toward a conception of culture for cross-cultural psychology. *Journal of Cross-Cultural Psychology, 15,* 111-138.

Rosaldo, M. (1973). I have nothing to hide: The language of Ilongot oratory. *Language in Society, 11,* 193-223.

Rosaldo, M. (1980). *Knowledge and passion: Ilongot notions of self and social systems.* Cambridge, UK: Cambridge University Press.

Smith, P., & Bond, M. H. (1993). *Social psychology across cultures.* New York: Harvester.

Triandis, H. C. (1972). *The analysis of subjective culture.* New York: John Wiley.

Triandis, H. C. (1977). *Interpersonal behavior.* Monterey, CA: Brooks/Cole.

Triandis, H. C. (1984). A theoretical framework for the more efficient construction of culture assimilators. *International Journal of Intercultural Relations, 8,* 301-330.

Triandis, H. C. (1994). *Culture and social behavior.* New York: McGraw-Hill.

Triandis, H. C. (1995). *Individualism-collectivism.* Boulder, CO: Westview.

Triandis, H. C., Malpass, R., & Davidson, A. (1973). Cross-cultural psychology. *Biennial Review of Anthropology, 24,* 1-84.

PART

II

ETIC PERSPECTIVES

CHAPTER

2

Cross-Cultural Variability of Communication in Personal Relationships

William B. Gudykunst
Yuko Matsumoto

In order to understand similarities and differences in communication across cultures, it is necessary to have a way of talking about how cultures differ and how they are similar. It does not explain cultural differences to say that "Yuko communicates indirectly because she is Japanese" or that "Bill communicates directly because he is from the United States." This only tells us *how* people in Japan and the United States communicate, it does not tell us *why* there are differences between the way people communicate in the United States and Japan. There has to be some aspect of the cultures in Japan and the United States that are different and this difference, in turn, explains why Japanese communicate indirectly and people from the United States communicate directly. In other words, there are variables on which cultures can be different or similar that can be used to explain communication across cultures. We refer to these variables as dimensions of cultural variability. The dimensions of cultural variability (e.g., individualism-collectivism) can be used to explain and predict systematic similarities and differences in communication across cultures. In individualistic cultures, for example, individuals take precedence over groups, whereas in collectivistic cultures, groups take precedence over individuals (Triandis, 1988). There are systematic variations in communication that can be explained by cultural differences in individualism and collectivism. To illustrate, members of individualistic cultures emphasize person-based information to predict each others' behavior, and members of collectivistic cultures emphasize group-based information to predict each others' behavior (Gudykunst & Nishida, 1986a).

There are general patterns of behavior that are consistent in individualistic cultures, and there are general patterns of behavior that are consistent in collectivistic cultures. Individualism and collectivism, however, are manifested in unique ways in each culture. In the Japanese culture, for example, collectivism involves a focus on the concepts of *wa* (roughly translated as harmony), *amae* (roughly translated as dependency), and *enryo* (roughly translated as reserve or restraint; Gudykunst & Nishida, 1994). Other collectivistic cultures emphasize different cultural constructs as part of their collectivistic tendencies (see the chapters in this volume for examples). Understanding communication in any culture, therefore, requires culture general information (i.e., where the culture falls on the various dimensions of cultural variability) and culture specific information (i.e., the specific cultural constructs associated with the dimension of cultural variability). Our purpose in this chapter is to focus on the general patterns and to illustrate how the dimensions of cultural variability can be used to explain and predict communication in personal relationships across cultures. We begin by looking at the general argument for how culture and communication are related.

Culture and Communication Behavior

Keesing (1974) argues that culture provides its members with an implicit theory about how to behave in different situations and how to interpret others' behavior in these situations. He contends that culture is shared in "its broad design and deeper principles," but "that not every individual shares precisely the same theory of the cultural code" (p. 89). Through the socialization process members of various cultures learn their implicit theories of their cultures.

Members of different cultures learn different implicit theories to guide their behavior. Cross-cultural researchers (e.g., Chinese Culture Connection, 1987; Hofstede, 1980; Kluckhohn & Strodtbeck, 1961) suggest dimensions that can be used to explain similarities and differences in these implicit theories across cultures. Individualism-collectivism is the major dimension of cultural variability isolated by theorists across disciplines to explain similarities and differences in behavior (e.g., Chinese Culture Connection, 1987; Gudykunst & Ting-Toomey, 1988; Hofstede, 1980, 1991; Ito, 1989; Kluckhohn & Strodtbeck, 1961; Mead, 1967; Parsons & Shils, 1951; Triandis, 1988, 1990, 1995). Although both individualism *and* collectivism exist in all cultures, one pattern tends to predominate.

As members of individualistic cultures are socialized into their culture, they learn the major values of their culture (e.g., independence, achievement) and learn preferred ways for how members of the culture are expected to view themselves (e.g., as unique persons). Members of collectivistic cultures learn different major values (e.g., harmony, solidarity) and different preferred ways to conceive of themselves (e.g., as interconnected with others). Members of individualistic and collectivistic cultures, however, do not just learn one set of values or just one way to conceive of themselves. Because individualism *and* collectivism exist in all cultures, members of individualistic cultures learn some collectivistic values and learn interdependent self construals, and members of collectivistic cultures learn some individualistic values and learn interdependent self construals (e.g., see Bellah, Madsen, Sullivan, Swidler, & Tipton, 1985, for a discussion of collectivism in the United States and Miyanaga, 1991, for a discussion of individualism in Japan).

Cultural individualism-collectivism has a direct influence on behavior (e.g., through norms/rules used to guide behavior), but it also influences behavior indirectly through the personalities, values, and self construals that individual members learn when being socialized into their culture. To understand individual behavior, both cultural level individualism-collectivism and individual level factors that mediate the influence of cultural individualism-collectivism must be taken into consideration. Cultural level tendencies alone, therefore, do not predict the behavior of all individual members of a culture. To understand individuals' behavior, it is necessary to understand the individual characteristics that mediate the influence of cultural level tendencies on individual communication.

We examine the four dimensions of cultural variability isolated by Hofstede (1980) in this chapter: individualism-collectivism, uncertainty avoidance, power distance, and masculinity-femininity. There are numerous other dimensions of cultural variability that also could be included (e.g., Kluckhohn & Strodtbeck's, 1961, value orientations; Parsons & Shils's, 1951, pattern variables; see Gudykunst & Ting-Toomey, 1988, for presentations of alternative dimensions). We focus on Hofstede's dimensions because they have been linked most clearly to communication behavior. Because the most research has been conducted on individualism-collectivism, we begin with it.

Individualism-Collectivism

We begin our discussion of individualism-collectivism by looking at cultural level tendencies. Next, we look at the individual-level factors that mediate the influence of cultural individualism-collectivism on communication behavior. Following this, we examine low- and high-context communication, the major ways that communication varies in individualistic and collectivistic cultures. In the remainder of this section, we illustrate the influence of individualism-collectivism on self-disclosure/social penetration, uncertainty, communication rules, face-negotiation, and communication in romantic relationships (there also is extensive work on conflict not included here; see Ting-Toomey, 1994b, 1994c, in press, for summaries).

Cultural-Level Individualism-Collectivism

Individuals' goals are emphasized more than group's goals in individualistic cultures. Group goals, in contrast, take precedence over individuals' goals in collectivistic cultures. In individualistic cultures, "people are supposed to look after themselves and their immediate family only," whereas in collectivistic cultures, "people belong to ingroups or collectivities which are supposed to look after them in exchange for loyalty" (Hofstede & Bond, 1984, p. 419). The emphasis in individualistic cultures is on individuals' initiative and achievement, whereas emphasis is placed on belonging to groups in collectivistic cultures.

Triandis (1988) argues that the relative importance of ingroups is one of the major factors that differentiate individualistic and collectivistic cultures. Ingroups are "groups of people about whose welfare one is concerned, with whom one is willing to cooperate without demanding equitable returns, and separation from whom leads to discomfort or even pain" (Triandis, 1988, p. 75). People in individualistic cultures have many specific ingroups (e.g., family, religion, social clubs, profession, to name only a few) that might influence their behavior in any particular social situation. Because there are many ingroups, individual ingroups, therefore, exert relatively little influence on individuals' behavior. In collectivistic cultures people have a few general ingroups (e.g., work group, university, family, to name the major ingroups that influence behavior in collectivistic cultures) that have a strong influence on their behavior across situations. People in individualistic cultures tend to be universalistic and apply the same value standards to all. People in collectivistic cultures, in contrast, tend to be particularistic and apply different value standards to ingroups and out-groups.

Although the ingroup may be the same in individualistic and collectivistic cultures, the sphere of its influence is different. The sphere of influence in an individualistic culture is very specific (e.g., the ingroup affects behavior in very specific circumstances), whereas the sphere of influence in a collectivistic culture is very general (e.g., the ingroup affects behavior in many different aspects of a person's life). To illustrate, in the individualistic culture of the United States, the university people attend generally influences their behavior only when they are at the university or at an alumni event. In some collectivistic cultures like Japan and Korea, in contrast, the university people attend influences their behavior throughout their adult lives.

Collectivistic cultures emphasize goals, needs, and views of the ingroup over those of the individual; the social norms of the ingroup, rather than individual pleasure; shared ingroup beliefs, rather than unique individual beliefs; and a value on cooperation with ingroup members, rather than maximizing individual outcomes. Ingroups have different rank-orders of importance in collectivistic cultures; some, for example, put family ahead of all other ingroups, while others put their companies ahead of other ingroups (Triandis, 1988). To illustrate, the company often is considered the primary ingroup in Japan, while the family is the primary ingroup in many other collectivistic cultures (e.g., Latin America).

Triandis (1995) argues that individualistic and collectivistic cultures can differ in whether relations among people in the culture are horizontal or vertical. People are not expected to stand out from others in horizontal cultures. In horizontal cultures, people tend to see themselves as the same as others, and there is an emphasis on valuing equality. People are expected to try to stand out from others in vertical cultures. In vertical cultures, people tend to see themselves as different from others, and equality is not valued highly.

In the horizontal, collectivistic cultures high value is placed on equality, but little value placed on freedom (Triandis, 1995). To illustrate, in Japan there is a saying, "The nail that sticks out, gets hammered down," that illustrates that members of the culture are not expected to stand out. In vertical, collectivistic cultures (e.g., India) individuals are expected to fit into the group and, at the same time, they are allowed or expected to try to stand out in the group. People in vertical, collectivistic cultures do not value equality or freedom. In vertical, individualistic cultures (e.g., United States, Britain, France, Germany), people are expected to act as individuals and try to stand out from others. People in these cultures place low value on equality and high value on freedom. In horizontal, individualistic cultures (e.g., Sweden, Norway), people are expected to act as individuals but, at the same time, not stand out from others. People in these cultures place high value on equality and freedom.

Individualism and collectivism exist in all cultures, but one tends to predominate. Cultures that tend to be individualistic include, but are not limited to: Australia, Belgium, Canada, Denmark, France, Germany, Great Britain, Ireland, Israel, Italy, the Netherlands, New Zealand, Norway, Sweden, Switzerland, and the United States (Hofstede, 1991). Cultures that tend to be collectivistic include, but are not limited to: Brazil, China, Colombia, Egypt, Greece, India, Japan, Kenya, Korea, Mexico, Nigeria, Pakistan, Panama, Peru, Saudi Arabia, Thailand, Venezuela, and Vietnam.

To summarize, individualism-collectivism has been used widely to explain cultural differences in behavior (see Triandis, 1990, for a summary). Kashima (1989), however, points out that there are problems with using individualism-collectivism to explain individual-level behavior. One area in which there are problems is the area of developing causal explanations: It is impossible to test causal explanations of behavior based on cultural level explanations (e.g., culture cannot be controlled in an experiment). The second area in which there are problems is in mapping individualistic and collectivistic cultures. Hofstede (1980) and the Chinese Culture Connection (1987) present cultural level scores regarding various dimensions of cultural variability, including individualism-collectivism. When specific samples are collected, however, they do not necessarily correspond with the cultural-level scores. To illustrate, when college students are sampled in Japan and the United States, the Japanese college students often are more individualistic than the college students in the United States (Gudykunst, Nishida, Chung, & Sudweeks, 1992; Triandis, Bontempo, Villareal, Asai, & Lucca, 1988). To overcome these problems, individual-level factors that mediate the influence of individualism-collectivism on communication behavior also must be examined.

Individualism-Collectivism at the Individual Level

There are at least three different aspects of the self that mediate the influence of cultural individualism-collectivism on communication behavior: individuals' personalities, individuals' values, and self construals. We begin with personality orientations.

Personality Orientations. The first factor that mediates the influence of cultural individualism-collectivism on communication behavior is individuals' personality orientations. Triandis, Leung, Villareal, and Clack (1985), for example, propose idiocentrism and allocentrism as the personality factors that mediate the influence of individualism and collectivism, respectively. They found that allocentrism is correlated positively with social support and negatively with alienation and anomie in the United States. Idiocentrism, in contrast, is correlated positively with an emphasis on achievement and perceived loneliness in the United States.

Gudykunst, Gao, Nishida, Nadamitsu, and Sakai (1992) found that idiocentrism correlates negatively with sensitivity to others' behavior in the United States. They also observed that idiocentrism is correlated negatively with sensitivity to others' behavior, attention to social comparison information, attention to others' status characteristics, and concern for social appropriateness in Japan. Gudykunst, Gao, and Franklyn-Stokes (1996) discovered that idiocentrism is correlated negatively with attention to others' status characteristics and concern for social appropriateness in England and China.

Idiocentric individuals in individualistic cultures see it as natural to "do their own thing" and disregard needs of their ingroups, whereas allocentric individuals in individualistic cultures are concerned about their ingroups (Triandis et al., 1988). Allocentric individuals in collectivistic cultures "feel positive about accepting ingroup norms and do not even raise the question of whether or not to accept them," whereas idiocentric individuals in collectivistic cultures "feel ambivalent and even bitter about acceptance of ingroup norms" (Triandis et al., 1988, p. 325).

Yamaguchi (1994) argues that collectivism at the individual level involves the tendency to give priority to the collective self over the private self, especially when the two are in conflict. He found that collectivism at the individual level is associated positively with affiliative tendencies and sensitivity to others, and negatively associated with need for uniqueness in Japan. Yamaguchi, Kuhlman, and Sugimori (1995) discovered that these tendencies also generalize to Korea and the United States.

Individual Values. The second way that the influence of cultural individualism-collectivism on communication is mediated is through the values individuals hold. Ball-Rokeach, Rokeach, and Grube (1984) argue that values are the core to individuals' personalities and that values help individuals maintain and enhance their self-esteem. Feather (1995) found that the values individuals hold influence the valences they attach to different ways to behave.

Schwartz (1992) isolated 11 motivational domains of values. Value domains specify the structure of values and consist of specific values [example values are given in brackets below]:

1. *Self-direction.* "Independent thought and action—choosing, creating, and exploring" (p. 5). [independent, freedom, curious]

2. *Stimulation.* "Excitement, novelty, and challenge in life" (p. 8). [exciting life, daring]

3. *Hedonism.* "Pleasure or sensuous gratification for oneself" (p. 8). [pleasure, enjoy life]

4. *Achievement.* "Personal success through demonstrated competence" (p. 8). [social recognition, capable, ambitious]

5. *Power.* "attainment of social status and prestige, and control or dominance over people" (p. 9). [authority, wealth, social recognition]

6. *Security.* "Safety, harmony, and stability of society, of relationships, and of self" (p. 9). [family security, social order, healthy]

7. *Conformity.* "Restraint of actions, inclinations, and impulses likely to upset or harm others and to violate social expectations or norms" (p. 9). [obedient, politeness, self-discipline]

8. *Tradition.* "Respect, commitment and acceptance of the customs and ideas that one's culture or religion impose on the individual" (p. 10). [respect for tradition, humble, moderate]

9. *Spirituality.* "Endow life with meaning and coherence in the face of seeming meaninglessness of everyday existence" (p. 10). [meaning in life, inner harmony, devout]

10. *Benevolence.* "Preservation and enhancement of the welfare of people with whom one is in frequent social contact" (p. 11). [helpful, loyal, responsible]

11. *Universalism.* "Understanding, appreciation, tolerance, and protection for the welfare of *all* people and for nature" (p. 12). [equality, world at peace, social justice]

Schwartz argues that the interests served by the 11 value domains can be individualistic, collectivistic, or mixed. The value domains of stimulation, hedonism, power, achievement, and self-direction serve individual interests; the value domains of tradition, conformity, and benevolence serve collective interests; and the value domains of security, universalism, and spirituality serve mixed interests.

Schwartz (1990) contends that individualistic and collectivistic values do not necessarily conflict. Individuals can hold both individualistic and collectivistic tendencies. Although people can hold both individualistic and collectivistic values, one tends to predominate. In the United States, for example, there are collective tendencies and some subcultures tend to be collectivistic, but most people hold individualistic values.

Self Construals. The third factor that mediates the influence of cultural individualism-collectivism on communication behavior is self construals (e.g., Kashima, 1989; Markus & Kitayama, 1991, 1994a, 1994b; Triandis, 1989). Triandis, for example, argues that cultural variations in individualism-collectivism can be linked directly to the ways members of cultures conceive of themselves. The focus on self construal is important because how individuals conceive of the self is one of the major determinants of their behavior. The most widely used conceptualization of self construal is Markus and Kitayama's (1991) distinction between independent and interdependent self construals.

People in individualistic cultures emphasize an independent construal of the self. The independent construal of self involves the view that an individual's self is a unique, independent entity. Geertz (1975), for example, describes the Western self "as a bounded, unique, more or less integrated motivational and cognitive universe, a dynamic center of awareness, emotion, judgment, and action organized into a distinctive whole and set contrastively both against other such wholes and against a social and natural background" (p. 48). Individualists' cultural "goal of independence requires construing oneself as an individual whose behavior is organized and made meaningful primarily by reference to one's own internal repertoire of thoughts, feelings, and action, rather than by reference to the thoughts, feelings, and actions of others" (Markus & Kitayama, 1991, p. 226).

The important tasks for people emphasizing an independent self construal are to be unique, to strive for their own goals, to express themselves, and to be direct (e.g., "say what you mean"; Markus & Kitayama, 1991). Individuals' self-esteem is based on their ability to express themselves and their ability to validate their internal attributes (Markus & Kitayama, 1991).

People in collectivistic cultures (e.g., Asian, African, Latino-American, and southern European cultures) emphasize an interdependent construal of the self. Markus and Kitayama (1991) point out that "experiencing interdependence entails seeing oneself as part of an encompassing social relationship and recognizing that one's behavior is determined, contingent on, and, to a large extent organized by what the actor [actress] perceives to be the thoughts, feelings, and actions of *others* in the relationship" (p. 227). The self-in-relation to specific others guides behavior in specific social situations. Depending on the situation, different aspects of the interdependent self will guide people's behavior. If the behavior is taking place at home, the family interdependent self guides behavior; if the behavior is taking place on the job, the co-worker interdependent self guides behavior.

The important tasks for people emphasizing an interdependent self construal are to fit in with the ingroup, act in an appropriate fashion, promote the ingroup's goals, occupy their proper place, be indirect, and to read other people's minds (Markus & Kitayama, 1991). Markus and Kitayama also point out that "giving in is not a sign of weakness, rather it reflects tolerance, self-control, flexibility, and maturity" (p. 229). Self-esteem is based on people's ability to adjust to others and on their ability to maintain harmony in the social context when an interdependent self construal predominates (Markus & Kitayama, 1991).

Extensive research supports the contention that independent self construals predominate in individualistic cultures, and interdependent self construals predominate in collectivistic cultures (e.g., Bouchner, 1994; Cousins, 1989; Driver & Driver, 1983). Bond and Cheung's (1983) research, however, suggests that other dimensions of cultural variability must be taken into consideration to understand fully the patterns that emerge. Their research revealed that Hong Kong Chinese and North Americans mention family roles more than Japanese, whereas Japanese mention sex and age more than the other two groups. These differences appear to be related to masculinity-femininity (see below).

Everyone has both an independent and an interdependent construal of the self. Further, people with predominately interdependent construals of the self exist in individualistic cultures and people with predominately independent construals of the self exist in collectivistic cultures. The critical issue is which self construal predominates to influence individuals' behavior and which self construal individuals use in guiding their behavior in a particular situation.

Low-Context and High-Context Communication

Individualism-collectivism provides a powerful explanatory framework for understanding cultural similarities and differences in interpersonal communication. There are cultural differences in the communication processes that predominate in individualistic and collectivistic cultures.

Characteristics of Low- and High-Context Communication. Hall (1976) differentiates between low- and high-context communication. A high-context communication or message is one in which "most of the information is either in the physical context or internalized in the person, while very little is in the coded, explicit, transmitted part of the message (Hall, 1976, p. 79). A low-context communication or message, in contrast, is one in which "the mass of information is vested in the explicit code" (p. 70). Hall points out that,

> People raised in high-context systems expect more of others than do the participants in low-context systems. When talking about something that they have on their minds, a high-context individual will expect his [or her] interlocutor to know what's bothering him [or her], so that he [or she] doesn't have to be specific. The result is that he [or she] will talk around and around the point, in effect putting all the pieces in place except the crucial one. Placing it properly—this keystone—is the role of his [or her] interlocutor. (p. 98)

These expectations clearly are different from those used in low-context communication where information is embedded mainly in the messages transmitted.

Members of individualistic cultures predominately use low-context communication and tend to communicate in a direct fashion, whereas members of collectivistic cultures predominately use high-context messages and tend to communicate in an indirect fashion. Levine (1985) describes communication in the collectivistic Amhara culture in Ethiopia:

> The Amhara's basic manner of communicating is indirect, often secretive. Amharic conversation abounds with general, evasive remarks, like *Min yeshallal?* ("What is better?") when the speaker has failed to indicate what issue he [or she] is referring to, or *Setagn!* ("Give me!") when the speaker fails to specify what it is he [or she] wants. When the speaker then is quizzed about the issue at hand or the object he [or she] desires, his [or her] reply still may not reveal what is really on his [or her] mind; and if it does, his [or her] interlocutor will likely as not interpret that response as a disguise. (p. 25)

Levine goes on to describe communication in the individualistic culture of the United States:

> The [North] American way of life, by contrast, affords little room for the cultivation of ambiguity. The dominant [North] American temper calls for clear and direct communication. It expresses itself in such common injunctions as "Say what you mean," "Don't beat around the bush," and "Get to the point." (p. 28)

These descriptions suggest that high-context communication is ambiguous and indirect, while low-context communication is direct and unambiguous.

Conversational Maxims. Grice (1975) isolates four assumptions regarding coordinated social interaction that are characteristic of low-context communication. First, individuals should not give others more or less information than necessary (quantity maxim). Second, people should state only that which they believe to be true with sufficient evidence (quality maxim). Third, individuals' contributions should be pertinent to the context of conversations (relevancy maxim). Fourth, people should avoid obscure expressions, ambiguity, excessive verbosity, and disorganization (manner maxim). These conversational maxims are not characteristic of high-context communication.

Direct communication (Grice's, 1975, manner maxim) involves transmitting verbal messages that "embody and invoke speakers' true intentions," while indirect communication involves transmitting verbal messages that "camouflage and conceal speakers' true intentions" (Gudykunst & Ting-Toomey, 1988, p. 100). Indirect communication emphasizes listeners' abilities to infer speakers' intentions, whereas direct communication emphasizes speakers' ability to express their intentions (K. Okabe, 1987; R. Okabe, 1983; Yum, 1988). To illustrate, K. Okabe (1987) points out that someone being direct might say, "The door is open" when asking someone to close the door, whereas someone being indirect might say, "It is somewhat cold today."

R. Okabe (1983) suggests that low-context communication involves the use of categorical words such as *certainly, absolutely,* and *positively.* High-context communication, in contrast, is expressed through the use of qualifiers such as *maybe, perhaps,* and *probably* in conversations (Okabe, 1983, p. 34). Qualifier words are used to avoid leaving an assertive impression with the listener.

High-context communication involves the use of indirect, implicit, ambiguous words when speaking. When individuals' responses to others' messages are indirect and ambiguous, the responses may not appear to be relevant to what others said (e.g., they appear to violate Grice's, 1975, relevancy maxim). In order to communicate successfully using high-context communication, listeners must infer how what speakers say is relevant to what they said. Listeners also must infer speakers' intentions accurately to understand utterances correctly. Yum (1988) contends that to be competent high-context communicators, people must "hear one and understand ten" (p. 384). This saying emphasizes the importance of receivers' sensitivity and abilities to capture the nonverbal aspect of indirect communication.

Consistent with Grice's (1975) quality maxim, speaking one's mind and telling the truth are "characteristic of a sincere and honest person" using low-context communication (Hofstede, 1991). People using low-context communication are expected to communicate in ways that are consistent with their feelings (Hall, 1976). People using high-context communication, in contrast, are expected to communicate in ways that maintain harmony in their ingroups. This may involve people transmitting messages that are inconsistent with their true feelings (Hall, 1976).

Speaking one's mind and telling the truth in low-context communication requires that individuals be open with others. Openness involves revealing "personal information about the self in communicative interactions" (Norton, 1978, p. 101). Personal information is necessary to predict behavior when low-context communication is being used (Gudykunst & Ting-Toomey, 1988). When individuals are open, they are not reserved and they are approachable. Open communicators also are not secretive, and they are relatively frank with others (Norton, 1978).

Openness is not characteristic of high-context communication. In high-context communication, individuals do not reveal large amounts of personal information about themselves. Personal information is not used to predict behavior in high-context communication. Rather, group-based information is needed (Gudykunst & Nishida, 1986a). Communicators perceived as competent high-context communicators tend to be reserved (Okabe, 1983). Being reserved, however, is not viewed as a passive activity as it is in low-context communication; rather, it is viewed as an active activity.

Low-context communication also involves being precise (Grice's, 1975, quantity maxim), while high-context communication involves the use of understatements. As indicated earlier, Grice's (1975) quantity maxim states that individuals' contributions to conversations should provide neither more nor less information than is required. High-context communication, in contrast, is not precise. Rather, high-context communication involves using understatements, or providing the least amount of information possible to allow listeners' to infer speakers' intentions, and using pauses and silences in everyday conversation. Okabe (1983) argues that high-context communication requires transmitting messages through understatement and hesitation rather than through superlative expression (the opposite of Grice's, 1975, quantity maxim). In high-context communication, there is a negative association between the amount of spoken words people use and the images other people have of them, especially in terms of their trustworthiness. People who use few words are viewed as more trustworthy than people who use many words (Lebra, 1987).

Closely related to the lack of emphasis on spoken words is the use of silence. In low-context communication, silence is space to be filled (Mare, 1990). People using low-context communication tend to experience a general discomfort with silence because it interrupts the flow of conversations. Silence often is interpreted by people using low-context communication as violating the quantity maxim. Silence also can be viewed as violating the relevancy maxim when individuals are using low-context communication. In high-context communication, in contrast, "silence is a communicative act rather than a mere void in communicational space" (Lebra, 1987, p. 343). Lebra argues that silence can be used to indicate truthfulness, disapproval, embarrassment, and disagreement.

Individualism-Collectivism and Low-Context Versus High-Context Communication

High-context communication is characterized as being indirect, ambiguous, and understated with speakers being reserved and sensitive to listeners. Low-context communication, in contrast, is characterized as being direct, explicit, open, precise, and as being consistent with one's feelings. As indicated earlier, these patterns of communication are compatible with collectivism and individualism, respectively.

Individuals use low- and high-context messages depending upon their relationship with the person with whom they are communicating. To illustrate, people in the individualistic culture of the United States use low-context communication in the vast majority of their relationships (Hall, 1976). They may, however, use high-context messages when communicating with a twin or their spouse of 20 years. In these relationships, it is unnecessary to be direct and precise to be clearly understood. People in Asian, African, and Latin collectivistic cultures, in contrast, tend to use high-context messages when they communicate most of the time. They, nevertheless, also use low-context messages in some relationships (e.g., close friendships).

Research on cultural differences in communication supports Gudykunst and Ting-Toomey's (1988) argument that low- and high-context communication are a function of individualism-collectivism. Members of individualistic cultures, for example, have been found to be more affect oriented (i.e., base their behavior on their feelings; Frymier, Klopf, & Ishii, 1990) and more inclined to talk (Gaetz, Klopf, & Ishii, 1990) than members of collectivistic cultures. Members of individualistic cultures are motivated to communicate interpersonally to achieve affection, pleasure, and inclusion more than members of collectivistic cultures (Fernandez-Collado, Rubin, & Hernandez-Sampieri, 1991). Members of collectivistic cultures pay more attention to others' behavior and more attention to others' status characteristics than do members of individualistic cultures (Gudykunst, Gao, Nishida, et al., 1992). Members of collectivistic cultures are more concerned with avoiding hurting others and imposing on them than are members of individualistic cultures (Kim, 1994). Members of individualistic cultures are more concerned with clarity in conversations (Kim, 1994) and view clarity as necessary for effective communication (Kim & Wilson, 1994) more than members of collectivistic cultures. Members of individualistic cultures perceive direct requests as the most effective strategy for accomplishing their goals, while members of collective cultures perceive direct requests the least effective (Kim & Wilson, 1994).

As indicated earlier, not all members of individualistic cultures are individualists, and not all members of collectivistic cultures are collectivists (Triandis et al., 1985). Further, individuals' communication styles are dependent upon the degree to which they have internalized the values of the culture in which they are socialized, and the way they see themselves, and the way their culture socializes people to see themselves (e.g., as independent, unique individuals or as individuals embedded in social groups). It, therefore, is necessary to link individual level variations in individualism-collectivism to communication styles.

Markus and Kitayama (1991) argue that, at the individual level, an independent self construal (one individual-level aspect of individualism) is associated with being unique, expressing the self, realizing internal attributes, and being direct. They suggest that an interdependent self construal (one individual-level component of collectivism), in contrast, is associated with belonging (fitting in), occupying one's proper place, engaging in appropriate action, and being indirect. Individuals use independent and interdependent self construals in different situations, and depending on their culture/ethnicity, they tend to use one more than the other.

Gudykunst and Nishida (1994) point out that "when a person's goal is to assert him or herself as a unique person (individualism), he or she must be direct so that others will know where he or she stands" (p. 40). Kim, Sharkey, and Singelis (1994) observed that using interdependent self construals is associated with concern for others' feelings and using independent self construals is associated with a concern for clarity in conversations. Singelis and Brown (1995) found that interdependent self construals are related to using high-context communication styles, while independent self construals are not related to using high-context communication styles. Singelis and Sharkey (1995) found that independent self construals are correlated negatively with embarrassability, and Sharkey and Singelis (1993) observed that independent self construals are correlated negatively with social anxiety.

Gudykunst et al. (1996) found that independent self construals and individualistic values positively predict use of dramatic communication, use of feelings to guide behavior, openness of communication, and preciseness of communication. Interdependent self construals and collectivistic values positively predict the tendency to use indirect communication and being interpersonally sensitive.

Individualism-Collectivism and Self-Disclosure/Social Penetration

Self-disclosure involves individuals telling information about themselves to others that the other people do not know (Altman & Taylor, 1973). Closely related to self-disclosure is Altman and Taylor's notion of social penetration. They argue that as relationships become more intimate, there is an increase in social penetration; that is, participants engage in self-disclosure on a larger variety of topics and with more intimacy.

Generally, self-disclosure is associated with direct communication styles that predominate in individualistic cultures, rather than with the indirect communication styles that predominate in collectivistic cultures (Gudykunst & Ting-Toomey, 1988). Intuitively, it appears that individualists would engage in more self-disclosure than would collectivists. Barnlund's (1975) research in Japan and the United States supports this contention. Similarly, Ting-Toomey's (1991) research in France, Japan, and the United States, as well as Chen's (1995) research in China and the United States, supports this position. Wheeler, Reis, and Bond (1989), however, discovered that Chinese in Hong Kong report engaging in more self-disclosure in everyday communication than do North Americans. On the surface, this finding appears inconsistent with the claim that self-disclosure is associated with direct communication, but this is not necessarily the case. Wheeler et al. point out that most of the Chinese respondents' contacts were with members of their ingroup and communication in ingroups in collectivistic cultures tends to be intimate (e.g., involves high levels of self-disclosure). Most of the North American respondents' contacts, in contrast, were with superficial acquaintances where high levels of self-disclosure are not expected.

Gudykunst, Gao, Schmidt, et al. (1992) found more self-disclosure with ingroup members than with outgroup members in two Chinese samples, both high in collectivism. There was, however, no difference in ingroup and outgroup self-disclosure in the Australia and United States samples, both high in individualism. The Japan data, in contrast, did not fit the expected pattern. Wheeler et al. (1989) argue that this reversal of expectation may be due to other dimensions of self-disclosure mediating the process of self-disclosure. To illustrate, the expected findings might not be observed in collectivistic cultures, like Japan, that are high in masculinity-femininity and/or uncertainty avoidance (discussed later in the chapter). Alternatively, Wheeler et al. point out that the findings for Japan may be due to the homogeneity of the Japanese culture. Barnlund (1975) contends that "the greater the cultural homogeneity, the greater the meaning conveyed in a single word, the more that can be implied rather than stated" (p. 162). This implies that explicit self-disclosure is not needed to convey intimate information.

Gudykunst and Nishida's (1986b) data on social penetration are consistent with Triandis's description of the focus on ingroup relationships in collectivistic cultures. The Japanese respondents in this study reported greater differences in personalization (e.g., knowing personal information), synchronization (e.g., coordination), and difficulty of communication between ingroup (classmate) and outgroup (stranger) relationships than the North American respondents. Gudykunst, Yoon, and Nishida (1987) also examined the influence of individualism on social penetration in ingroup and outgroup relationships in Japan, Korea, and the United States. They found that the greater the degree of collectivism present in a culture, the greater the differences between ingroup (i.e., classmate) and outgroup (i.e., stranger) communication in terms of amount of personalization (e.g., intimacy of communication) and synchronization (e.g., coordination of communication) and of difficulty in communication.

Individualism-Collectivism and Uncertainty

Anxiety/uncertainty management (AUM) theory (Gudykunst, 1995) suggests that effective interpersonal and intergroup communication is a function of the amount of anxiety and uncertainty individuals experience when communicating with others. Uncertainty involves individuals' ability to predict and/or explain others' feelings, attitudes, and behavior (Berger & Calabrese, 1975). Managing uncertainty is a cognitive process. Anxiety is the affective equivalent of uncertainty. It stems from feeling uneasy, tense, worried, or apprehensive about what might happen and is based on a fear of potential negative consequences (Stephan & Stephan, 1985).

Consistent with the conclusions from the social penetration studies, Gudykunst and Nishida (1986a) found that Japanese students have more attributional confidence (the inverse of uncertainty) regarding classmates (members of an ingroup in Japan) than do students in the United States, while the reverse pattern exists for strangers (potential members of an outgroup in Japan).

Gudykunst, Nishida, and Schmidt (1989) found differences in uncertainty reduction processes between ingroup and outgroup relationships in the Japan sample, but not in the United States sample. Gudykunst, Gao, Schmidt, et al.'s (1992) study of uncertainty reduction processes in ingroup and outgroup relationships in Australia, Japan, Hong Kong, and the United States support the earlier findings. There was a main effect for group membership (ingroup vs. outgroup) in the Japan and Hong Kong samples, but not in the United States and Australia samples. As expected, uncertainty was lower for communication with members of ingroups than for communication with members of outgroups in

Japan and Hong Kong, but there was no difference in Australia and the United States.

The ways that individuals gather information to reduce uncertainty differs in individualistic and collectivistic cultures. Members of individualistic cultures seek out person-based information to reduce uncertainty about strangers, and members of collectivistic cultures seek out group-based information to reduce uncertainty (Gudykunst & Nishida, 1986a). The focus on person-based information leads members of individualistic cultures to search for personal similarities when communicating with outgroup members more than do members of collectivistic cultures (Gudykunst, 1995). The focus on group-based information, in contrast, leads members of collectivistic cultures to search for group similarities when communicating with outgroup members more than do members of individualistic cultures.

There also are differences in how members of individualistic and collectivistic cultures explain others' behavior. Members of collectivistic cultures emphasize the importance of context in explaining others' behavior more than members of individualistic cultures do (e.g., Kashima, Siegel, Tanaka, & Kashima, 1992). The emphasis on context in collectivistic cultures affects other aspects of their communication as well. To illustrate, adapting and accommodating to the context in which they are communicating is an important part of the high-context communication patterns used in collectivistic cultures (Hall, 1976).

Individualism-Collectivism and Communication Rules

Rules for intergroup communication differ across cultures. Noesjirwan (1978), for example, found that the rule for behavior with respect to the ingroup in Indonesia is that members of the ingroup should adapt to the group, so that the group can present a united front. In Australia, in contrast, the rule is that members of the ingroup are expected to act as individuals, even if it means going against the ingroup. Argyle, Henderson, Bond, Iizuka, and Contarelo (1986) also found that rules regarding ingroups (e.g., maintaining harmony) are endorsed more highly in collectivistic cultures, like Japan and Hong Kong, than in individualistic cultures, like Britain and Italy.

Mann, Mitsui, Beswick, and Harmoni (1994) examined respect rules for interaction with father, mother, teacher, best friend, adult neighbor, and same-age neighbor used by Japanese and Australian children. They found that Australian children endorsed rules for greeting targets respectfully, did what the target told them, and stuck up for the target more than did Japanese children. The Japanese children differentiated their endorsement of rules with respect to parents and teachers compared with friends and neighbors. Mann et al. argue that Japanese rules are person- and situation-specific and that lapses of politeness are tolerated in the family because of the strong ingroup bond.

Individualism-Collectivism and Face-Negotiation

Face involves the projected image of one's self in a relational situation. More specifically, face is conceptualized as the interaction between the degree of threats or considerations a member offers to another party, and the degree of claim for a sense of self-respect (or the demand of respect) by the other party in a given situation (Ting-Toomey, 1988). Ting-Toomey (1988) developed theoretical propositions to account for the relationship between individualism-collectivism and face-management. Ting-Toomey contends that members of individualistic cultures emphasize self-face maintenance more than do members of collectivistic cultures. Members of collectivistic cultures, in comparison, emphasize mutual-face and other-face maintenance more than do members of individualistic cultures.

Ting-Toomey et al.'s (1991) results for Japan and the United States were not consistent with the theoretical predictions. They found that students in the United States are concerned more with other-face than are students in Japan, whereas students in Japan are concerned more with self-face than are students in the United States. These findings may be due to the measurement of facework used in the study (i.e., it was a measure developed in the United States and not modified for use in Japan), or the respondents from the collectivistic cultures may have been more individualistic than the respondents from the United States.

Other research supports Ting-Toomey's (1988) theoretical propositions (see Ting-Toomey, 1994a, for alternative conceptualizations of face across cultures). Holtgraves and Yang (1992), for example, found that Koreans are influenced by others' power and the relational distance more than North Americans are. Cocroft and Ting-Toomey (1994) discovered that North Americans use anti-social, self-presentation, and self-attribution face-maintenance strategies more than Japanese do, whereas Japanese use indirect face-maintenance strategies more than North Americans. Cupach and Imahori (1993) found that North Americans are more likely to use humor and aggression to deal with social predicaments than Japanese are, while Japanese are more likely than North

Americans to use apologies and remediation. Imahori and Cupach (1994) observed that North Americans use humor as a way to maintain face in embarrassing situations more than Japanese. Japanese, in contrast, use remediation (e.g., the correction of behavior) as a way to manage face more than North Americans do.

Holtgraves (1992) argues that the relative power two people have and the relationship between them influences the amount of politeness behavior across cultures. Even though the factors that contribute to politeness behavior are consistent across cultures, cultural differences in the way people look at these factors can lead to intercultural misunderstandings. He argues, for example, that people in the United States emphasize the distance between themselves and others less than Koreans do. North Americans, therefore, may assume a closer distance than Koreans when they interact and use less politeness behavior than Koreans expect. Koreans may interpret the lack of politeness as a claim to greater power in the relationship. Scollon and Scollon (1981) reported that European Americans are less polite than Athabascan Indians when members of the two groups interact. European Americans' politeness behavior is guided by how close they think they are to the other person. They often use less politeness than Athabascan Indians expect. The Athabascan Indians interpret the lack of politeness as being due to the European Americans thinking they are culturally superior.

Individualism-Collectivism and Romantic Relationships

Dion and Dion (1988) suggest that individualism-collectivism is the major dimension of cultural variability that influences similarities and differences in romantic relationships across cultures. They point out that in individualistic cultures like the United States the idea of being "dependent" upon someone else either is viewed negatively or receives a neutral response. This, however, is not the case in collectivistic cultures. Doi (1973), for example, relates the Japanese concept of *amae,* to love. *Amae* refers to the tendency to depend upon another person and/or presume upon that person's benevolence. Doi claims that "*amae,* generally speaking, is an inseparable concomitant of love" (p. 118). Hsu (1981) makes a similar observation about love in Chinese culture.

Dion and Dion (1988) isolate several problems that arise in individualistic cultures regarding love relationships:

First, one can "lose" one's self and the feeling of personal autonomy in a love relationship, feeling used and exploited as a result. Second, satisfying the autonomous needs of two "separate" individuals in a love relationship obviously becomes a balancing act. Third, the spirit of [North] American individualism makes it difficult for either partner in a relationship to justify sacrificing or giving to the other more than one is receiving. Finally, and inevitably, [North] Americans confront a fundamental conflict trying to reconcile personal freedom and individuality, on the one hand, with obligations and role requirements of marital partner and parent, on the other. (p. 286)

These problems would not necessarily arise in collectivistic cultures where dependence on others is valued.

Dion and Dion (1993) suggest that romantic love is less likely to be considered an important reason for marriage in collectivistic cultures than in individualistic cultures. Romantic love is considered the main reason for marriage in individualistic cultures, whereas having a family tends to be the most important reason for marriage in collectivistic cultures. In collectivistic cultures, acceptance of the potential mate by the family is important. Dion and Dion (1993) also contend that psychological intimacy is more important to marital satisfaction in individualistic cultures than in collectivistic cultures.

Dion and Dion's research (cited in 1993) suggests that the greater individuals' psychological individualism, the less positive their attitudes toward marriage. Dion and Dion (1991) found that the greater individuals' self-contained individualism (e.g., a tendency to dislike any form of dependency), the less love, care, trust, and physical attraction experienced with their partners in romantic relationships. Doherty, Hatfield, Thompson, and Choo's (1994) research indicated that individual level individualism correlated negatively with passionate love among members of different ethnic groups in Hawaii.

Dion, Pak, and Dion (1990) suggested that individualism-collectivism influences the stereotyping of members of the opposite sex based on physical attractiveness. They contended that collectivism leads individuals to stereotype members of the opposite sex on group-related attributes (e.g., the other person's position in a social network and family memberships) rather than individual attributes such as physical attractiveness. Their research with Chinese in Canada supported their speculation.

Sprecher et al. (1994) reported that North Americans emphasize romantic love, passionate love, and love based on friendship more than do Japanese and Russians. North Americans and Russians scored higher on romantic beliefs than Japanese. North Americans also rated physical appearance, similarity, family and friend approval, personality, affection, and mystery as more important than did Russians and Japanese. With the exception of friend and family approval, these findings support Dion and Dion's (1993) speculations.

Gao (1993) found that individualism-collectivism influences love, intimacy, and communication in romantic relationships. Specifically, European American partners in romantic relationships reported more passion than did partners in romantic relationships in China. Partners in Chinese romantic relationships, in contrast, reported more "intellectual" intimacy and uncertainty reduction than did partners in European American relationships.

Gao and Gudykunst (1995) found greater high-context attributional confidence (i.e., reducing uncertainty indirectly) in Chinese romantic relationships than in European American romantic relationships. They also discovered that perceived attitude similarity is higher among European Americans than Chinese (note that perceived background similarity would be reversed). Finally, they observed that others socially reacted to European American romantic partners as a couple more than Chinese. These differences are compatible with cultural variability in individualism-collectivism.

In addition, there is research on the use of power strategies (i.e., ways of persuading others to do something) in romantic relationships that is consistent with individualism-collectivism. Belk et al. (1988) found that individuals in the United States use direct power strategies such as persistence, persuasion, and telling more than Mexicans. Mexicans, in contrast, used bilateral-indirect strategies more than people in the United States did. They also discovered that Mexican men use more indirect-unilateral power strategies than men in the United States. This last difference may be a function of masculinity-femininity (see below).

Given the preceding review of the influence of individualism-collectivism on communication in personal relationships, we turn our attention to other dimensions of cultural variability. Our emphasis in the following discussion is on the cultural level of analysis because not much research on the individual level factors that mediate the influence of these dimensions on communication has been conducted. We focus on Hofstede's (1980) dimensions of cultural variability.

Hofstede's Dimensions of Cultural Variability

Hofstede (1980, 1991) empirically derived four dimensions of cultural variability in his large-scale study of a multinational corporation. The first dimension isolated in his study, individualism, already has been discussed. The other three dimensions were uncertainty avoidance, power distance, and masculinity-femininity.

Uncertainty Avoidance

In comparison to members of cultures low in uncertainty avoidance, members of cultures high in uncertainty avoidance have a lower tolerance "for uncertainty and ambiguity, which expresses itself in higher levels of anxiety and energy release, greater need for formal rules and absolute truth, and less tolerance for people or groups with deviant ideas or behavior" (Hofstede, 1979, p. 395). In high uncertainty avoidance cultures, aggressive behavior of self and others is acceptable; however, individuals prefer to contain aggression by avoiding conflict and competition.

Characteristics of Uncertainty Avoidance. There is a strong desire for consensus in cultures high in uncertainty avoidance; deviant behavior is therefore not acceptable. Members of high uncertainty avoidance cultures also tend to display emotions more than do members of low uncertainty avoidance cultures. Members of low uncertainty avoidance cultures have lower stress levels and weaker superegos, and accept dissent and taking risks more than do members of high uncertainty avoidance cultures.

Hofstede (1991) points out that uncertainty avoidance should not be equated with risk avoidance. People in

> uncertainty avoiding cultures shun ambiguous situations. People in such cultures look for a structure in their organizations, institutions, and relationships which makes events clearly interpretable and predictable. Paradoxically, they are often prepared to engage in risky behavior to reduce ambiguities, like starting a fight with a potential opponent rather than sitting back and waiting. (p. 116)

Hofstede summarizes the view of people in high uncertainty avoidance cultures as "what is different, is dangerous," (p. 119) and the credo of people in low uncertainty avoidance cultures as "what is different, is curious" (p. 119).

Hofstede (1980) found that in comparison to members of low uncertainty avoidance cultures, members of high uncertainty avoidance cultures resist change more, have higher levels of anxiety, have higher levels of intolerance for ambiguity, worry about the future more, see loyalty to their employer as more of a virtue, have a lower motivation for achievement, and take fewer risks. In organizations, workers in high uncertainty avoidance cultures prefer a specialist career, prefer clear instructions, avoid conflict, and disapprove of competition among employees more than do workers in low uncertainty avoidance cultures.

Different degrees of uncertainty avoidance exist in every culture, but one tends to predominate. Cultures that tend to be high in uncertainty avoidance include, but are not limited to: Argentina, Belgium, Chile, Egypt, France, Greece, Guatemala, Japan, Korea, Mexico, Peru, Portugal, and Spain (Hofstede, 1991). Cultures that tend to be low in uncertainty avoidance include, but are not limited to: Canada, Denmark, England, Hong Kong, India, Jamaica, Sweden, and the United States.

Uncertainty Avoidance and Communication. Uncertainty avoidance is useful in understanding differences in how strangers are treated. People in high uncertainty avoidance cultures try to avoid ambiguity and, therefore, develop rules and rituals for virtually every possible situation in which they might find themselves, including interacting with strangers. Interaction with strangers in cultures high in uncertainty avoidance may be highly ritualistic and/or very polite. If people from high uncertainty avoidance cultures interact with strangers in a situation where there are not clear rules, they may ignore the strangers—treat them as though they do not exist.

Because outgroup members may deviate from expectations, members of high uncertainty avoidance cultures tend to have less positive expectations for interacting with outgroup members than do members of low uncertainty avoid-ance cultures (Gudykunst, 1995). Interaction with outgroup members may be avoided in informal situations where there are not clear norms to guide behavior in high uncertainty avoidance cultures. The rituals that are developed in high uncertainty avoidance cultures provide clear scripts for interaction and allow individuals to attune their behavior with outgroup members. The scripts for interacting with outgroup members, however, are much more complex in high uncertainty avoidance cultures than in low uncertainty avoidance cultures (Gudykunst, 1995).

Uncertainty avoidance also influences affective reactions, one of the major by-products of interaction with others (Pettigrew, 1986). Bobad and Wallbott's (1986) cross-cultural research in eight cultures reveals that there is greater fear associated with interactions with people who are unfamiliar (outgroup mem-bers) than with people who are familiar (ingroup members), and that there is less verbalization of and less control over expressing anger with people who are unfamiliar across cultures. Gudykunst and Ting-Toomey (1988) argue that differences across the eight cultures are linked to uncertainty avoidance. Members of low uncertainty avoidance cultures appear to engage in more vocalization of anger toward outgroup members and to control their anger toward outgroup members less than do members of high uncertainty avoidance cultures.

Individual-Level Uncertainty Avoidance. Uncertainty orientation is one factor that mediates the influence of cultural uncertainty avoidance on communication behavior (Gudykunst, 1995). Uncertainty orientation influences whether or not individuals try to gather information about others. Individuals' orientations toward uncertainty are based on the degree to which they have an open or closed mind. People with an open mind "need to know and understand" themselves and others (Rokeach, 1960, p. 67), and they are uncertainty oriented. People with a closed mind, in contrast, "need to ward off threatening aspects of reality" (p. 67), and they are certainty oriented. This often is accomplished by ignoring new information made available.

Uncertainty-oriented people are interested in reducing uncertainty, whereas certainty-oriented people try to avoid looking at uncertainty when it is present (Sorrentino & Short, 1986). Uncertainty-oriented people integrate new and old ideas and change their belief systems accordingly. They evaluate ideas and thoughts on their own merit and do not necessarily compare them with others. Uncertainty-oriented people want to understand themselves and their environment. The more uncertainty oriented individuals are, the more likely they are willing to question their own behavior and its appropriateness when communicating with strangers. Also, the more uncertainty oriented individuals are, the more they would try to gather information about strangers when they communicate with them. Certainty-oriented people, in contrast, like to hold on to traditional beliefs and have a tendency to reject ideas that are different. Certainty-oriented people maintain a sense of self by not examining themselves or their behavior.

A certainty orientation at the individual level is the equivalent of high uncertainty avoidance at the cultural level, while an uncertainty orientation at the individual level is equivalent of low uncertainty avoidance at the cultural level. Although it is clear that uncertainty orientation is one individual-level equivalent of cultural level uncertainty avoidance, no research has linked the two levels systematically.

Power Distance

Power distance is defined as "the extent to which the less powerful members of institutions and organizations accept that power is distributed unequally" (Hofstede & Bond, 1984, p. 419). Cultures vary from emphasizing low to high degrees of power distance.

Characteristics of Power Distance. Individuals from high power distance cultures accept power as part of society. As such, superiors consider their subordinates to be different from themselves and vice versa. Members of high power distance cultures see power as a basic fact in society, and stress coercive or referent power, while members of low power distance cultures believe power should be used only when it is legitimate and prefer expert or legitimate power.

In summarizing the differences between cultures low in power distance and cultures high in power distance, Hofstede (1991) points out that

> in small power distance countries there is limited dependence of subordinates on bosses, and a preference for consultation, that is, *interdependence* between boss and subordinate. The emotional distance between them is relatively small: subordinates will quite readily approach and contradict their bosses. In large power distance countries there is considerable dependence of subordinates on bosses. Subordinates respond by either *preferring* such dependence (in the form of autocratic or paternalistic boss), or rejecting it entirely, which in psychology is known as *counterdependence:* that is dependence, but with a negative sign. (p. 27)

The power distance dimension clearly focuses on the relationships among people of different statuses (e.g., superiors and subordinates in organization).

Hofstede (1980) found that parents in high power distance cultures value obedience in their children, and students value conformity and display authoritarian attitudes more than do those in low power distance cultures. In organizations, close supervision, fear of disagreement with supervisor, lack of trust among co-workers, and directed supervision are all manifested more in high power distance cultures than in low power distance cultures. Further, Hofstede discovered that members of low power distance cultures see respect for the individual and equality as antecedents to "freedom," whereas members of high power distance cultures view tact, servitude, and money as antecedents to "freedom." Antecedents to "wealth" in low power distance cultures include happiness, knowledge, and love. Inheritance, ancestral property, stinginess, deceit, and theft, in contrast, are viewed as antecedents to "wealth" in high power distance cultures.

Low and high power distance tendencies exist in all cultures, but one tends to predominate. Cultures in which high power distance tends to predominate include, but are not limited to: Egypt, Ethiopia, Ghana, Guatemala, India, Malaysia, Nigeria, Panama, Saudi Arabia, and Venezuela (Hofstede, 1991). Cultures in which low power distance tends to predominate include, but are not limited to: Austria, Canada, Denmark, Germany, Ireland, Israel, New Zealand, Sweden, and the United States.

Power Distance and Communication. Power distance is useful in understanding strangers' behavior in role relationships, particularly those involving different degrees of power or authority. People from high power distance cultures, for example, do not question their superiors' orders. They expect to be told what to do. People in low power distance cultures, in contrast, do not necessarily accept superiors' orders at face value; they want to know why they should follow them. When people from the two different systems interact, misunderstanding is likely unless one or both understand the other person's system.

The degree to which cultural rules require cooperation with outgroup members appears to be a function of power distance. Power differences are expected in high power distance cultures. People with less power are expected to do what people with more power tell them to do. This interaction logic leads to low levels of egalitarian cooperation between people with different amounts of power. Because outgroup members are outsiders, they generally have less power than insiders. Gudykunst (1995), therefore, suggests that cultural rules require less cooperation with outgroup members in high power distance cultures than in low power distance cultures.

Power distance also influences perceptions of emotions. Matsumoto (1989) concludes that

> cultures high in power distance and low in individualism stress hierarchy and group cohesion ("collectivity"), while individuality is minimized. In these cultures, the communication of negative emotions threatens group solidarity and interpersonal social structure. On the other hand, cultures low in power distance and high in individualism may sanction the communication of these emotions more, as they relate to individual freedom to express and perceive negative emotions. As such,

they do not threaten social structures and groups to the same extent found in high power distance, low individualism cultures. (p. 101)

Matsumoto (1991) argues that because subjugating individuals' goals to group goals is more important in collectivistic cultures than individualistic cultures, members of collectivistic cultures will emphasize emotional displays that facilitate group cooperation, harmony, and cohesion more than members of individualistic cultures will. Members of individualistic cultures also display a wider variety of emotional behaviors than members of collectivistic cultures. Members of collectivistic cultures are not "tolerant of wide ranges of individual variations, and thus frown upon such variation" (p. 132).

Individual-Level Power Distance. Gudykunst (1995) argues that egalitarianism mediates the influence of cultural power distance on communication behavior. Egalitarianism involves treating other people as equals. Low levels of egalitarianism at the individual level would be equated with high power distance at the cultural level, and high levels of egalitarianism at the individual level would be equated with low power distance at the cultural level. To the best of our knowledge, no research has been conducted on this construct.

Masculinity-Femininity

High masculinity involves a high value placed on things, power, and assertiveness, whereas systems in which people, quality of life, and nurturance prevail are low on masculinity or high on femininity (Hofstede, 1980). Cultural systems high on the masculinity index emphasize differentiated sex roles, performance, ambition, and independence. Conversely, systems low on masculinity value fluid sex roles, quality of life, service, and interdependence.

Characteristics of Masculinity-Femininity. Hofstede (1980) found that in comparison to people in feminine cultures, people in masculine cultures have stronger motivation for achievement; view work as more central to their lives; accept their company's "interference" in their private lives; have higher job stress; have greater value differences between men and women in the same position; and view recognition, advancement, or challenge as more important to their satisfaction with their work.

As with the other dimensions of cultural variability, both masculinity and femininity tendencies exist in all cultures. One tendency, however, tends to predominate. Cultures in which masculinity tends to predominate include, but are not limited to: Austria, Italy, Jamaica, Japan, Mexico, Switzerland, and Venezuela (Hofstede, 1991). Cultures in which femininity tends to predominate include, but are not limited to: Chile, Costa Rica, Denmark, Finland, the Netherlands, Norway, and Sweden. The United States falls in the middle on this dimension.

Masculinity-Femininity and Communication. Masculinity-femininity is useful in understanding cultural differences and similarities in opposite-sex and same-sex relationships. People from highly masculine cultures, for example, tend to have little contact with members of the opposite sex when they are growing up. They tend to see same-sex relationships as more intimate than opposite-sex relationships. The greater the masculinity in a culture, the less intimate and the more problematic members of the culture see opposite-sex relationships to be. Wheeler (1988), for example, found that opposite-sex relationships are considered problematic by Chinese students in Hong Kong. Gudykunst and Nishida (1986b) found that North Americans view opposite-sex relationship terms (i.e., lover, fiance, mate, spouse, boy-/girlfriend, steady) as more intimate than Japanese do. Similarly, Gudykunst and Nishida (1993) discovered that students in the United States are most likely to select a romantic relationship as the closest relationship, while Japanese students are most likely to select a same-sex friend.

Gudykunst et al. (1989) argue that members of masculine cultures draw a sharper distinction between same-sex and opposite-sex relationships than members of feminine cultures. They found significant differences in the amount of self-disclosure, attraction, perceived similarity, nonverbal affiliative expressiveness, shared networks, and attributional confidence in opposite-sex and same-sex relationships in Japan, but not in the United States. Further, unreported data from Gudykunst, Yang, and Nishida's (1985) research supports this conclusion. They found significant differences in communication between same-sex friends and dates in Japan and Korea, but not in the United States.

Individual-Level Masculinity-Femininity. Psychological sex roles mediate the influence of cultural masculinity-femininity on communication behavior (Gudykunst, 1995). Psychological sex roles are the traits and behaviors that traditionally are called masculine or feminine. They are "the psychological traits and the social responsibilities that individuals have and feel are appropriate for them because they are male or female" (Pleck, 1977, p. 182). The traits and behaviors associated with being female or male are based on stereotypes learned growing up. Females, for example, are viewed as more nurturing than males. Some males, however, are nurturing. The stereotype nevertheless persists that females are more nurturing than males.

Masculinity and femininity are opposite ends of a continuum; both males and females exhibit masculine and feminine traits (Bem, 1974). Four psychological sex role orientations can be isolated. First, individuals have a masculine sex role if they exhibit a high degree of masculine traits and behaviors and a low degree of feminine traits and behaviors. Second, individuals have a feminine sex role if they exhibit a high degree of feminine traits and behaviors and a low degree of masculine traits and behaviors. Third, individuals have an androgynous sex role if they exhibit a high degree of masculine traits and behaviors and a high degree of feminine traits and behaviors. Finally, individuals have an undifferentiated sex role if they exhibit a low degree of masculine traits and behaviors and a low degree of feminine traits and behaviors. There is extensive research on individual-level psychological sex roles, but it has not been linked systematically to cultural level masculinity-femininity.

Conclusion

We have demonstrated that dimensions of cultural variability can be used to explain similarities and differences in communication in personal relationships across cultures. There are, however, problems with the use of dimensions of cultural variability that must be addressed in future research.

First, to date there has been too much emphasis on the dimension of individualism-collectivism. Part of the problem is that individualism-collectivism has been treated as a dichotomy rather than a continuum. To increase the accuracy of predictions and explanations, individualism-collectivism needs to be treated as a continuum. The difficulty in doing this is that all cultural-level scores (e.g., Chinese Culture Connection, 1987; Hofstede, 1980, 1991) are biased in some way or another. Another part of the problem is that researchers have assumed that either individualism *or* collectivism exists in any culture. We contend that both exist in all cultures, but one tends to predominate in different spheres of life. The tendency that does not predominate, however, may be the major tendency that influences certain types of communication behavior. To illustrate, although Japan tends to be collectivistic, communication in close friendships is guided by individualistic values.

One way to overcome the problem with focusing on the dichotomous distinction between individualism and collectivism is to incorporate another distinction. As indicated earlier, Triandis (1995) proposes that individualistic and collectivistic cultures can be further distinguished in whether they are vertical or horizontal cultures. He argues that people are not expected to stand out from others in horizontal cultures (e.g., see themselves as similar to others), while they are expected to stand out from others in vertical cultures (e.g., see themselves as different from others). In the horizontal, collectivistic culture of Japan there is a saying, "The nail that sticks out gets hammered down," that illustrates that members of the ingroup are expected not to stand out. There are, however, vertical, collectivistic cultures (e.g., India) where individuals are expected to fit into the group and, at the same time, they are allowed or expected to stand out from the group. In vertical, individualistic cultures like the United States people are expected to act as individuals and to try to stand out from others. In horizontal, collectivistic cultures (e.g., Norway), in contrast, individuals are expected to act as individuals, but not to try to stand out from others.

Another way to deal with the problem of focusing on individualism-collectivism is to incorporate a second dimension of cultural variability that separates individualistic and/or collectivistic cultures. To illustrate, though collectivistic cultures share many common attributes, they also differ in terms of the degree to which they try to avoid uncertainty (especially Asian collectivistic cultures). By differentiating collectivistic cultures that are high on uncertainty avoidance from those that are low on uncertainty avoidance, better explanations and predictions can be made.

The vast majority of research on individualism-collectivism has focused on comparing the United States (and sometimes England or Australia) with Asian cultures. The generalizations developed, therefore, may be limited to these cultures. Extensive research is needed that examines non-Asian collectivistic cultures (e.g., African, Arab, Latin cultures). In addition, this research needs to include at least four cultures (two individualistic and two collectivistic) so critical comparisons can be made.

Finally, there is need for more research on the individual-level factors that mediate the influence of the various dimensions of cultural variability on communication behavior. This research must involve the development of derived etic measures of the individual-level constructs that are used (e.g., measures of independent and interdependent self construals that are applicable across cultures). Research at the individual level also needs to address the issue of which individual-level factors are the best predictor of different types of behavior. To illustrate, which types of behavior influenced by cultural-level individualism-collectivism can be predicted best by personality orientations (e.g., idiocentrism-allocentrism), individual values, or self construals.

To conclude, although extensive research has been conducted in recent years on cultural variability of communication in personal relationships, extensive research is still needed. This need can only be met by multicultural research teams conducting systematic lines of inquiry across cultures.

References

Altman, I., & Taylor, D. (1973). *Social penetration*. New York: Holt, Rinehart & Winston.

Argyle, M., Henderson, M., Bond, M., Iizuka, Y., & Contarelo, A. (1986). Cross-cultural variations in relationship rules. *International Journal of Psychology, 21,* 287-315.

Ball-Rokeach, S., Rokeach, M., & Grube, J. (1984). *The great American value test*. New York: Free Press.

Barnlund, D. (1975). *Public and private self in Japan and the United States*. Tokyo: Simul.

Belk, S., Snell, W., Garcia-Falconi, R., Hernandez-Sanchez, J., Hargrove, L., & Holzman, W. (1988). Power strategy use in the intimate relationships of women and men from Mexico and the United States. *Personality and Social Psychology Bulletin, 14,* 439-447.

Bellah, R., Madsen, R., Sullivan, W., Swidler, A., & Tipton, S. (1985). *Habits of the heart: Individualism and commitment in American life*. Berkeley: University of California Press.

Bem, S. (1974). The measurement of psychological androgyny. *Journal of Consulting and Clinical Psychology, 42,* 155-162.

Berger, C., & Calabrese, R. (1975). Some explorations in initial interaction and beyond. *Human Communication Research, 1,* 99-112.

Bobad, E., & Wallbott, H. (1986). The effects of social factors on emotional reactions. In K. Scherer, H. Wallbott, & A. Summerfield (Eds.), *Experiencing emotions* (pp. 154-172). Cambridge, UK: Cambridge University Press.

Bond, M., & Cheung, T. (1983). College students' spontaneous self-concepts: The effects of culture among respondents in Hong Kong, Japan, and the United States. *Journal of Cross-Cultural Psychology, 14,* 153-171.

Bouchner, S. (1994). Cross-cultural differences in the self concept. *Journal of Cross-Cultural Psychology, 25,* 273-283.

Chen, G. (1995). Differences in self-disclosure patterns among Americans versus Chinese. *Journal of Cross-Cultural Psychology, 26,* 84-91.

Chinese Culture Connection. (1987). Chinese values and the search for culture-free dimensions of culture. *Journal of Cross-Cultural Psychology, 18,* 143-146.

Cocroft, B., & Ting-Toomey, S. (1994). Facework in Japan and the United States. *International Journal of Intercultural Relations, 18,* 469-506.

Cousins, S. (1989). Culture and self perception in Japan and the United States. *Journal of Personality and Social Psychology, 56,* 124-131.

Cupach, W., & Imahori, T. (1993). Managing social predicaments created by others. *Western Journal of Communication, 57,* 431-444.

Dion, K. K., & Dion, K. L. (1991). Psychological individualism and romantic love. *Journal of Social Behavior and Personality, 6,* 17-33.

Dion, K. K., & Dion, K. L. (1993). Individualistic and collectivistic perspectives on gender and the cultural context of love and intimacy. *Journal of Social Issues, 49*(3), 53-59.

Dion, K. K., Pak, A., & Dion, K. L. (1990). Stereotyping and physical attractiveness. *Journal of Cross-Cultural Psychology, 21,* 378-398.

Dion, K. L., & Dion, K. K. (1988). Romantic love: Individual and cultural perspectives. In R. Sternberg & M. Barnes (Eds.), *The psychology of love* (pp. 264-289). New Haven, CT: Yale University Press.

Doherty, R. W., Hatfield, E., Thompson, K., & Choo, P. (1994). Cultural and ethnic influences on love and attachment. *Personal Relationships, 1,* 391-398.

Doi, T. (1973). *The anatomy of dependence.* Tokyo: Kodansha.

Driver, E., & Driver, A. (1983). Gender, society, and self conceptualization. *International Journal of Comparative Sociology, 24,* 200-217.

Feather, N. (1995). Values, valences, and choice. *Journal of Personality and Social Psychology, 68,* 1135-1151.

Fernandez-Collado, C., Rubin, R., & Hernandez-Sampieri, R. (1991, May). *A cross-cultural examination of interpersonal communication motives in Mexico and the United States.* Paper presented at the International Communication Association convention.

Frymier, A., Klopf, D., & Ishii, S. (1990). Japanese and Americans compared on the affect orientation construct. *Psychological Reports, 66,* 966-985.

Gaetz, L., Klopf, D., & Ishii, S. (1990, June). *Predispositions toward verbal behavior of Japanese and Americans.* Paper presented at the Communication Association of Japan convention, Tokyo.

Gao, G. (1993, May). *A test of the triangular theory of love in Chinese and European American romantic relationships.* Paper presented at the International Communication Association convention.

Gao, G., & Gudykunst, W. B. (1995). Attributional confidence, perceived similarity, and network involvement in Chinese and European American romantic relationships. *Communication Quarterly, 43,* 431-445.

Geertz, C. (1975). On the nature of anthropological understanding. *American Scientist, 63,* 42-53.

Grice, H. (1975). Logic and conversation. In P. Cole & J. Morgan (Eds.), *Syntax and semantics: Vol. 3. Speech acts* (pp. 107-142). New York: Academic Press.

Gudykunst, W. B. (1995). Anxiety/uncertainty management (AUM) theory: Current status. In R. Wiseman (Ed.), *Intercultural communication theory* (pp. 8-57). Thousand Oaks, CA: Sage.

Gudykunst, W. B., Gao, G., & Franklyn-Stokes, A. (1996). Self-monitoring and concern for social appropriateness in China and England. In J. Pandy, D. Sinha, & D. Bhawuk (Eds.), *Asian contributions to cross-cultural psychology* (pp. 255-267). New Delhi: Sage.

Gudykunst, W. B., Gao, G., Nishida, T., Nadamitsu, Y., & Sakai, J. (1992). Self-monitoring in Japan and the United States. In S. Iwawaki, Y. Kashima, & K. Leung (Eds.), *Innovations in cross-cultural psychology* (pp. 185-194). Amsterdam: Swets & Zeitlinger.

Gudykunst, W. B., Gao, G., Schmidt, K., Nishida, T., Bond, M., Leung, K., Wang, G., & Barraclough, R. (1992). The influence of individualism-collectivism on communication in ingroup and outgroup relationships. *Journal of Cross-Cultural Psychology, 23,* 196-213.

Gudykunst, W. B., Matsumoto, Y., Ting-Toomey, S., Nishida, T., Kim, K., & Heyman, S. (1996). The influence of cultural individualism-collectivism, self construals, and individual values on communication styles across cultures. *Human Communication Research, 22,* 510-543.

Gudykunst, W. B., & Nishida, T. (1986a). Attributional confidence in low- and high-context cultures. *Human Communication Research, 12,* 525-549.

Gudykunst, W. B., & Nishida, T. (1986b). The influence of cultural variability on perceptions of communication behavior associated with relationship terms. *Human Communication Research, 13,* 147-166.

Gudykunst, W. B., & Nishida, T. (1993). Closeness in interpersonal relationships in Japan and the United States. *Research in Social Psychology, 8,* 76-84.

Gudykunst, W. B., & Nishida, T. (1994). *Bridging Japanese/North American differences.* Thousand Oaks, CA: Sage.

Gudykunst, W. B., Nishida, T., Chung, L., & Sudweeks, S. (1992, January). *The influence of strength of cultural identity and perceived typicality on individualistic and collectivistic values in Japan and the United States.* Paper presented at the Asian Regional Congress of the International Association for Cross-Cultural Psychology, Kathmandu, Nepal.

Gudykunst, W. B., Nishida, T., & Schmidt, K. (1989). Cultural, relational, and personality influences on uncertainty reduction processes. *Western Journal of Speech Communication, 53,* 13-29.

Gudykunst, W. B., & Ting-Toomey, S., with Chua, E. (1988). *Culture and interpersonal communication.* Newbury Park, CA: Sage.

Gudykunst, W. B., Yang, S., & Nishida, T. (1985). A cross-cultural test of uncertainty reduction theory. *Human Communication Research, 11,* 407-454.

Gudykunst, W. B., Yoon, Y., & Nishida, T. (1987). The influence of individualism-collectivism on perceptions of communication in ingroup and outgroup relationships. *Communication Monographs, 54,* 295-306.

Hall, E. T. (1976). *Beyond culture.* Garden City, NY: Doubleday.

Hofstede, G. (1979). Value systems in forty countries. In L. Eckensberger, W. Lonner, & Y. Poortinga (Eds.), *Cross-cultural contributions to psychology* (pp. 389-407). Amsterdam: Swets & Zeitlinger.

Hofstede, G. (1980). *Culture's consequences.* Beverly Hills, CA: Sage.

Hofstede, G. (1991). *Cultures and organizations: Software of the mind.* London: McGraw-Hill.

Hofstede, G., & Bond, M. (1984). Hofstede's culture dimensions. *Journal of Cross-Cultural Psychology, 15,* 417-433.

Holtgraves, T. (1992). The linguistic realization of face management. *Social Psychology Quarterly, 55,* 141-159.

Holtgraves, T., & Yang, J. (1992). The interpersonal underpinnings of request strategies: General principles and differences due to culture and gender. *Journal of Personality and Social Psychology, 62,* 246-256.

Hsu, F. (1981). *Americans and Chinese* (3rd ed.). Honolulu: University of Hawaii Press.

Imahori, T., & Cupach, W. (1994). A cross-cultural comparison of the interpretation and management of face. *International Journal of Intercultural Relations, 18,* 193-219.

Ito, Y. (1989). Socio-cultural background of Japanese interpersonal communication. *Civilisations, 39,* 101-137.

Kashima, Y. (1989). Conceptions of person: Implications in individualism/collectivism research. In C. Kagitcibasi (Ed.), *Growth and progress in cross-cultural psychology* (pp. 104-112). Amsterdam: Swets & Zeitlinger.

Kashima, Y., Siegel, M., Tanaka, K., & Kashima, E. (1992). Do people believe behaviors are consistent with attitudes? *British Journal of Social Psychology, 31,* 111-124.

Keesing, R. (1974). Theories of culture. *Annual Review of Anthropology, 3,* 73-97.

Kim, M. S. (1994). Cross-cultural comparisons of the perceived importance of conversational constraints. *Human Communication Research, 21,* 128-151.

Kim, M. S., Sharkey, W., & Singelis, T. (1994). The relationship between individuals' self construals and perceived importance of interactive constraints. *International Journal of Intercultural Relations, 18,* 117-140.

Kim, M. S., & Wilson, S. R. (1994). A cross-cultural comparison of implicit theories of requesting. *Communication Monographs, 61,* 210-235.

Kluckhohn, F., & Strodtbeck, F. (1961). *Variations in value orientations.* New York: Row, Peterson.

Lebra, T. S. (1987). The cultural significance of silence in Japanese communication. *Multilingua, 6,* 343-357.

Levine, K. (1985). *The flight from ambiguity.* Chicago: University of Chicago Press.

Mann, L., Mitsui, H., Beswick, G., & Harmoni, R. (1994). A study of Japanese and Australian children's respect for others. *Journal of Cross-Cultural Psychology, 25,* 133-145.

Mare, L. D. (1990). *Ma* and Japan. *The Southern Communication Journal, 55,* 319-328.

Markus, H. R., & Kitayama, S. (1991). Culture and the self: Implications for cognition, emotion, and motivation. *Psychological Review, 98,* 224-253.

Markus, H. R., & Kitayama, S. (1994a). A collective fear of the collective: Implications for selves and theories of selves. *Personality and Social Psychology Bulletin, 20,* 568-579.

Markus, H. R., & Kitayama, S. (1994b). The cultural construction of self and emotion. In S. Kitayama & H. R. Markus (Eds.), *Culture, self, and emotion* (pp. 89-130). Washington, DC: American Psychological Association.

Matsumoto, D. (1989). Cultural influences on perceptions of emotions. *Journal of Cross-Cultural Psychology, 20,* 92-104.

Matsumoto, D. (1991). Cultural influences on the facial expression of emotion. *Southern Communication Journal, 56,* 128-137.

Mead, M. (1967) *Cooperation and competition among primitive peoples.* Boston: Beacon.

Miyanaga, K. (1991). *The creative edge: Individualism in Japan.* New Brunswick, NJ: Transaction Books.

Noesjirwan, J. (1978). A rule-based analysis of cultural differences in social behavior. *International Journal of Psychology, 13,* 305-316.

Norton, R. (1978). Foundations of a communicator style construct. *Human Communication Research, 4,* 99-112.

Okabe, K. (1987). Indirect speech acts of the Japanese. In D. L. Kincaid (Ed.), *Communication theory from Eastern and Western perspectives* (pp. 127-136). New York: Academic Press.

Okabe, R. (1983). Cultural assumption of East and West: Japan and the United States. In W. Gudykunst (Ed.), *Intercultural communication theory* (pp. 21-44). Beverly Hills, CA: Sage.

Parsons, T., & Shils, E. A. (1951). *Toward a general theory of action.* Cambridge, MA: Harvard University Press.

Pettigrew, T. (1986). The intergroup contact hypothesis revisited. In M. Hewstone & R. Brown (Eds.), *Contact and conflict in intergroup encounters* (pp. 169-195). London: Basil Blackwell.

Pleck, J. (1977). The psychology of sex roles. *Journal of Communication, 26,* 173-200.

Rokeach, M. (1960). *The open and closed mind.* New York: Basic Books.

Schwartz, S. (1990). Individualism-collectivism. *Journal of Cross-Cultural Psychology, 21,* 139-157.

Schwartz, S. (1992). Universals in the content and structure of values. In M. Zanna (Ed.), *Advances in experimental social psychology* (Vol. 25, pp. 1-65). New York: Academic Press.

Scollon, R., & Scollon, S. (1981). *Narrative, literacy, and face in interethnic communication.* Norwood, NJ: Ablex.

Sharkey, W. F., & Singelis, T. M. (1993, June). *Embarrassability and relational orientation.* Paper presented at the International Network on Personal Relationships conference, Milwaukee.

Singelis, T. M., & Brown, W. J. (1995). Culture, self, and collectivist communication: Linking culture to individual behavior. *Human Communication Research, 21,* 354-389.

Singelis, T. M., & Sharkey, W. F. (1995). Culture, self construal, and embarrassability. *Journal of Cross-Cultural Psychology, 26,* 622-644.

Sorrentino, R., & Short, J. (1986). Uncertainty orientation, motivation, and cognition. In R. Sorrentino & E. Higgins (Eds.), *Handbook of motivation and cognition* (pp. 379-403). New York: Guilford.

Sprecher, S., Aron, A., Hatfield, E., Cortese, A., Potapova, E., & Levitskaya, A. (1994). Love: American style, Russian style, and Japanese style. *Personal Relationships, 1,* 349-369.

Stephan, W., & Stephan, C. (1985). Intergroup anxiety. *Journal of Social Issues, 41*(3), 157-166.

Ting-Toomey, S. (1988). Intercultural conflict styles: A face-negotiation theory. In Y. Y. Kim & W. B. Gudykunst (Eds.), *Theories in intercultural communication* (pp. 213-238). Newbury Park, CA: Sage.

Ting-Toomey, S. (1991). Intimacy expression in three cultures: France, Japan, and the United States. *International Journal of Intercultural Relations, 15,* 29-46.

Ting-Toomey, S. (Ed.). (1994a). *The challenge of facework: Cross-cultural and interpersonal issues.* Albany: State University of New York Press.

Ting-Toomey, S. (1994b). Managing conflict in intimate intercultural relationships. In D. Cahn (Ed.), *Intimate conflict in personal relationships* (pp. 47-77). Hillsdale, NJ: Lawrence Erlbaum.

Ting-Toomey, S. (1994c). Managing intercultural conflicts effectively. In L. Samovar & R. Porter (Eds.), *Intercultural communication: A reader* (pp. 360-372). Belmont, CA: Wadsworth.

Ting-Toomey, S. (in press). Intercultural conflict competence. In W. Cupach & D. Canary (Eds.), *Competence in interpersonal conflict.* New York: McGraw-Hill.

Ting-Toomey, S., Gao, G., Yang, Z., Trubisky, P., Kim, H., Lin, S., & Nishida, T. (1991). Culture, face maintenance, and styles of handling interpersonal conflict. *International Journal of Conflict Management, 2,* 275-296.

Triandis, H. C. (1988). Collectivism vs. individualism: A reconceptualization of a basic concept in cross-cultural psychology. In G. Verma & C. Bagley (Eds.), *Cross-cultural studies of personality, attitudes, and cognition* (pp. 60-95). London: Macmillan.

Triandis, H. C. (1989). The self and social behavior in differing cultural contexts. *Psychological Review, 96,* 506-517.

Triandis, H. C. (1990). Cross-cultural studies of individualism-collectivism. In J. Berman (Ed.), *Nebraska Symposium on Motivation 1989* (Vol. 37, pp. 41-133). Lincoln: University of Nebraska Press.

Triandis, H. C. (1995). *Individualism and collectivism.* Boulder, CO: Westview.

Triandis, H. C., Bontempo, R., Villareal, M., Asai, M., & Lucca, N. (1988). Individualism-collectivism: Cross-cultural studies on self-ingroup relationships. *Journal of Personality and Social Psychology, 54,* 323-338.

Triandis, H. C., Leung, K., Villareal, M., & Clack, F. (1985). Allocentric versus idiocentric tendencies. *Journal of Research in Personality, 19,* 395-415.

Wheeler, L. (1988). My year in Hong Kong: Some observations about social behavior. *Personality and Social Psychology Bulletin, 14,* 410-420.

Wheeler, L., Reis, H., & Bond, M. (1989). Collectivism-individualism in everyday social life. *Journal of Personality and Social Psychology, 57,* 79-86.

Yamaguchi, S. (1994). Collectivism among the Japanese: A perspective from the self. In U. Kim, H. Triandis, C. Kagitcibasi, S. Choi, & G. Yoon (Eds.), *Individualism and collectivism* (pp. 175-188). Thousand Oaks, CA: Sage.

Yamaguchi, S., Kuhlman, D., & Sugimori, S. (1995). Personality correlates of allocentric tendencies in individualistic and collectivistic cultures. *Journal of Cross-Cultural Psychology, 26,* 658-672.

Yum, J. O. (1988). The impact of Confucianism on interpersonal relationships and communication patterns in East Asia. *Communication Monographs, 55,* 374-388.

CHAPTER

3

Elementary Structures
of Social Interaction

Angela K. Hoppe
Lisa Snell
Beth-Ann Cocroft

I never once made a discovery. . . . I speak without exaggeration that
I have constructed three thousand different theories in connection
with the electric light. . . . Yet in only two cases did my experiment
prove the truth of my theory.

Thomas A. Edison

This statement by Thomas Edison is a perfect illustration of the value behind
the laborious process of constructing and testing theories. The crucial point
is that Edison kept trying and discovered electric light. In the same light (no
pun intended), social scientists have attempted, again and again, to create
theories explaining human relations. The result is myriad theoretical explanations that have not been synthesized. Consequently, many scholars, from
different disciplines, are unaware that they have duplicated and overlapped

AUTHORS' NOTE: An earlier version of this chapter was presented at the Intercultural and
Development Communication Division convention, International Communication Association,
Washington D.C., May, 1993. The authors wish to thank Bill Gudykunst for his review and
helpful comments on an earlier version of this chapter.

one another. Fiske (1991) recognized this discrepancy and attempted to integrate diverse bodies of research into a coherent theory of social relations. The result is *Structures of Social Life: The Four Elementary Forms of Human Relations,* in which Fiske presents a theory of social relations.

Fiske (1991) isolated four elementary structures that people use to guide their action and to make sense of and respond to the social action of other people. Fiske calls the four structures that guide the human cognitive process authority ranking, communal sharing, equality matching, and market pricing. According to Fiske, the four structures of social interaction are similar to the social scripts that people use to guide their behavior. The purpose of this chapter is to explain Fiske's four structures of social relations and to demonstrate how the structures can be used to understand cross-cultural interpersonal communication. First, we will provide an overview of Fiske's four structures. Second, we will examine the structures across cultures using the dimensions of cultural variability. Finally, we will illustrate the link among interpersonal relationships, culture, and the four social structures using Burgoon and Hale's (1987) relational topoi and Fitzpatrick's (1990) marital typology.

Fiske's Typology

Fiske (1991) maintains that because the four structures cut across all social domains, the models must be generated from something that gives the same order to all social process. That something, according to Fiske, is the human mind. The four structures are shared psychological models that people use to coordinate their actions with others.

What is unique about the four relational structures is that they go beyond the realm of traditional consistency and balance theories to incorporate the complex network of relationships beyond the dyadic level. "These models organize the contingent links among social relationships" (Fiske, 1991, p. 174). The basis of this perspective is that relationships are intricate networks governed by the four models, so that "the action of any person in a social relationship has potential ramifications for all the relationships linked to the primary relationship" (p. 174).

A second unique feature of Fiske's theory is that, unlike other Western-based relational theories that exclude culture as a factor, the theory incorporates culture as a key dimension in determining the expression of the four elementary models. The rules of any given culture will determine how the models are played out.

The basic structure of each model remains the same. What varies is that the "cultural rules determine the domains in which they operate and that assign persons to positions in each kind of relationship" (Fiske, 1993, p. 467).

The third distinguishing feature of Fiske's typology is that he incorporates economic, ethnographic, psychological, sociological, and anthropological evidence, as well as classical social theory, in support of his theory.

Communal Sharing

The first model Fiske (1991) describes is that of communal sharing. Relationships in communal sharing are characterized by people who perceive themselves in terms of the group to which they belong. Group membership is important and so are the boundaries that differentiate insiders from outsiders. People have a sense of belonging, and they identify with the collectivity of the group. The model is characterized by sharing according to group membership regardless of individual contributions. Fiske explains how communal sharing shapes groups:

> people may constitute a group because they have a sense of common substance (flesh and blood), a feeling of being the same kind, of unity of belonging—whether to a family, town, college, club, team, gang, ethnic group, or nation. Members' identities . . . involve a merging of self into the greater whole that is the group. (p. 83)

In other words, individuals in interpersonal relationships that are organized based on communal sharing see themselves in terms of "we" instead of "I."

Several social psychologists have identified and isolated relational types that Fiske refers to as communal sharing; relationships operating within this structure are referred to as "communal relationships" (Clark & Mills, 1979). According to Clark and Mills (1993), friendships, romantic relationships, and family relationships are typical of relationships guided by a communal structure. The defining characteristic that sets communal relationships apart from other relational structures is that "each person has a concern for the welfare of the other" (Clark & Mills, 1979, p. 12). This orientation, which places an emphasis on the well-being of others, is a root feature in guiding other behaviors such as decision making, persuasion, and group identity.

Decision making as communal sharing is a process by which the individual adheres to the wisdom of the group. Decision making is characterized by each individual sharing his or her thoughts and experiences; the ultimate goal of the decision-making process is to reach consensus. The jury system in the United States is based in part on communal sharing. Twelve individuals are brought together to discuss, deliberate, and to reach a decision regarding the issue at hand. In the case of a murder trial, the goal of the jury is to reach a consensus regarding the guilt or innocence of the defendant. In turn, lack of consensus is discouraged by the declaration of a hung jury.

A second example of decision making by communal sharing is the Japanese practice of *consensus,* where unanimous agreement stands as the foundation for decision-making practices (Doi, 1982). The Japanese recognize that individuals may have their own perspective; however, contradiction is viewed with disdain. "Subtlety in speech permits the Japanese to express, accommodate to, and resolve implicit differences without any disagreements. Doi reports that when it is appropriate, Japanese will speak gracefully for hours without ever coming to the point or taking a definite, clear position" (Fiske, 1991, p. 75). Thus, rather than stressing individual judgments, individuals operating from the communal sharing structure place value on decisions made by the group.

Persuasion in communal sharing is produced by the desire to be similar to others. According to Fiske (1991), similarity compliance occurs in two situations: (a) People try to be similar to avoid the embarrassment of standing out; and (b) as perceived similarity increases, the more likely it becomes that influence will occur. The former is clearly illustrated by a traditional Japanese saying: The nail that sticks out will be promptly hammered down. The latter situation has been documented by several communication researchers (see Berschied, 1966; Brock, 1965). For example, in a landmark study, Brock (1965) found an interesting trend in the behaviors of customers seeking tools and supplies to paint their homes. The study revealed that when customers were seeking information on the amount of paint to use on their homes, the painters were more likely to follow the advice of a salesclerk who had just had a similar experience (used the same amount of paint for a similar job) than that of an expert (e.g., to use 20 times the amount of paint for a large job). According to Brock, the results of the study indicate that in many situations people are more likely to be influenced by someone whom they perceive to be similar than someone who is an expert. Individuals may believe that they can trust someone who is similar.

This is often the aim of advertisers, who seek to develop a form of identification between their spokesmodels and their customers. If the customers believe that they are similar to the spokesperson, they are more likely to buy the product. Many popular celebrities have lost product endorsements when their public image became less than favorable because of personal scandal or failed enter-tainment projects. Advertisers believe that the public will have a hard time identifying with someone who has just divorced for the fifth time or who claims to be unable to live on palimony of $20,000 a month. Within the communal sharing structure, similarity extends beyond social influence to be one of the determining factors of identity.

The construal of self within the communal sharing structure is predominately shaped by group membership, whether in an ethnic group, age group, family, sports team, or religious affiliation. Not only experiencing a sense of belonging with a particular group, but also being recognized as a member of the group by outsiders, plays a part in developing an individual's sense of self. Roosens's (1989) description of ethnic identity is a fitting representation of how identity operates within the communal sharing structure:

> If I see and experience myself as a member of an ethnic category or group, and others—fellow members and outsiders—recognize me as such, ways of being become possible for me that set me apart from the outsiders. These ways of being contribute to the content of my self-perceptions. In this sense I become my ethnic allegiance; I experience any attack on the symbols, emblems, or values (cultural elements) that define my ethnicity as an attack on myself. (p. 18)

Thus, as reflected by Roosens's statement, identity in communal sharing is established by the groups that one associates oneself with. An example of this is the use of labels to describe one's ethnicity.

Group membership as characterized by communal sharing is often a central factor in shaping an individual's identity. A Mexican student in one of our classes recently explained why she gets upset if people mislabel her a Hispanic or Latina. She said that calling her Hispanic would mean that she is from Spain; calling her a Latina would mean that she is from Central America; however, labeling herself Mexican acknowledges her Spanish as well as Indian ancestry. It is not only necessary to be accepted as part of a group, it is also important for outsiders to acknowledge group membership.

The communal sharing structure operates on the basis that "all the members of some group or category are the same and that the group transcends its individual members" (Fiske, 1993, p. 464). This behavior is motivated by the belief that the welfare of others is most important (Clark & Mills, 1993). This group orientation that guides the communal sharing structure is evident in the expression of all elements of human relations.

Authority Ranking

The authority ranking model involves hierarchy, in contrast to communal sharing, which is guided by group membership. In authority ranking, people perceive each other as different in terms of status. High-ranking people control more resources (power, money, time) than lower-ranking people and have more choices. Typically, subordinates accept their role as a subordinate as their proper place in life. Followers are loyal and obedient, and leaders provide them with protection and help.

The power that superiors hold in authority ranking is not a domination by force or by threat of punishment; it is perceived by subordinates as a legitimate power that comes from the superior position of the other. The manner in which control is exercised varies according to culture. Language use is one way that indicates what type of authority may be operating in the Authority Ranking structure. For example, Fitch (1991) reports that *mamá,* one variation of the Colombian term *madre,* is used in particular situations to indicate respect owed to authority figures who are also nurturing and affectionate. In this case, the term used denotes a particular type of authority that is also caring and self-sacrificing.

Groups are created when authority ranking is formed around a popular or appointed leader. Members of the group may strongly identify with the leader or may just obey him or her. Dedication to a common superior or leader forms a bond among members of the group, who are otherwise unrelated. These groups are typically organized hierarchically with members of varying ranks; the higher the rank of an individual, the more power and control he or she legitimately possesses.

In authority ranking, the self is perceived in terms of either a respected leader or a dedicated follower. Identity is derived from one's position in the hierarchy; the leader's identity is based, in part, on his or her perceived ability to take the initiative and to make appropriate choices. The follower's identity relates to his or her ability to serve the leader or superior.

Decision making in authority ranking follows a strict chain of command. The decisions of superiors are communicated to subordinates through each level of the hierarchy. Although superiors can delegate decisions, they are still held responsible for any consequences. In organizations where authority ranking operates, certain people may be designated to collect information on which decisions may be based.

It is the rules of each particular culture that determine the criteria for achieving rank and the domains in which authority can be exercised. In some cultures, rank may be achieved through age, seniority, or gender. In other cultures it may be dependent upon achievement in particular areas such as education, ancestry, or ethnicity. Depending on the culture, authority ranking may apply to anything from relationships to work. Fiske argues that by the age of 3, a child has begun to externalize the model of authority ranking.

Throughout his theory, Fiske (1991) provides evidence that supports the existence of authority ranking. Fiske describes McAdams's (1988) research, which indicates that authority ranking is one of two independent relational concerns (communal sharing is the other) that make up the identity individuals report in narrating their lives. Berger, Cohen, and Zelditch (1972) show that power and prestige within small decision-making groups are determined by status differences among members. In supporting the existence of authority ranking, Fiske (1991) also states that Weber (1922/1978) analyzed authority in the decision-making process of charismatic leaders. In addition, Cialdini (1988) identifies authority as one of three major psychological persuasive tools in influencing others.

Lebra (1969) provides additional support for authority ranking. She describes the Japanese belief that, "Filial piety toward parents and services to superiors will be balanced by matching loyalty from one's own children and subordinates" (Lebra, 1969, cited in Fiske, 1991, p. 54). This demonstrates both authority ranking and equality matching. In addition, Lebra states that the strong obligation to reciprocate is easily changed to authority ranking when that which was given is impossible to repay.

Equality Matching

Equality matching is a model of social relations in which "people are separate, but equal" (Fiske, 1991, p. 15). This relationship is characterized by a desire for balance. According to Clark and Mills (1979), equality matching is set apart from communal sharing because "members assume that benefits are given with the expectation of receiving a benefit in return. The receipt of a benefit incurs a debt or obligation to return a comparable benefit" (p. 12). Equality matching may be manifested in turn taking, reciprocity of same or like items, eye-for-an-eye revenge, or equal distribution. It may also take the form of equal reciprocity in which the actual items exchanged may be different but the categories are perceived as the same or very similar. It is irrelevant who gets or gives which portion as long as everything comes out even. For example, individuals may send birthday cards to people who remembered their birthdays. In relationships characterized by equality matching, "a person may think of himself [or herself] as one of a set of equals who reciprocate fairly, share and contribute equally, a partner on a par with his [or her] fellows" (Fiske, 1991, p. 89). In other words, I will scratch your back if you will scratch mine.

Equality matching groups are peer groups in which all members are of equal status. The groups are made up of people who reciprocate things or services such as gifts or favors. One example of an equality matching group is the babysitting groups formed among some families. One day a week Susanne babysits Katie's children so that Katie can have some time alone. In return, Katie takes Susanne's children one day a week. There is no money involved; it is simply a system of reciprocation.

Individuals involved in the equality matching model of social relations perceive their self as separate from their peers, but also as equal to them. Their social identity revolves around staying even and keeping up with their reference group (the groups most important to them). For example, in order to be equal to their co-workers or family members, individuals may feel they must own a house or a certain type of car.

In equality matching, decision making follows a one-person, one-vote format. Each individual's contribution to the decision-making process carries equal weight. Sometimes turn taking is implemented in decision making. For example, on one occasion the husband may decide which movie the couple will see, and on the next occasion the wife will decide. A lottery may also be used to determine a particular outcome. According to Cialdini (1988), in the United States, reciprocity is an important and often used tool. One way reciprocity is used is with the "free gifts or samples" provided at the grocery store. The free gift serves two purposes: (a) to introduce the consumer to a new product, and (b) to activate feelings of obligation. When people are given a free gift, they feel obligated to return the favor and reciprocate by buying the product. The need to reciprocate, and the rules that guide the behavior, vary depending upon the culture in which the equality matching model is operating.

Cultural rules determine who and what is considered equal. The specific procedures used for maintaining balance and for matching are also dependent on the particular culture in which equality matching is operating. For example, Lebra (1969) explains the Japanese concept of *on* (reciprocity). Japanese try to reciprocate similar gifts in the same exact circumstances in which the gift was given. Culture determines how turn taking is initiated and what is perceived as an appropriate delay before reciprocating. In addition, research by Lerner (1974) demonstrates that children distribute rewards equally. In the United States, children are generally taught that they should take turns, and should reciprocate gifts and slumber parties. According to Fiske (1991), children first begin to externalize equality matching at approximately 4 years of age.

The example that Fiske (1991) cites most often in support of equality matching is the existence of rotating credit associations (RCAs). People contribute equal amounts of money periodically. Each person has a turn to obtain the entire sum of money. During a round, each member pays the exact amount that he or she receives. There are no interest or ratio calculations involved in RCAs.

Market Pricing

Unlike equality matching, the market pricing model entails exchange of unlike items or services that are traded in proportion to the market value or to the contribution made. This structure is based on a market system in which people evaluate commodities in ratio terms, which includes a cost-benefit analysis. In market pricing, therefore, relationships are entered into as a contract. As Fiske (1991) explains, relationships are characterized by "the idea that civil society in general and the state in particular is the product of a voluntary contract between autonomous individuals who bind themselves to a circumscribed compact to further their individual self-interest" (p. 89). One theory in speech communication that is similar to the notion of market pricing is social exchange theory (Thibaut & Kelley, 1959). The social exchange model of a relationship argues that individuals "buy" the best type of relationship they can get. As Fitzpatrick (1987) explains, individuals look for a relationship that is "the most rewarding, the least costly, and the best value relative to other relationships" (p. 579).

Decision making within the market pricing structure is influenced by the principle of supply and demand. For example, *Billboard's* Top 20 selection is determined by the sale of a particular album. The song with the highest sales during a particular time period is ranked as number one. Likewise, a computer software firm may base decisions regarding production of its software line, as well as additional accessories, on the demand for the product, such as Microsoft did with Windows 95.

According to the market pricing structure, the attempt to influence individuals, as well as groups, is governed by cost and reward enticements. Turn on the television and tune in to a late night infomercial and you will be bombarded with such claims as "If you act now, not only will you receive this valuable item, but we will throw in a free gift too!" or "Act now, while supplies last!" According to Bettinghaus and Cody (1994),

Marketers actually plan shortage of certain desirable products so that customers will pay for the hard-to-find objects. At Christmas, some dolls, video games, race car sets, and many other products are frequently advertised, but a shortage of the items means that more parents are looking for the products than there are products available. (p. 303)

According to Fiske (1991), within the market pricing structure the self is governed by economic rules. People's occupation, personal financial success, and independent contracts shape their self-concept. Within the market pricing structure, people are motivated by achievement, as this is a defining characteristic identity. Achievement consists of the need to try to do everything well, to be stimulated to excel by the presence of others, to enjoy competition (Murray, 1938).

Comparison of Models

Determination of which model is operating depends on the participant's point of view; the standard for determining what kind of social structure is operative is the perception each individual has of the relational structure. The actual structures that are operating may or may not correspond to the structure that an outside observer determines from looking at behavior. Here is an example to help clarify the differences among the four models. Families can use one or all of the four structures to organize the process of preparing dinner. In the mode of communal sharing, cooking dinner is a family effort. Every member of the family contributes whatever he or she does best to prepare the dinner. Alternatively, within the authority ranking structure, dinner preparation is based on traditional roles in the household. In this case, the mother, who is in charge of the kitchen, delegates responsibilities to her children. When equality matching is operating, the responsibility for dinner preparation is distributed equally. For example, people may take turns doing the dishes, or each member of the family may have one specific duty at each meal time. Market pricing is similar to eating out. The family pays someone else to prepare the dinner for them.

Fiske (1991) argues that the four social structures operate at all social levels, from interactions among individuals to interactions among nations. In addition, he states that as the level of analysis moves from the dyad to more complex groups, institutions, and societies, two or more models can combine to structure the relationship. In order to clarify this point, Fiske provides an example of how the models combine and influence the functioning of the United Nations' interactions with other institutions. First, equality matching is operating in the United Nations because each country has one vote in the General Assembly.

Second, communal sharing is represented in the United Nations in that aid to developing countries is often distributed based on need. Profits from the United Nations are often pooled to solve world problems that affect all nations. Third, authority ranking operates in the United Nations through the status of nations that have permanent seats on the Security Council and consequently more influence and power. Finally, market pricing controls aspects of the United Nations that deal with contracting work to nations to provide services for the United Nations and other countries.

In summary, the four structures operate in all social relationships in all cultures. Some models may be predominant in some cultures and in certain domains of behavior within any culture. Fiske (1991) argues that "the same model may look somewhat different in different domains of social action and cognition, and in diverse realizations within any domain" (p. 23).

Dimensions of Cultural Variability

Fiske's (1991) structures can be associated with the different dimensions of cultural variability. The following provides examples of how the dimensions of cultural variability are evident within each of Fiske's four structures of social relations. Though there are dominant structures evident in certain types of cultures, based on the dimensions of cultural variability, the examples provided are not universal because any culture contains all of the four structures in some domains of behavior.

One way to utilize the dimensions of cultural variability in theory is through the use of the individualism-collectivism dimension. Researchers have identified individualism-collectivism as a major dimension of cultural variability (Hofstede, 1980; Hui & Triandis, 1986; Triandis, 1988). Individualism-collectivism refers to attitudes, beliefs, and behaviors that differentiate clusters of cultures (Triandis, 1988). In addition to individualism-collectivism, we will include three other dimensions of cultural variability: power distance, femininity-masculinity, and uncertainty avoidance (Hofstede, 1980). The dimension of power distance refers to differences in views and practices of skills, wealth, status, and power that differentiate clusters of cultures. The femininity-masculinity dimension refers primarily to the expression of emotions, roles of men and women, and the dominant values of a society. The dimension of uncertainty avoidance refers to the degree of tolerance for ambiguity that is expressed by members of a culture.

Communal sharing structures are predominantly collectivistic in that the structure emphasizes the importance of the ingroup and of shared group goals. The communal sharing system is feminine in that the relationships in the structure value interdependence and guarding the relationship. The market pricing structure is predominantly individualistic in that the emphasis is placed on individual achievement. In addition, market pricing is masculine in nature because money, achievement, and independence are valued. Relationships in market pricing prescribe rules and formal settings, which is standard of high uncertainty avoidance cultures. Alternatively, equality matching is more accepting of differences and ambiguity, therefore the culture is characterized by a low uncertainty avoidance orientation. Equality matching depicts a low power distance culture, because everyone is considered equal though separate. Equality matching is predominantly individualistic in that individual status is emphasized: The self is considered separate but equal. The authority ranking structure is a high power distance culture because of the emphasis on status and the separation of superiors and subordinates. Triandis (1990) notes that collectivistic cultures tend to see a big difference between those with power and those without, and that the emphasis on hierarchy is a characteristic of collectivism. Hofstede (1980) found that power distance and collectivism were highly correlated. Authority ranking is therefore characterized as a collectivistic culture.

Burgoon and Hale's Relational Topoi

Burgoon and Hale (1984), in a review of literature from a variety of disciplines that related to relational communication, delineated aspects that are significant and distinct to interpersonal relationships. The six overriding categories derived from the investigation are (a) control, (b) intimacy, (c) composure, (d) formality, (e) task-social orientation, and (f) equality. The dimensions identified "may be viewed simultaneously as primary themes for relational discourse and as the dimensions along which partners interpret and define their interpersonal relationship" (p. 194).

The schemata have been derived from a compilation of research from a variety of fields. Control consists of the dominance-submission dimension, and the distribution of power and influence in relationships. Intimacy is made up of five dimensions: (a) affection-hostility, (b) inclusion-exclusion, (c) intensity of involvement, (d) trust, and (e) depth-similarity. Composure has to do with an individual's self-control, degree of comfort, and relaxation. Formality "is the degree of personalism, reserve, and decorum being exhibited" (Burgoon & Hale, 1984, p. 209). The task-social factor includes the degree to which tasks influence the relationship. Equality is related to the equity in the relationship.

The six topoi will be applied to each model in order to illustrate the link among interpersonal relationships, culture, and the four social structures. Each theme will vary according to the structure that provides the framework for the relationship. To some extent, each theme exists in each model, although certain themes predominate in certain models.

Authority Ranking

According to Fiske (1991), authority ranking is motivated by power. The motivation of power and influence of a hierarchy create a theme based on the complementary relationship of dominance-submission. The dominant individuals control the upper levels of the hierarchy, whereas the subordinates possess lower levels of the hierarchy. Power, however, is evident in both roles. For example, the dominant individual may posses power based on personal status, whereas the subordinate may control power by using passive-aggressive strategies to get a superior to comply. Of importance is that power is outside of the individual and, in the case of authority ranking, individuals with low status respect the status of those who dominate them. High-ranking individuals control many people.

Intimacy levels in this structure can be high, based on the complementarity of the relationship. Because the relationship is complementary in nature, each partner attempts to meet the needs of the other based on each one's dominant or submissive role. Relationships that are complementary are more intimate than those that are not (Berg & Clark, 1986). A specific example of this phenomenon is evident in the traditional marital type, which is based on complementary roles in which the husband is dominant and the wife is submissive. This couple type reports a higher degree of sharing and intimacy than any of the other types Fitzpatrick (1990) has isolated.

Similarity, a component of intimacy (Burgoon & Hale, 1987), is apparent in the attempt of subordinates to emulate the behaviors of their superiors. In this case similarity is often based on "hero-worship." This is "based on idealistic loyal admiration . . . people orient their behavior to others . . . and modify their behavior accordingly" (Fiske, 1991, p. 76).

Fiske (1991) provides a specific description of task relationships in authority ranking. "Superiors direct and control the work of subordinates, while often doing less of the arduous or menial labor. Superiors control product of subordinates' labor" (p. 42). The role of the task in relationships is controlled by the dominant members of the structure. This is manifested in high power distance cultures where higher status individuals closely supervise subordinates and subordinates fear disagreeing with the superior (Hofstede, 1980).

As noted earlier, levels of formality will vary depending on the intimacy level of the relationship. Primarily, authority ranking is characterized by formal roles for interaction that are dictated by the status of the individuals in a relationship. The dominant member of the relationship would control the level of formality and the submissive member would follow the dominant member's example. For instance, a child's level of formality or informality with its parents would be dependent on how the parents expect the child to behave. If the parents are very expressive and intimate toward the child, then the child would be allowed to act informally in the presence of its parents.

The degree of composure exhibited by individuals in the authority ranking structure is determined by the comfort they find in their role in society. Fiske points out that in authority ranking, individuals are comfortable with the status differences and accept them as natural, so the degree of composure would be high. "Subordinates believe that their subordination is legitimate" (Fiske, 1991, p. 14). This is true as well in high power distance cultures, where power is viewed as part of everyday life (Hofstede & Bond, 1984). Fiske continues, however, to say that subordinates "may take issue with any given aspect of their subordination" (p. 14). In this case, levels of composure would falter.

Equality is distributed according to status. Whereas equality coexists on the same levels of status, in authority ranking the higher the status, the more privileges individuals have. The higher an individual's rank the more opportunity, choice, or items she or he is provided with. Individuals at the lower end of the hierarchy are provided with what is left over or not of equal quality. In addition, only people who have the same status and authority would consider themselves as equals.

Equality Matching

According to the equality matching model there is an equal distribution of power and control. The relationships are characterized by mutual respect. Hofstede (1980) clarified this notion with his example of the qualities of a low power distance culture. He demonstrated that respect for the individual and equality are precursors to freedom (Gudykunst & Ting-Toomey, 1988).

The equality matching model is characterized by intimacy of a reciprocal nature. For example, self-disclosure would be moderated by the level of intimacy in a relationship, but the amounts of self-disclosure provided would be equal.

The task-social element is moderated in a number of ways. Under equality matching, individuals may take turns doing a specific job, do different jobs that require equal effort, or align themselves by completing the same task.

Levels of composure would be at their highest when individuals believe that their roles are distributed equally. For instance, a husband and wife share household duties that are different, such as the wife mowing the lawn and the husband taking care of sewing. If both were satisfied that they were completing equal amounts of work, they would display a high degree of comfortableness and be relaxed. "Contributions match each other's donations equally" (Fiske, 1991, p. 43). If they did not feel that the contributions to the relationship were equally matched, the amount of composure would decrease.

According to the equality matching model, everyone is equal. This is evident in the distribution of goods, where everyone is given identical shares regardless of need (Fiske, 1991). Work is distributed equally and individuals are viewed as equal, although they may be different. Fiske maintains that the primary motivation of the equality matching structure is equality.

Communal Sharing

In the communal sharing structure, power is centered within the group. The group, collectively, has control. This structure displays the more submissive aspects of the control dimension in that relationships in this structure attempt to conform to what is acceptable according to the group's standards. Triandis (1988) argues that the number of ingroups affects the amount of influence that a particular group has on an individual. The fewer the number of ingroups, the more influence that each group will have on the individual. Thus the communal structure, when operating in a collectivistic culture, is characterized by fewer ingroups in comparison to individualistic cultures.

Fiske (1991) categorizes intimacy as the main motivation of the communal sharing relational model. Relationships in this structure are characterized by more listening, more self-disclosure, more references to "us" and "we," and by displaying more concern for friends and family. A primary concern is the protection of intimate relationships. Similarity, a component of intimacy, is the main social influence in the communal sharing structure. Relationships guided by communal sharing are based on conformity and unanimity. In the "CS orientation . . . people may go along with others when they fear the derision and embarrassment of standing out as disparate or opposed to the group" (Fiske, 1991, p. 76). Relationships in the communal sharing structure are based on similarity for establishing intimacy. This is supported by research that states that people are more likely to choose partners from the same race, social class, intelligence level, religion, and so on (Kerckhoff, 1974).

Inclusion-exclusion, a subcategory of intimacy, is evident in the communal sharing structure because of the distinction between ingroups and outgroups. According to Triandis (1988), members of collectivistic societies perceive their ingroup relationships to be more intimate than do members of individualistic cultures. Therefore, because the ingroup is stressed in communal sharing, inclusion in the group would be high, and, in turn, so would the level of intimacy.

Task-social dimension is determined by the collectivity of the relationship. "Tasks are treated as [the] collective responsibility of the group, without dividing the job or assigning specific individual duties" (Fiske, 1991, p. 42). There are no checks or balances to determine if the contributions of work are equal. Everybody does what they can. Relationships in this structure are more influenced by the social aspect of the dimensions than by the task aspect. There is a sense of unity in the relationships that people want to maintain. People may participate in a group project in order to ensure fulfilling needs of affiliation (Fiske, 1991).

Formality is determined by the collectivity of the relationship. The relationship is based on sharing and common goals; therefore, a high degree of formality is necessary to maintain the structure of the relationship. This is characteristic of a low tolerance for ambiguity, so relationships in communal sharing would rate high on uncertainty avoidance.

The measure of composure would be determined by how comfortable individuals are with their group associations. Are they familiar with the formal rules of the group, and are these rules being carried out by the members of the group? Individuals in this structure would have a higher level of composure when dealing with members of their own group. Who is "us" and who is "other" is important to individuals defining their roles. This is similar to collectivism. Research supports that individuals from collectivistic societies deal more successfully with members of their ingroup than with members of an outgroup. People guided by the communal sharing structure would therefore display higher degrees of composure when dealing with members of their ingroup than if they were dealing with outsiders.

Relationships in communal sharing are based on the notion of "one for all." Equity and reciprocity are not based on status or pure equality, but on need. What an individual receives is not based on his or her contributions but on what he or she needs.

Market Pricing

Control is negotiated in the structure of market pricing. Power and control are negotiated using a cost-benefit rationale. The "market decides, governed by supply and demand for expected utilities" (Fiske, 1991, p. 45). The market is the dominant force that controls the power in the structure; for example, by determining prices.

Intimacy levels are determined in part by the costs/benefits of the relationship. Individuals are willing to stay in their relationships as long as the rewards outweigh the costs (Thibaut & Kelley, 1959). Intimate resources such as time spent together and affection are allocated according to the value placed on them by the relational partners. The task-social dimensions incorporate into the market pricing structure in several ways. First, tasks, or work assignments, are performed for a wage that is determined to be of value equal to the effort. Second, the individualistic nature of this structure is apparent by the delegation of tasks. Even when there is a group project, the responsibilities are eventually delegated into individual subtasks. "The joint task divides neatly into independent individual subtasks, and the collective outcome depends on the most competent (. . . productive) members" (Fiske, 1991, p. 165). Finally, the task-social dimension is essential to this structure because individuals' roles are defined by their economic status, achievement, and/or profession.

In market pricing, there are formal rules for behavior, such as rules that determine proper business etiquette. Because this structure often operates in the arena of business, formal rules are enacted. This is further supported by high uncertainty avoidance cultures, where there is a need for formal rules.

Under the market pricing structure, the self is presented in such a way as to achieve maximum rewards. Composure may falter with lack of success or with the agony of defeat. Degree of comfort would be highest when individuals maximize their entrepreneurial skills.

Equality, based on equity and distribution, is determined by market value. In return for pay, an equal proportion of goods is supplied. Inequality, or demand for a product, creates value. The relationships in this structure are not based on maintaining harmony but function through rivalry. "People are assessed according to a fixed ratio or percentage (e.g., tithing, sales or real estate taxes)" (Fiske, 1991, p. 43).

The synthesis of Fiske's four structures of social relations and Burgoon and Hale's (1987) relational topoi demonstrates that the relational themes are an integral part of the structures. The themes will vary depending on the structure in which they operate. The application of Burgoon and Hale's relational topoi provides additional validation for Fiske's (1991) structures of social life.

Fitzpatrick's Marital Typology

In the field of speech communication, Fitzpatrick (1987, 1990) has proposed a relational typology that is similar to Fiske's (1991) four relational structures. Fitzpatrick (1987) argues that within any sample of couples there are a limited number of marital types that can be isolated. Couples within the same type will communicate in a manner similar to other couples in the same type, as opposed to couples in different types (Fitzpatrick, 1990).

The three types of marital definitions that Fitzpatrick (1990) discusses are traditional, independent, and separate. Traditionals value conventional ideas about marriage and the family, and the marriage partners are very interdependent. Independents display a more liberal approach toward marriage and family. "Separates are ambivalent about their family values, not very interdependent in their marriage, and tend to avoid marital conflict" (Fitzpatrick, 1990, p. 441).

As a foundation for her theory, Fitzpatrick (1990) explains the concept of schemata. She views schemata as an individual's cognitive representation of the world. The function of marital schemata is compatible with the function of Fiske's (1991) four structures. Specifically, Fiske's structures provide a shared psychological schema that people use to coordinate their actions with others. Likewise, Fitzpatrick (1990) argues that relationship partners coordinate their interaction with one another based on their marital schemata.

Traditionals can be classified under authority ranking, because these marital couples score high on the ideology of traditionalism (Fitzpatrick, 1988). The interaction in the marriage is based on the marital partners' complementary roles, in which one partner is dominant and the other is submissive. Fiske (1991) argues that within the authority ranking structure, one relational partner has control over the other partner. The relationship is complementary in nature. Thus, in a traditional marital type, relational partners may interact with one another based on the structure of authority ranking. This is consistent with high power distance cultures in that emphasis is placed on hierarchy and status.

In addition, traditional marital types can be typed as Fiske's structure of communal sharing, in which people feel a sense of belonging. Traditional couples score high on the factors of sharing and undifferentiated space (Fitzpatrick, 1988). Sharing refers to a high level of intimacy, and undifferentiated space refers to the limited privacy of the relational partners. In general, these two factors combine and the relational partners begin to view the world in terms of "we" rather than "I" (Fitzpatrick, 1990). There is a sense of unity and oneness in the relationship. To carry the notion a step farther, one can conceptualize the relationship in terms of a collectivistic culture, where relational partners would emphasize meeting the needs of the relationship rather than focusing on individual needs. This is consistent with Fiske's (1991) description of a prototype communal sharing marriage, which is "based on love that involves a merging of selves, a desire for intimacy, . . . together with indefinite and potentially unlimited obligations, desire to serve, and selfless mutual caring" (p. 93). Therefore, traditional couples are evident in Fiske's (1991) communal sharing structure.

Alternatively, independents score high on sharing and have moderate intimacy in the relationship, and they score the highest on the factor of autonomy (Fitzpatrick, 1988). Therefore, these couples interact with one another based on Fiske's model equality matching, in which relational partners are viewed as separate but equal. The individual goals are just as important as the shared goals of the marriage. Independents score lower on undifferentiated space, which means that they make more provisions for privacy in the relationship than traditionals do. Finally, because independents score low on the ideology of traditionalism, their view of the marriage is not based on complementary roles; instead, they view themselves as equal partners in the marriage. This is compatible with low power distance cultures in that the individual is respected and consequently the power is distributed equally. Fiske (1991) notes that "many contemporary marriages in principle are based on Equality Matching ideals, in which each spouse should have equal rights and equal say in decisions, take turns with onerous tasks . . . and have distinct, coequal personalities" (p. 93). Equality, a guiding force in independent relationships, is the main theme present in the equality matching structure.

Independents score high on the factor of assertiveness and are habituated to conflict (Fitzpatrick, 1988). Therefore, the independent couple is also characterized by Fiske's structure of market pricing, because these couples organize their relationships based on competition and cost-benefit value exchanges. This reflects the value placed on success and ambition in an individualistic culture. These factors reflect the couples' tendency to compete with one another and continually renegotiate their marital roles. As Kelley and Burgoon (1991) point out, the traditionals show more competitive symmetry than either of the other couple types. According to Fiske (1991), in the market pricing structure marriage is treated as a negotiated contract in which "everything has its price and is commensurable with everything else in terms of potential or actual exchange ratios" (p. 93).

Separates are similar to the traditionals in that they score high on the factor of ideology of traditionalism (Fitzpatrick, 1988). Separates' marriages are also made up of the structure of authority ranking. Their marriages are characterized by traditional roles in which the male is dominant and the female is submissive. In the authority ranking structure the marriage is typically characterized by "the husband having proprietary control over and pastoral responsibility for his wife and family. Men have made the fundamental decisions, exercised broad powers, and had much higher status than their wives" (Fiske, 1991, p. 93). Similar to the traditional marriage, this is consistent with high power distance cultures in that it is characterized by dominant and submissive roles.

Separates do not score high on the factors for sharing. A separate marriage may be based on market pricing, in which marital partners view the marriage as a contract similar to a business contract in which each partner receives some financial or other type of gain besides personal sharing and intimacy. Separates appear to stay married based on Johnson's (1982) notion of social commitment in which they stay married to fulfill social roles rather than for personal fulfillment. Separates may therefore stay married for economic reasons such as saving on taxes, buying a home, or to raise children. The need for formality in the marriage can be explained by the uncertainty avoidance dimension. Specifically, separates would be high in uncertainty avoidance because they would avoid conflict and have clear instructions for the marital roles.

Conclusion

In this chapter we have examined Fiske's four structures of social interaction as a means of explaining cultural differences and interpersonal relationships.

Fiske's four structures enhance our understanding of why interpersonal relationships vary within and across cultures.

Future research should develop an empirical method for testing the four structures. Although Fiske's attempt at presenting a grand theory falls short in some areas, he has created a theory based on the integration of a wide range of theories and research. The theory is an integration of the work of classical social theorists (e.g., the work of Marx, Mead, Piaget, Ricoeur, and Weber) and research by sociologists; economists; social, cultural, and psychological anthropologists; theologians; cross-cultural, developmental, and social psychologists; and social linguists.

Integration of many different theories and research is a desirable goal because it yields a theory that can provide greater understanding of the human experience. For example, some of the areas of human behavior this theory attempts to explain include human motivation, social influence, justice, distribution processes, decision making, reciprocal exchange, social identity, aggression, conflict, and morality. The theory therefore has a broad scope because it applies to a diverse range of events.

References

Berg, J. H., & Clark, M. S. (1986). Differences in social exchange between intimate and other relationships: Gradually evolving or quickly apparent? In V. J. Derlega & B. A. Winstead (Eds.), *Friendship and social interaction*. New York: Springer.

Berger, J., Cohen, B. P., & Zelditch, M. (1972). Status characteristics and social interaction. *American Sociological Review, 37,* 241-255.

Berscheid, E. (1966). Opinion change and communicator-communicatee similarity and dissimilarity. *Journal of Personality and Social Psychology, 4,* 670-680.

Bettinghaus, E. P., & Cody, M. J. (1994). *Persuasive communication* (5th ed). Orlando, FL: Harcourt Brace.

Brock, T. C. (1965). Communicator-recipient similarity and decision change. *Journal of Personality and Social Psychology, 1,* 650-654.

Burgoon, J. K., & Hale, J. L. (1984). The fundamental topoi of relational communication. *Communication Monographs, 51,* 193-214.

Burgoon, J. K., & Hale, J. L. (1987). Validation and measurement of the fundamental themes of relational communication. *Communication Monographs, 55,* 58-79.

Cialdini, R. B. (1988). *Influence: Science and practice* (2nd ed.). Glenview, IL: Scott, Foresman.

Clark, M. S., & Mills, J. (1979). Interpersonal attraction in exchange and communal relationships. *Journal of Personality and Social Psychology, 37,* 12-24.

Clark, M. S., & Mills, J. (1993). The difference between communal and exchange relationships: What it is and is not. *Personality and Social Psychology Bulletin, 19,* 684-691.

Doi, K. (1982). A two dimension theory of achievement motivation: Affiliative and non-affilitative. *Japanese Journal of Psychology, 52,* 344-350.

Fiske, A. P. (1991). *Structures of social life: The four elementary forms of human relations.* New York: Free Press.

Fiske, A. P. (1993). Social errors in four cultures: Evidence about universal forms of social relations. *Journal of Cross-Cultural Psychology, 24,* 463-494.

Fitch, S. (1991) The interplay of linguistic universals and cultural knowledge in personal address: Colombian *madre* terms. *Communication Monographs, 58,* 254-271.

Fitzpatrick, M. A. (1987). Marital interaction. In C. R. Berger & S. M. Chaffee (Eds.), *Handbook of communication science.* Newbury Park, CA: Sage.

Fitzpatrick, M. A. (1988). *Between husbands and wives: Communication in marriage.* Newbury Park, CA: Sage.

Fitzpatrick, M. A. (1990). Models of marital interaction. In H. Giles & W. P. Robinson (Eds.), *Handbook of language and social psychology.* New York: John Wiley.

Gudykunst, W. B., & Ting-Toomey, S. (1988). *Culture and interpersonal communication.* Newbury Park, CA: Sage.

Hofstede, G. (1980). *Culture's consequences: International differences in work-related values.* Beverly Hills, CA: Sage.

Hofstede, G., & Bond, M. (1984). Hofstede's culture dimensions: An independent validation using Rokeach's value survey. *Journal of Cross-Cultural Psychology, 15,* 417-433.

Hui, C., & Triandis, H. (1986). Individualism-collectivism: A study of cross-cultural researchers. *Journal of Cross-Cultural Psychology, 17,* 248-255.

Johnson, M. P. (1982). Social and cognitive features of the dissolution of commitment to relationships. In S. W. Duck (Ed.), *Personal relationships: Vol. 4. Dissolving personal relationships.* London: Academic Press.

Kelley, D. L., & Burgoon, J. K. (1991). Understanding marital satisfaction and couple type as functions of relational expectations. *Human Communication Research, 18*(1), 40-69.

Kerckhoff, A. C. (1974). The social context of interpersonal attraction. In T. L. Huston (Ed.), *Foundations of interpersonal attraction.* New York: Academic Press.

Lebra, T. S. (1969). Reciprocity and the asymmetric principle. An analytical reappraisal of the Japanese concept of On. *Psychologia, 12,* 129-138.

Lerner, M. J. (1974). The justice motive: "Equity" and "parity" among children. *Journal of Personality and Social Psychology, 29,* 539-550.

McAdams, D. P. (1988). *Power, intimacy, and the life story: Personalogical inquiries into identity.* New York: Guilford.

Murray, H. A. (1938). *Explorations in personality.* New York: Oxford University Press.

Roosens, E. (1989). *Creating ethnicity.* Newbury Park, CA: Sage.

Thibaut, J. W., & Kelley, H. H. (1959). *The social psychology of groups.* New York: John Wiley.

Triandis, H. C. (1988). Collectivism vs. individualism: A reconceptualization of a basic concept in cross-cultural psychology. In C. Bagley & G. Verma (Eds.), *Personality, cognition, and values: Cross-cultural perspectives of childhood and adolescence.* London: Macmillan.

Triandis, H. C. (1988). Cross-cultural studies of individualism and collectivism. In J. Berman (Ed.), *Nebraska Symposium on motivation 1989* (vol. 37). Lincoln: University of Nebraska.

Weber, M. (1978). *Economy and society.* Berkeley: University of California Press. (Original work published 1922)

PART

III

EMIC PERSPECTIVES

CHAPTER

4

Self and OTHER:
A Chinese Perspective
on Interpersonal Relationships

Ge Gao

Arlene, a Chinese woman, has been living in the United States for 13 years and has been married to an American for 10 years. For the past 10 years, Arlene has been trying to find a fit between her husband's American culture and her Chinese culture. She has been successful in achieving balance in many areas of her life, but she is constantly caught in one area—differences between the two cultures in approaching interpersonal relationships.

Arlene has been indebted to her sisters over the years, because when their parents passed away it was her elder sisters who assumed the responsibility of taking care of her and the family. When Arlene's niece, Meiling, decided to pursue a higher

AUTHOR'S NOTE: This research was supported in part by an Affirmative Action Faculty Development Grant from San Jose State University. I thank Bill Gudykunst and Stella Ting-Toomey for their insightful suggestions and comments. My thanks also go to the interlibrary loan staff at San Jose State University for making all the articles available to me. An earlier version of this research was presented at the International Communication Association Convention, Sydney, Australia, July 1994.

education in the United States a few years ago, Arlene was very pleased that, finally, she was given an opportunity to repay her sister. She offered Meiling free accommodation while in school. As a result, her own nuclear family was extended. Arlene's other sister decided to buy a new house and needed to borrow some money for the down payment. Arlene gave her sister the money and told her not to worry about returning it. "We are all family. If she needs help, I should help her," was what she said.

Reflecting upon the past and the present during our conversations, Arlene feels that she has done nothing for her husband's family and she is very unsettled about that. Accounts such as this are typical and commonly given among my circle of Chinese friends. Trying to understand why Chinese behave the way they do, I searched for answers in various interpersonal theories, but I could not find a satisfactory explanation. My numerous questions and puzzlement compelled me to start exploring explanations indigenous to the Chinese culture.

It is important to recognize that "All things under heaven are born of Existence; Existence is born of Nonexistence" (Lao Zi).[1] Lao Zi's statement tells us that everything originated from somewhere and that somewhere may at times not be overt (B. Wang, 1990). To understand ways of relating in the Chinese culture, one needs to inquire into the interconnected nature of personal relationships and to uncover some of the guiding principles embedded in those relationships. The purpose of this chapter, therefore, is to explore both covert and manifest sources of communication in Chinese interpersonal relationships. It attempts to unravel indigenous themes of Chinese interpersonal relationships by examining both the present and the past. Specifically, two questions will be addressed: (a) How are personal relationships conceptualized in the Chinese culture? (b) What are some of the rules and norms that guide personal relationships in the Chinese culture?

In this chapter, a Chinese perspective on interpersonal relationships is presented in five sections. The basic concepts of self and OTHER, as well as their relational implications, will be introduced first. Second, the importance of family and the distinction between insiders and outsiders will be analyzed. Third, the notion of hierarchy and role relationships will be presented. Fourth, specific relational principles, such as *lian* 脸 and *mian* 面 (face and image, respectively), *ren qing* 人情 (human feeling), and *bao* 报 (reciprocation), as well as *gan qing* 感情 (emotional love), will be discussed. Finally, implications of the Chinese relational perspective for the study of communication will be outlined. Throughout, the discussion is based on analyses in the context of the Chinese culture.

The Self and OTHER Perspective

Self-concept is important in explaining and interpreting many aspects of human behavior. It affects a person's relational development and the meaning of family, hierarchy, and role relationships as well as other specific relational properties such as face and reciprocity. In the Chinese culture, the notion of self is formulated and expressed in a unique way. In this section, a Chinese concept of self and its relational implications are presented.

Conceptualizations of Self and OTHER

In the Western world, an "individual" signifies an independent entity with free will, emotions, and personality. An individual, however, is not conceptualized in this way in the Chinese culture. Sun (1991) argues that an individual is not a complete entity in the Chinese culture; an individual implies only a physical "body." An exchange of "hearts" (*xin* 心) between two "bodies" completes a person (*ren* 人), as exemplified in the Chinese language. A *ren* (人) is written with the character for "two" with a "human" radical (Sun, 1991).

The incomplete nature of the Chinese self is supported by both Taoism and Confucianism even though they differ in many fundamental ways. Taoism defines self as part of nature. Self and nature together complete a harmonious relationship. Self in the Confucian sense is defined by a person's surrounding relations, which often are derived from kinship networks and supported by cultural values such as filial piety, loyalty, dignity, and integrity. Given that, traditionally, the Chinese self involves multiple layers of relations with others, a person in this relational network tends to be sensitive to his or her position as being above, below, or equal to others (e.g., Chu, 1985; Fairbank, 1991; King & Bond, 1985). A male Chinese, for example, would view himself as a son, a brother, a husband, a father, but hardly as himself (Chu, 1985). Moreover, according to Confucius the "civilized" person should always be a responsible self, aware of his or her position in society and the world, and perform his or her duty accordingly (Chiu, 1984). In essence, a person can never separate him- or herself from obligations to others (King & Bond, 1985).

The position of self in Chinese interpersonal relationships is further articulated in Chinese writings. The late, contemporary Chinese philosopher, *Hu Shi* 胡适, asserted that "in the Confucian human-centered philosophy, man [or woman] cannot exist alone; all actions must be in a form of interaction between man [woman] and man [woman]" (cited in King & Bond, 1985, p. 31). *Zhuang Zi* 庄子, who was believed to have written *Dao De Jing* 道德经 with *Lao Zi* 老子 and lived in the fourth and third centuries B.C., wrote, "When you look at yourself as *part* of the natural scheme of things, you are equal to the most minute insignificant creature in the world, but your existence is great because you are in *unity* with the whole universe" (emphasis added; cited in Dien, 1983, p. 282).

The present conceptualization of the Chinese self appears to correspond to the discussion of the interdependent construal of self (see Markus & Kitayama, 1991, for a review). According to Markus and Kitayama, an interdependent self—as opposed to an independent self—is defined by the person's relations with others in specific contexts. The other-orientation thus is key to an interdependent self. Congruous with the notion of an interdependent self, the Chinese self also needs to be recognized, defined, and completed by others. The self's orientation to others' needs, wishes, and expectations is essential to the development of the Chinese self. Consequently, the other-orientation is inseparable from the Chinese self; it permeates all indigenous concepts of Chinese interpersonal relationships.

Relational Implications

Each culture has a set of norms and rules that provides guidance for acceptable behavior and communication. As defined by Olsen (1978), norms involve standards with moral or ethical connotations, whereas rules involve standards without moral or ethical connotations. An understanding of the distinctive way of defining *self* in the Chinese culture provides explanations for both rules and norms of interaction in interpersonal relationships.

Chinese conceptions of the self set boundaries for appropriate interaction in interpersonal relationships. As Yang (1981) points out, the importance of others in defining the Chinese self "represents a tendency for a person to act in accordance with external expectations or social norms, rather than with internal wishes or personal integrity, so that he [or she] would be able to protect his [or her] social self and function as an integral part of the social network" (p. 161). He further elaborates on the specific consequences of this other orientation as

> the Chinese's submission to social expectations, social conformity, worry about external opinions, and non-offensive strategy in an attempt to achieve one or more of the purposes of reward attainment, harmony maintenance, impression management, face protection, social acceptance, and avoidances of punishment, embar-

rassment, conflict, rejection, ridicule, and retaliation in a social situation. (Yang, 1981, p. 161)

Research findings appear to be consistent with Yang's assertions. Following a person's success, Chinese college students in Hong Kong, for example, have been documented to like humble or self-effacing attributions better than self-enhancing ones (Bond, Leung, & Wan, 1982). Chinese are less likely to take pride in their success than are their North American counterparts (Stipek, Weiner, & Li, 1989). Chinese American graduate students and professionals report themselves less active, flexible, attractive, sharp, and beautiful than do white American graduate students and professionals (White & Chan, 1983). The de-emphasis on self thus has an impact on the Chinese self-concept.

The importance of "other" in defining the Chinese self also is reflected in cultural norms such as modesty and humility (Bond et al., 1982; White & Chan, 1983), reserve, and formality, as well as restraint and inhibition of strong feelings (Sue & Sue, 1973). These cultural norms, along with the use of shame and guilt to control behavior (Devos & Abbot, 1966), all serve to reinforce the other-orientation in personal relationships. To be modest is to treat oneself strictly and others leniently. Values such as tolerance of others (*rong ren* 容忍), harmony with others (*sui he* 随和), and solidarity with others (*tuan jie* 团结) further demonstrate the importance of "other" in one's relational development (Chinese Culture Connection, 1987). The concern for others first and then for oneself is reflected in marital relationships as well. The most persuasive argument for the reconciliation of broken marriages appeals to the needs and wishes of others, including the family, children, and friends. To illustrate, in a well-publicized divorce trial in Shanghai in 1979, one broken marriage was reconciled for the sake of the child, the family, and the state. The judge even criticized the woman who initiated the divorce for lack of self-control (Dien, 1983).

Family and Insider Versus Outsider Distinction

In the Chinese culture, family serves as the most significant and influential environment in which people learn to develop their self-concepts, to interact with others, and to conduct appropriate communication. The importance of family dynamics and distinctions between insiders and outsiders are discussed in this section.

Family

Family provides an important context for the development of the Chinese self. It orients the self to others in terms of role obligations, status differences, and ingroup/outgroup distinctions. In the Chinese culture, family is the center of everything (e.g., Smith, 1991; Tseng & Wu, 1985; Whyte, 1991). Although the structure of the traditional extended family has continued to decline in Taiwan, Hong Kong, and many places in China, the importance of family in many aspects of a person's life still remains. Family as the prototype of Chinese social organizations has significance in the study of family relationships in particular and interpersonal relationships in general. The rules and norms that guide family relationships tend to hold true in a larger social context.

Family is viewed as the foundation of a society (Whyte, 1991). Its impact on the Chinese culture is demonstrated clearly in a passage from the *Great Learning,* one of the "Four Books" of Confucian teaching:

> By inquiring into all things, understanding is made complete; with complete understanding, thought is made sincere; when thought is sincere, the mind is as it should be; when the mind is as it should be, the individual is morally cultivated; when the individual is morally cultivated, the family is well regulated; when the family is well regulated, the state is properly governed; and when the state is properly governed, the world is at peace. (Whyte, 1991, p. 297)

To the Chinese, family is both a home and a community. Family serves as the primary and ongoing unit of socialization of each person. It is in the family that one acquires various skills, such as relating to and communicating with others. To illustrate, when friends become very close, Chinese say they're like members of the family (*peng you ru jia ren* 朋友如家人). Another example involves the adoption of such kinship forms of address as uncle, aunt, brother, and sister in one's social relations; kinship terms are utilized to serve as guidance for appropriate interpersonal interaction. Thus principles of friendship development in a larger social context are derived from those in the family. In the meantime, the Chinese self also has an obligation to the family. Chinese children are taught to remember themselves as members of the family and to remember that what they do, good or bad, will affect the family (Chiu, 1984).

Family as the center of everything also has its limitations. Cheng (1990) argues that the Five Cardinal Relationships place too much emphasis on family and one-on-one relationships (e.g., sister and brother, mother and daughter, father and son), and thus fail to address the broader aspect of human relationship, such as that between a person and the community at large. Liang (1936; *Liang Qi Chao* 梁启超 was a prominent thinker in modern Chinese history) attributed a person's lack of "civic morality" (*gong de* 公德) and sense of obligation to society to the Confucian ethic. Examples to support this contention are not uncommon in the Chinese culture. For instance, the Chinese are most likely to put family and one-on-one relationships before group or society. The charity patterns of the Chinese tend to center around kinship lines rather than the general public. Stories are told about wealthy relatives helping extended families residing all over the world, but little, if any, support is given to the local community.

Zi Ji Ren 自己人 (Insider)
Versus *Wai Ren* (Outsider)

Chinese make clear distinctions between insiders and outsiders, and this distinction exists on all levels of interpersonal interactions. As defined by Gu (1990), insiders consist of people from two categories: automatic and selected. Automatic insiders include one's parents, siblings, relatives, colleagues, and classmates, whereas selected ones are special relations that one has developed over time at work or elsewhere. For example, a person is considered an insider at work after he or she has developed a special relationship by helping each other and sharing information with the other. The five common criteria of an insider are nice, trustworthy, caring, helpful, and empathetic (Gu, 1990).

The distinction between an insider and an outsider provides specific rules of interaction in Chinese interpersonal relationships. Insiders often are treated differently from outsiders (Gu, 1990) and a person with insider status often enjoys privileges and special treatment beyond an outsider's comprehension. To illustrate, a Chinese person may go beyond his or her means to help an insider, but an outsider has to follow the rules. The same principle pertains to other collectivistic cultures in which members make clear distinctions between in-groups and outgroups and apply different standards to ingroups (Hofstede, 1980; Triandis, 1988). The insider-outsider distinction also involves moral implications. In the Chinese culture, moral judgments are not only cognitively but affectively based. According to Hwang (1990), moral standards tend to vary from one relationship to another.

Family-centered "insider" relationships have two important implications for relationship development with strangers (i.e., outsiders). First, as King and Bond (1985) argue, the importance of family and the sense of dependency built up in the Chinese family system make it difficult to develop personal relationships with strangers. In the Chinese culture, the transformation from a *wai ren* (outsider) to a *zi ji ren* (insider) involves an arduous and time-consuming process, because personal relationships often take a long time to develop. After relationships have been developed, however, they tend to stay very solid. As a result, in order to overcome the inherent difficulty in relationship development, intermediaries are widely used for social relational construction (King & Bond, 1985). Second, the Chinese and other collectivistic cultures tend to be particularistic in their utilization of value standards toward ingroups and outgroups (Hofstede, 1980; Triandis, 1988). That is, members of ingroups and outgroups are granted different value standards. This particularistic principle of interpersonal relationships hinders interactions with outsiders because value standards applied to ingroups may not be readily adapted to outgroups, and most Chinese do not feel knowledgeable about dealing with outsiders.

Hierarchy and Role Relationships

The notion of hierarchy permeates every aspect of Chinese society (Bond & Hwang, 1986; Taylor, 1989); thus, it is central to an investigation of Chinese interpersonal relationships. In a hierarchical structure, each person is presumed to have a fixed role in society and to enact that role accordingly. In addition, statuses are specified clearly and behaviors are guided by the principle of *li* 礼 (ritual propriety), that is, doing the proper things with the right people in the appropriate relationships (Bond & Hwang, 1986). Based on the Confucian paradigm, the most important relationships in the Chinese culture involve the Five Cardinal (*Wu Lun* 五伦) Relationships, which are ordered by the rule of hierarchy. The Five Cardinal Relationships are those between ruler and subject, father and son, husband and wife, elder brother and younger brother, and between friends (Cheng, 1990). The appropriate role behaviors associated with people at the lower rank, such as subject, son, and wife, are those of obedience, respect, and submission (MacCormack, 1991).

The moral or social order in any culture, as Confucian belief notes, is maintained through the fundamental social roles played by parent and child as well as by husband and wife (MacCormack, 1991). In the Chinese culture, even the most intimate relationships, such as the relationship between husband and wife, convey a role-directed dimension. Ordering relationships by status and observing this order (*zun bei you xu* 尊卑有序), for example, is considered a very important Chinese value (Chinese Culture Connection, 1987). As Cheng (1990) argues, the role, not the self, determines the behavior in most East Asian cultures. Personal choices, therefore, are based on prescribed roles. This argument is supported by the observation that a Chinese person still identifies strongly with the nuclear family and work-unit (*dan wei* 单位) at the concrete level, and the nation and the state instead of the extended family at the abstract level (Sun, 1991).

A Chinese person's identity is therefore connected closely with the social role he or she plays. The Chinese social code is of "acting a human being" (*zuo ren* 做人), instead of "being" one (Sun, 1991, p. 20). A recent study shows that the Chinese report paying greater attention to social comparison information and others' status characteristics than do the English. The English, in contrast, report greater ability to modify their self-presentations, tendency to avoid public performances, sensitivity to others' expressive behavior, and self-monitoring than the Chinese (Gudykunst, Gao, & Franklyn-Stokes, 1996).

The importance of hierarchy and role relationships can be attributed to the other-orientation of the self in the Chinese culture. Differences in hierarchy and role relationships help position a person in relation to others and thereby provide guidance for him or her to function appropriately in society.

Specific Principles of
Interpersonal Relationships

The indigenous perspective on self and OTHER in connection with family, hierarchy, and role relationships provides a general framework for understanding and explaining Chinese personal relationships. This framework not only helps generate specific relational principles operating in various forms of relationships, but also offers a conceptual context in which these principles can be interpreted and understood. Given the limited space here, only three major relational principles will be examined. They include *gan qing* 感情 (feeling), *ren qing* 人情 (human feeling), and *bao* 报 (reciprocity), as well as *lian* 脸 and *mian* 面 (face and image, respectively). The indigenous concepts of *gan qing, ren qing* and *bao* as well as *lian* and *mian* play very important roles in the everyday life of the Chinese: They operate in the context of the self and OTHER perspective. The other-orientation accounts for how feeling is developed and nurtured, how reciprocity is utilized, as well as how face is managed in Chinese interpersonal relationships. The basis of Chinese personal relationships, *gan qing,* will be presented first. Then two major relational mechanisms, *ren qing/bao* and *lian/mian* will be discussed.

Gan Qing 感情: The Basis of Chinese Personal Relationships

Gan qing is an important relational concept that is congruent with the other-oriented self. The Chinese word *gan qing* does not correspond to the Western concept of "emotions" (Sun, 1991); rather, it symbolizes mutual good feelings, empathy, friendship and support, and love between two people with little emphasis on the sexual aspect. *Gan qing* can be cultivated and nurtured in a relational context by means of "mutual aid" (*hu xiang bang zhu* 互相帮助 and "mutual care" (*hu xiang guan xin* 互相关心). Although mutual aid and mutual care are found in personal relationships universally, the Chinese use them to establish good feelings and love between people as well as to affirm and symbolize relationships (Potter, 1988). Thus *gan qing,* as an emotional concept, conveys a sense of interdependency. For the Chinese, emotional love is mediated through helping and caring for one another; one expresses love by showing care for and helping the other. To illustrate, fixing someone's bicycle, helping someone learn a subject matter, and cooking someone dinner are common ways to initiate a personal relationship and to express love. In personal relationships, whether they be social, romantic, or marital relationships, "the [Chinese] expressive forms that validate the relationship are not enacted in an idiom of emotional love but in an idiom of work and mutual aid" (Potter, 1988, pp. 201-202). Potter (1988) continues, noting that "the West has used the capacity to love as the symbolic basis for social relationships; the Chinese have used the capacity to work" (p. 199). An account given by a Chinese husband regarding the basis of his marriage further demonstrates this approach:

> We were on the same team, and we met working together. In 1973, we began to have good feelings for one another. I helped her family, and she helped mine. I helped them to build a house, to weed their plots, and by taking them to the hospital when they were ill. When we were the right age, we registered the marriage. My wife's side did not ask for the little cakes the groom's family is supposed to contribute, but I gave them anyway. (Potter, 1988, p. 201)

Consequently, *pei yang gan qing* 培养感情 (to nurture feelings) becomes the basis for any type of relationship ranging from romantic to friendship (Sun, 1991).

Given that *gan qing* is achieved through helping and caring for one another, verbal expressions become less important. In the Chinese culture, the discussion of love is very subtle and indirect (Gao, Ting-Toomey, & Gudykunst, 1996; Potter, 1988). For many Chinese, it is almost embarrassing to say "I love you" (Yu & Gu, 1990). This lack of expressiveness of the Chinese is supported by research findings. North Americans, for example, report a greater degree of passion in romantic relationships than do their Chinese counterparts. Yet the Chinese and North Americans do not differ in their level of intimacy or commitment (Gao, 1993). As compared with people in other cultures, the Chinese are the least emotionally expressive, especially in matters regarding sex (Sun, 1991). The Chinese view love as an internal feeling that need not be expressed by words because actions have replaced words (Yu & Gu, 1990).

Observations in the everyday life of the Chinese further support this lack of expressiveness. Husband and wife, boyfriend and girlfriend, mother and daughter, father and son rarely hug or kiss one other in public or private settings. It often takes a long time for partners to develop intimacy in a romantic relationship. For the Chinese, it is not uncommon to ask a friend to go along on a date. Moreover, a Chinese is rarely seen to jump up and down, shout, and laugh upon receiving a piece of good news because, in the Chinese culture, control of emotional expressions is a sign of maturity.

The present analysis of *gan qing* as the basis of personal relationships affirms the importance of "other" in the development of the Chinese self. Attending and responding to others' needs and wishes appear to provide the foundation for a viable relationship. A relationship with *gan qing* is one that values mutuality and interdependence.

Ren Qing 人情 and *Bao* 报

Given that the Chinese self is relational in nature, smooth and harmonious interpersonal transactions become highly critical in a person's self-definition. *Ren qing* and *bao* represent two important dimensions of interpersonal transactions. The literal translation of *ren qing* is "human feeling." *Ren qing,* however, involves three layers of meanings: feelings between people, a person's natural inclinations, and interpersonal resources (Yang, 1990b). According to Yang (1990b), *ren qing* as interpersonal resources functions as an important mechanism in regulating Chinese personal relationships. A person can give and take *ren qing* as interpersonal resources. Once *ren qing* is presented, one immediately becomes indebted. This give-and-take helps build a relational bond among people. *Ren qing* also possesses both expressive and instrumental functions (Zhu, 1990). That is, *ren qing* can be used to express sincere feelings one has toward others, and at the same time it can be used as "social investments" for personal gains.

The Chinese word *bao* as a verb has multiple meanings ranging from "to report," "to respond," "to repay," to "to retaliate," and "to retribute" (Yang, 1957). In the Chinese culture, the relational principle of *bao* is very important and it is other-centered. Wen (1990) notes that *bao* takes two forms: The rational *bao* is native to the Chinese, and the irrational *bao* or fatalism originated in the Indian culture. The principle of *bao* covers many relational spheres. In modern Chinese societies, as Yang (1990a) contends, *bao* is less collectively oriented. That is, one does not need to pay back the debts one's parents or grandparents owed. One is only responsible for paying back one's own debt. The investment value of *bao* also is decreasing. *Bao* is considered a relational bond, and expectations of return are not as high. In addition, the obligation to reciprocate is not as strong but is determined by the individual. Finally, the Chinese fatalistic belief is declining. Although the Chinese concept of *bao* is becoming more individually oriented, its impact on personal relationships is still far-reaching (Yang, 1990a). The relational boundaries by which the self is surrounded involve a constant need for reciprocation.

In the Chinese culture *ren qing* coupled with *bao* operate in various forms of interpersonal transactions. *Ren qing* and *bao* are often used interchangeably. According to Y. Wang (1990), *ren qing* is the way of managing Chinese interpersonal relationships. The notion of *ren qing,* however, is based on the moral code of *bao* (e.g., Hsu, 1971; Yang, 1957). A person who understands *ren qing (dong ren qing* 懂人情) knows how to reciprocate (*bao*). Reciprocation of greetings, favors, and gifts (*li shang wang lai* 礼上往来) is perceived as a very important relational principle in the Chinese culture (Chinese Culture Connection, 1987). Moreover, a person who is indebted to *ren qing (qian ren qing* 欠人情) needs to pay back (*hu bao* 回报). A well-known Chinese saying, "You honor me a foot, and I will in return honor you ten feet" (*ni jing wo yi chi, wo jing ni yi zhang* 你敬我一尺, 我敬你一丈), attests to this principle of reciprocity.

In social and personal interactions, a Chinese becomes vulnerable or at least feels uneasy to be indebted to someone, and an immediate return is called for to achieve balance in the relationship. To illustrate, if one were given a gift, one would immediately be in a double-bind situation; rejecting the gift would be rude and disruptive to the harmony of the relationship, but accepting it would put one in a no "no" situation (i.e., unable to decline any request for a favor). If one fails to reciprocate, one is perceived as *mei you liang xin* 没有良心 (heartless). The code of reciprocity applies to all types of relationships. It is the basic principle of being a person. Personal accounts such as "xxx helped me and my family then. We'll do whatever to help xxx now"; "How could you walk away from someone who has been so good to you?" demonstrate the importance of reciprocity in Chinese personal relationships. One also hears that so and so is not a person anymore because the heart is not there.

Research findings also provide support for the intricate interchange between *ren qing* and *bao*. In a recent study in Taiwan, the concepts of *ren qing* and *bao* are significant in the informants' accounts of their personal relationships (Chang, 1992). The study further indicates that the indebtedness a person feels tends to differ on the basis of the scope of *ren qing* (e.g., big or small) and the nature of a relationship (e.g., expressive, instrumental, or expressive and instrumental). For instance, if a relationship is instrumentally based, one would not take on the burden of indebtedness but reciprocate in the form of a business transaction. A return also is carefully measured to be proportionate to *ren qing* owed (Chang, 1992). The value of one's return of a job offer hence should outweigh that of a dinner invitation.

For the Chinese, the basic virtue of *xiao* 孝 (filial piety) also finds its justification in the concept of *bao* (Yang, 1957). According to Sun (1991),

> in [the] Chinese culture, a person is motivated to serve and make sacrifices by means of [a] sense of indebtedness. The principle is that a person is already in debit [*sic*] before he [or she] is born; he or she owes a debt to the parents who conceive them, and who will raise them in the future. Indeed, paying back the benevolence of the parents becomes the prototype for all the reciprocal transactions in society. (p. 35)

The importance of *xiao* (filial piety), a special form of *bao*, is perceived to be not incompatible with the "modern" life. Results of recent studies in Hong Kong report that 85% of the respondents want a law to force people to care for elderly parents; 77% would voluntarily and happily support their parents (Wong & Stewart, 1990). In mainland China, Article 49 of the Constitution states, "Parents have the duty to rear and educate their minor children." "Children who have come of age have the duty to support and assist their parents" (cited in Wong & Stewart, 1990, p. 530). Consequently, it is not inconceivable for a Chinese person to feel indebted to parents, family, and friends, as well as to society. The feeling of indebtedness serves as a control mechanism in regulating a Chinese person's behavior.

The specific principles of *bao* are further delineated in Hwang's (1987) model of face and favor in Chinese society. Hwang conceptualizes principles of interpersonal transactions in the context of the petitioner and the resource allocator. The roles of the petitioner and the resource allocator are enacted upon rules unique in each of the three different resource distribution contexts: expressive tie, mixed tie, and instrumental tie (Hwang, 1987). Both the expressive and mixed ties appear to be governed by the relational mechanism of *bao* (reciprocation); the instrumental tie, however, is impersonal in nature and is based on the equity rule.

According to Hwang (1987), relationships among family members are considered as the most important expressive tie. The need rule applies to family members and dictates parents' responsibility in raising children and children's responsibility in taking care of parents in their elder years. Reciprocation in this relational context is accomplished through a specific form of *bao*—filial piety. The mixed tie is outside a person's immediate family; it is considered not as strong as the expressive tie. *Guan xi* 关系 (connection) is essential to the *ren qing* rule in this relational context. The establishment of connections in mixed tie relationships is regulated through strategies of reciprocation such as *ren qing* (e.g., doing favors) and *mian zi* (e.g., giving face).

In short, managing and negotiating relationships with others are truly important in the Chinese self-construal. The complex processes of relational exchanges and negotiations in the Chinese culture focus on how people position themselves in relation to others. A Chinese person is constantly reminded of the interdependent nature of the self through exercises of *ren qing, bao,* and a sense of indebtedness.

Lian 脸 (Face) and *Mian Zi* 面子 (Image)

The concept of *lian* (face) or *mian zi* (image) is not unique to the Chinese culture (e.g., Brown & Levinson, 1978; Goffman, 1955; Ho, 1976; Hu, 1944; Ting-Toomey, 1988). The definition and form of presentation of face or image, however, are influenced by premises of a particular culture. As Ting-Toomey (1988) indicates, facework is a culturally grounded concept that needs to be examined in a cultural context.

In the Chinese culture, face is conceptualized in two ways: as *lian* (face) and as *mian* or *mian zi* (image). Hu (1944) defines *lian* as something that "represents the confidence of society in the integrity of ego's moral character, the loss of which makes it impossible for him [or her] to function properly within the community" (p. 45). *Lian*, he notes, "is both a social sanction for enforcing moral standards and an internalized sanction" (p. 45). *Mian* or *mian zi*, however, "stands for the kind of prestige that is emphasized in [the United States]: a reputation achieved through getting on in life, through success and ostentation" (Hu, 1944, p. 45). In other words, *mian* concerns the projection and the claiming of public image (Ting-Toomey, 1988).

In the current literature, the concepts of *lian* and *mian* have been used interchangeably. Even though *lian* and *mian* convey similar messages in some communication contexts in the Chinese culture, they evoke very different meanings in others (Gao, 1994). For instance, the expression *bu yao lian* 不要脸 (no face need) is a specific and direct condemnation of one's personal integrity and moral character, which often has a very negative connotation in the Chinese culture. *Bu yao mian zi* 不要面子 (no image need), however, suggests one's lack of consideration for public image, which can be interpreted as being "down to earth." Areas of differences as such are potentially rich for further exploration.

Both *lian* and *mian zi* are central to the Chinese self-concept and relational development. In the Chinese culture, as Yu and Gu (1990) argue, *mian zi* and self-esteem are mixed together. *Ren yao lian; shu yao pi* 人要脸, 树要皮 (a person needs face like a tree needs bark) is an expression commonly used in the Chinese discourse. A person's self-esteem often is formed on the basis of others' remarks. If others' remarks are positive, one's self-esteem is boosted and, consequently, one has face (Yu & Gu, 1990). As Ting-Toomey (1988) asserts, members of collectivistic cultures are oriented to other-face concern.

Furthermore, one's need for face has several important implications for the everyday life of the Chinese. First, engaging in *appropriate* behavior is of concern to most Chinese because inappropriate behavior often results in others' negative remarks and thus brings a loss of face to the person (Gao, 1994). "Face need," therefore, serves to regulate a person's behavior. To illustrate, if one initiates a relationship, then terminating it becomes a face-threatening act for the initiator. The concern for face influences not only relationship initiation, but also its development and deterioration. The importance of "face need" also is supported by empirical research. Smith (1991), for example, notes that Chinese families in modern Taiwan constantly evaluate their behaviors because public ridicule in child-rearing practices, in husband-wife relationships, and in caring for the elderly can provoke a loss of face in the family.

Second, one's concern for face governs what to disclose and not to disclose in personal relationships. Clear boundaries of self-disclosure exist in the Chinese culture, as demonstrated in the expression, *jia chou bu ke wai yang* 家丑不可外扬 (family disgrace should not be revealed to the outsider). To avoid the threat of losing face, the Chinese will not reveal their personal or family disgrace to others. Incidents of misbehavior or wrongdoing often are concealed. Engaging in appropriate self-disclosure helps protect the face of the person and the family involved. As a result, one rarely hears a Chinese person discuss topics such as family dysfunction, poor relationships between parents, and sibling conflicts. Various face-saving strategies thus operate in Chinese personal relationships to protect the need for face.

Finally, "face need" is not only a personal concern but, more important, a collective concern (King & Bond, 1985). As King and Myers (1977) indicate, face is more a concern to the family than to the person and face-losing or face-gaining acts reflect both on persons themselves and on their families. To illustrate, one's failure threatens the face of the family; one's accomplishment, however, gains face for the family. Chinese parents often teach their children to behave appropriately by stating *bie diu zan jia de lian* 别丢咱家的脸 (don't make our family lose face). Facework management hence is essential to various aspects of personal and interpersonal relationship development in the Chinese culture.

Implications for Communication

The primary functions of communication in the Chinese culture are to maintain existing relationships among individuals, to reinforce role and status differences, and to preserve harmony within the group (Gao et al., 1996). The unique characteristics of Chinese interpersonal relationships delineated in this chapter have significant influence on communication processes. To illustrate, the concern for public image helps explain the discrepancy between public and private conversations. In the Chinese culture, public conversations are ritualized to avoid face-threatening situations; private conversations, in contrast, are substantive. Compatible with this line of reasoning, *yi lun* 议论 (making remarks behind one's back, or gossip) becomes an important communicative activity because it is the least face-threatening (Yu & Gu, 1990). As Yu and Gu indicate, the Chinese utilize the forum of *yi lun* to satisfy their curiosity about others' privacy and the need to speak their true feelings.

The substantial influence of family also has significant consequences in a Chinese person's relational communication. The tendency to rely on family and familiar surroundings makes it difficult for a Chinese to interact with strangers (Yu, 1990). Interactions with strangers often are initiated by a third person (an intermediary) who is known to both parties. Intermediaries both formal and informal play a very important role in Chinese personal relationships.

The hierarchical system provides the basis for nonsymmetric communication. That is, a person at a lower status is to complement communication of a person at a higher status. In Chinese parental education, a good child is one who shows an ability to listen (*ting hua* 听话) but never talks back (*bu ding zui* 不顶嘴). G. Wang (1990) argues that the younger generation's total withdrawal strategy is the solution to intergeneration conflicts in the Chinese culture. As a result, children pay a big price to preserve harmony in the family. This pattern of communication also applies to other types of relationships. A good employee, for instance, is one who shows an ability to listen (*ting hua*), follows orders, and is willing to meet others' expectations and accept others' criticism (Zhuang, 1990).

Conclusion

This chapter has responded to the need for an integrated approach to the study of Chinese personal relationships. The complexities involved in Chinese personal relationships have been examined in the framework of self and OTHER. By utilizing and combining indigenous concepts and perspectives, it is proposed that Chinese personal relationships are situated in an other-oriented, hierarchical, and role-directed context. For the Chinese, family is where personal relationships originate and end. Family relationships are thus the prototype for all social relationships. *Gan qing, ren qing,* and *bao,* as well as *mian zi,* are identified as important guiding principles of Chinese personal relationships. The conceptualizations presented in this chapter are readily available for understanding and explaining complex processes of interpersonal interactions in the Chinese culture. This chapter echoes a call for a "native" or "indigenous" approach to the study of interpersonal relationships (Baxter, 1992). It symbolizes a beginning of a departure from a Eurocentric approach in the field of communication.

This chapter also has responded to the need for broadening the scope of individualism and collectivism. Although the individualism-versus-collectivism framework is useful in understanding and explaining cultural similarities and differences (e.g., Gudykunst & Ting-Toomey, 1988; Hofstede, 1980; Triandis, 1988), the idiosyncrasies of each culture within each general characterization also needs consideration. The concepts and perspectives isolated in this chapter have not only reaffirmed the collective orientation of the Chinese, but also have suggested ways in which the Chinese differ from others.

Before concluding, a number of theoretical and research issues that surround an indigenous approach to the study of interpersonal relationships needs to be addressed. First, this chapter only attempts to propose working assumptions regarding Chinese personal relationships. The assumptions put forth need to be tested and verified empirically in future studies. Second, even though examples have been provided in the text to support various arguments, a systematic study is needed to enhance our understanding of processes of Chinese interpersonal relationships. Third, the relational principles isolated in this chapter are neither exclusive nor exhaustive. *Yuan* 緣 (destined affinity), *guan xi* (connections), and many other relational concepts, for example, await further investigation. Future theorizing needs to broaden the relational boundaries. Finally, research on Chinese interpersonal relationships will benefit tremendously from methods such as participant observation and in-depth interviews. Rich descriptions gained from those methods will help theorize Chinese personal relationships.

To conclude, the present analysis of Chinese relational framework of other-orientation, role-directedness, and hierarchy will provide a fertile ground for analyzing personal relationships in the Chinese culture. Our understanding of the relationships among various relational principles can be broadened when the influences of other, role, and hierarchy are examined.

Note

1. The indigenous Chinese concepts and names in this chapter are transliterated using the *pin-yin* 拼音 system of romanization. To illustrate, *bao* under the *pin-yin* system is equivalent to *pao* under the Wade-Giles system.

References

Baxter, L. A. (1992). Interpersonal communication as dialogue: A response to the "social approaches" forum. *Communication Theory, 2,* 330-337.

Bond, M. H., & Hwang, K. K. (1986). The social psychology of Chinese people. In M. H. Bond (Ed.), *The psychology of the Chinese people* (pp. 213-266). Oxford, UK: Oxford University Press.

Bond, M. H., Leung, K., & Wan, K. C. (1982). The social impact of self-effacing attributions: The Chinese case. *Journal of Social Psychology, 118,* 157-166.

Brown, P., & Levinson, S. (1978). Universals in language usage: Politeness phenomenon. In E. Goody (Ed.), *Questions and politeness: Strategies in social interaction* (pp. 56-289). New York: Cambridge University Press.

Chang, H. C. (1992, May). *The concepts of Pao and human emotional debt in Chinese interpersonal relationships and communication.* Paper presented at the Annual International Communication Association Convention, Miami, FL.

Cheng, S. K. (1990). Understanding the culture and behavior of East Asians—A Confucian perspective. *Australian and New Zealand Journal of Psychiatry, 24,* 510-515.

Chinese Culture Connection. (1987). Chinese values and the search for culture-free dimensions of culture. *Journal of Cross-Cultural Psychology, 18,* 143-164.

Chiu, M. M. (1984). *The Tao of Chinese religion.* New York: University Press of America.

Chu, G. C. (1985). The changing concept of self in contemporary China. In A. J. Marsella, G. DeVos, & F. L. K. Hsu (Eds.), *Culture and self: Asian and Western perspectives* (pp. 252-277). New York: Tavistock.

Devos, G., & Abbot, K. A. (1966). *The Chinese family in San Francisco.* Unpublished master's thesis, University of California, Berkeley.

Dien, D. S.-F. (1983). Big me and little me: A Chinese perspective on self. *Psychiatry, 46,* 281-286.

Fairbank, J. K. (1991). The old order. In R. F. Dernberger, K. J. DeWoskin, J. M. Goldstein, R. Murphey, & M. K. Whyte (Eds.), *The Chinese* (pp. 31-37). Ann Arbor: University of Michigan, Center for Chinese Studies.

Gao, G. (1993, May). *A test of the triangular theory of love in Chinese and American romantic relationships.* Paper presented at the Annual International Communication Association Convention, Washington, D.C.

Gao, G. (1994). *An initial analysis of the effects of face and concern for "other" in Chinese interpersonal communication.* Manuscript in preparation.

Gao, G., Ting-Toomey, S., & Gudykunst, W. B. (1996). Chinese communication processes. In M. H. Bond (Ed.), *Handbook of Chinese psychology* (pp. 280-293). Hong Kong: Oxford University Press.

Goffman, E. (1955). On face-work: An analysis of ritual elements in social interaction. *Psychiatry: Journal of the Study of International Processes, 18,* 213-231.

Gu, Y. J. (1990). Nei wai you bie, qi ke bu fen: "Zi ji ren" he "wai ren" de ren ji yun dong [How could you not make a distinction between an insider and an outsider?]. In *Zhong guo ren de xing li: Vol. 3. Zhong guo ren de mian ju xing ge: Ren qing yu mian zi* (pp. 28-39). Taipei, Taiwan: Zhang Lao Shi Chu Ban She.

Gudykunst, W. B., Gao, G., & Franklyn-Stokes, A. (1996). *Self-monitoring in China and England.* In J. Pandy, D. Sinha, & D. P. S. Bhawuk (Eds.), *Asian contributions to cross-cultural psychology* (pp. 255-267). New Delhi: Sage.

Gudykunst, W. B., & Ting-Toomey, S. (1988). *Culture and interpersonal communication*. Newbury Park, CA: Sage.

Ho, D. Y. F. (1976). On the concept of face. *American Journal of Sociology, 81,* 867-884.

Hofstede, G. (1980). *Culture's consequences: International differences in work-related values*. Beverly Hills, CA: Sage.

Hsu, F. L. K. (1971). Eros, affect, and pao. In F. L. K. Hsu (Ed.), *Kinship and culture* (pp. 439-75). Chicago: University of Chicago Press.

Hu, H. C. (1944). The Chinese concepts of "face." *American Anthropologist, 46,* 45-64.

Hwang, K. K. (1987). Face and favor: The Chinese power game. *American Journal of Sociology, 92,* 944-974.

Hwang, K. K. (1990). Gui fan xing guan xi he gong ju xing guan xi [Regulative and instrumental relations]. In *Zhong guo ren de xing li: Vol. 8. Zhong guo ren de shi jian you xi: Ren qing yu shi gu* (pp. 57-63). Taipei, Taiwan: Zhang Lao Shi Chu Ban She.

King, A. Y., & Bond, M. H. (1985). The Confucian paradigm of man: A sociological view. In W. S. Tseng & D. H. Wu (Eds.), *Chinese culture and mental health* (pp. 29-45). Orlando, FL: Academic Press.

King, A. Y., & Myers, J. T. (1977). *Shame as an incomplete conception of Chinese culture: A study of face* (Occasional paper). Social Research Center, The Chinese University of Hong Kong.

Liang, C. C. (1936). *Yin Ping Shih Wen Chi* (Collected works of Liang Chi Chao). Tai Pei, Taiwan: Culture Books.

MacCormack, G. (1991). Cultural values in traditional Chinese law. *Chinese Culture, 32*(4), 1-11.

Markus, H. R., & Kitayama, S. (1991). Culture and the self: Implications for cognition, emotion, motivation. *Psychological Review, 98,* 224-253.

Olsen, M. (1978). *The process of social organization* (2nd ed.). New York: Holt, Rinehart & Winston.

Potter, S. H. (1988). The cultural construction of emotion in rural Chinese social life. *Ethos, 16,* 181-208.

Smith, D. C. (1991). Children of China: An inquiry into the relationship between Chinese family life and academic achievement in modern Taiwan. *Asian Culture Quarterly, 14*(1), 1-29.

Stipek, D., Weiner, B., & Li, K. (1989). Testing some attribution-emotion relations in the People's Republic of China. *Journal of Personality and Social Psychology, 56,* 109-116.

Sue, D. W., & Sue, S. (1973). Understanding Asian Americans: The neglected minority, an overview. *Personnel and Guidance Journal, 51,* 387-389.

Sun, L. K. (1991). Contemporary Chinese culture: Structure and emotionality. *The Australian Journal of Chinese Affairs, 26,* 1-42.

Taylor, R. (1989). Chinese hierarchy in comparative perspectives. *The Journal of Asian Studies, 48,* 490-511.

Ting-Toomey, S. (1988). Intercultural conflict styles: A face-negotiation theory. In Y. Y. Kim & W. B. Gudykunst (Eds.), *Theories in intercultural communication* (pp. 213-235). Newbury Park, CA: Sage.

Triandis, H (1988). Collectivism vs. individualism: A reconceptualization of a basic concept in cross-cultural psychology. In C. Bagley & G. Verma (Eds.), *Cross-cultural studies of personality, attitudes, and cognition* (pp. 60-95). London: Macmillan.

Tseng, W. S., & Wu, D. Y. (Eds.). (1985). *Chinese culture and mental health*. Orlando, FL: Academic Press.

Wang, B. (1990). Lao Zi and the Xia culture. *Chinese Studies in Philosophy, 21*(4), 34-69.

Wang, G. H. (1990). Er sun zi you er sun fu: Zhong guo ren de dai jian guan xi [Sons and grandsons have their happiness]. In *Zhong guo ren de xin li: Vol. 3. Zhong guo ren de mian ju xing ge: Ren qing yu mian zi* (pp. 14-27). Taipei, Taiwan: Zhang Lao Shi Chu Ban She.

Wang, Y. L. (1990). Ren qing sheng suo, mian zi gong fu: Zhong guo ren de quan mou zhi dao [Ren qing and mian zi]. In *Zhong guo ren de xin li: Vol. 3. Zhong guo ren de mian ju xing ge: Ren qing yu mian zi* (pp. 40-52). Taipei, Taiwan: Zhang Lao Shi Chu Ban She.

Wen, C. Y. (1990). Bao de die ti liu bian [Bao and its turns/changes]. In *Zhong guo ren de xing li: Vol. 8. Zhong guo ren de shi jian you xi: Ren qing yu shi gu* (pp. 14-19). Taipei, Taiwan: Zhang Lao Shi Chu Ban She.

White, W. G., & Chan, E. (1983). A comparison of self-concept scores of Chinese and white graduate students and professionals. *Journal of Non-White Concerns, 11,* 138-141.

Whyte, M. K. (1991). Introduction. In R. F. Dernberger, K. J. DeWoskin, J. M. Goldstein, R. Murphey, & M. K. Whyte (Eds.), *The Chinese* (pp. 295-313). Ann Arbor: University of Michigan, Center for Chinese Studies.

Wong, G., & Stewart, S. (1990). Confucian family values: Lessons for the West. *The World & I, 5,* 523-535.

Yang, K. S. (1981). Social orientation and individual modernity among Chinese students in Taiwan. *Journal of Social Psychology, 113,* 159-170.

Yang, K. S. (1990a). Bao de gong neng yu bian qian [Bao's functions and changes]. In *Zhong guo ren de xing li: Vol. 8. Zhong guo ren de shi jian you xi: Ren qing yu shi gu* (pp. 28-34). Taipei, Taiwan: Zhang Lao Shi Chu Ban She.

Yang, K. S. (1990b). Xian dai she hui zhong de "Ren qing" [Ren qing in modern society]. In *Zhong guo ren de xing li: Vol. 8. Zhong guo ren de shi jian you xi: Ren qing yu shi gu* (pp. 101-104). Taipei, Taiwan: Zhang Lao Shi Chu Ban She.

Yang, L. S. (1957). The concept of *pao* as a basis for social relations in China. In J. K. Fairbank (Ed.), *Chinese thought and institutions* (pp. 291-309). Chicago: University of Chicago Press.

Yu, D. H. (1990). Zhong guo ren xin di de gu shi [The hidden stories of Chinese]. In *Zhong guo ren de xin li: Vol. 3. Zhong guo ren de mian ju xing ge: Ren qing yu mian zi* (pp. 63-107). Taipei, Taiwan: Zhang Lao Shi Chu Ban She.

Yu, D. H., & Gu, B. L. (1990). Zhong guo ren de qing mian jiao lu [Chinese face concerns]. In *Zhong guo ren de xin li: Vol. 3. Zhong guo ren de mian ju xing ge: Ren qing yu mian zi* (pp. 63-107). Taipei, Taiwan: Zhang Lao Shi Chu Ban She.

Zhu, R. L. (1990). Expressive and instrumental ren qing. In *The Chinese social game: Ren qing and shi gu* (Chinese Psychology Series), *8,* 120-127. Taipei, Taiwan: Professor Zhang Press. (In Chinese)

Zhuang, H. Q. (1990). Zhan sheng zi ji nei xin de di ren [Defeating the internal enemy]. In *Zhong guo ren de xin li: Vol. 3. Zhong guo ren de mian ju xing ge: Ren qing yu mian zi* (pp. 109-119). Taipei, Taiwan: Zhang Lao Shi Chu Ban She.

CHAPTER

5

Communication in
Personal Relationships in Japan

Tsukasa Nishida

Communication theories from other countries, mainly from the United States, have had a profound influence on the way communication is studied in Japan.[1] There have been many tests, criticisms, and evaluations of these theories (e.g., Nakanishi, 1986; Nishida, 1990; Yamaguchi, 1984). Conversely, there has been communication-oriented research in Japan that has paid little attention to these North American theories. This has resulted in arguments regarding general views about nature, human relations, and communication, and the unique characteristics of Japanese communication patterns.[2]

It is not an easy task to describe communication behaviors across cultures without biases such as cultural ethnocentrism. Even the most careful cultural comparisons or measuring scales can be culturally biased and thus give a distorted, one-sided description of the communication behaviors being observed. Therefore, in order to understand the communication behaviors of any culture, it is important to examine them in light of communication theories that have developed within the culture itself.

In this chapter I will review research that reflects the development of communication theories by Japanese researchers, both those that have been influenced by North American communication theories and those that have been developed independently of the work being done outside of Japan. My hope is that this will be a step toward the development of non-ethnocentric theories of communication in interpersonal relationships across cultures.

The North American Influence on Japanese Communication Studies

Professional journals and academic texts are filled with studies proposing various theories of communication. In this section, I will review some representative communication theories used by Japanese scholars in the study of personal relationships.

Takeuchi's (1973) model of the communication process utilizes components found in American models from the 1950s and 1960s, beginning with Shannon and Weaver (1949). According to Takeuchi, Person A functions both as receiver (decoding) and as sender (coding), and sends messages through a channel to Person B. Takeuchi's model includes self-feedback that arises within communicators. He called this a model of the social communication process. He pointed out that his model cannot be symmetrical in actual communication because the message flow is uneven, and because individual differences exist in encoding and decoding ability. Moreover, just as "noise" exists in the mathematical model, there will be interfering elements in this model of communication.

More recently, Takeuchi (1990) classified social communication circuits according to three variables. These take into account whether communication circuits are direct or transmitted, public or personal, and, finally, whether they are one-way or two-way. Combining these three kinds of circuits, he grouped communication into eight types: The first is direct, public, one-way communication, such as verbal messages from a boss to a subordinate. The second type is direct, public, two-way communication, as in discussions in meetings. The third, direct, personal, and one-way, is how Takeuchi characterizes communication such as rumors and old men's storytelling. The fourth, direct, personal, two-way communication, is found in conversations about club activities and about shared memories. The fifth type is indirect, public, and one-way, and can be found in mass communication and written messages of orders or directions. The sixth is indirect, public, and two-way, as in diplomatic statements and trade contracts. The seventh is indirect, personal, and one-way, such as spy reports. And the eighth style is indirect, personal, two-way communication, found in telephone conversations, and in private or circle publications. In addition, each type of communication is further defined according to three dimensions: face-to-face, personal, and interactive.

The development of models of the communication process has been one of the important practical guides in the study of communication in the United States. Bormann (1980) states that "communication models are thus one aspect of an extensive effort to depict human behavior by graphing, plotting, or diagraming the essential elements and fitting them into a structure" (p. 30). Accordingly, some Japanese researchers take the same stand. For example, Akutsu (1976) first quoted the Shannon and Weaver (1949) model, as well as one of Schramm's (1954) models that emphasizes the importance of the change of symbols, that is, the process of encoding and decoding. In addition, he discussed Osgood's (1952) model and Berlo's (1960) SMCR model. He also included a mention of Takeuchi's model. According to Akutsu, because Takeuchi's model is based on the above-mentioned U.S. models, it can be generalized to accommodate information processing and communication. This model, therefore, should apply not only to communication between individuals but also between groups and organizations. Senders and receivers can be individuals or groups. Moreover, the model is viewed as a circuit based on the interaction of message exchange. According to Takeuchi (1990), the model of communication process is open and thus forms social communication networks. This flexibility makes this model unique as a social communication model. Akutsu cautions, however, that such systems are not specified and might therefore create problems regarding levels of social systems.

Lastly, Akutsu (1976) introduced the role-based ABC model proposed by Wesley and MacLean (1957). Akutsu also discussed his own categories of communication. He suggested that communication can be classified according to levels of systems, functions of systems, characteristics of messages, and characteristics of channels. Commenting on Wesley and MacLean's model, Akutsu points out that individuals and social systems in the model are not clearly separated. Thus, according to Akutsu, the model attempts to explain communication phenomena solely by defining roles of interlocutors.

Because the study of mass communication was introduced to Japan prior to the study of human communication, it might be said that the latter has not flourished in Japan. In recent publications regarding communication, however, we find that the issues relating to human communication are covered, sometimes as chapters, or that entire chapters are devoted to the subject of human communication.

Pointing up the fact that communication studies are conducted in various fields, Akutsu (1976) introduced communication theories from North American psychological and sociological studies into Japan. From psychology he took up Hovland, Janis, and Kelley (1953) and Osgood (1952). In both lines of studies, however, persuasion is the theme and a view that one influences the other is very clear. From sociology the work of Cooley (1953), Schramm (1954), and Hartley and Hartley (1952) was also introduced by Akutsu. He reported that, in these studies, communication is discussed in the context of interactiveness, human relations, and commonality. Akutsu also referred to Takeuchi's study of information processing and social communication.

In the field of sociology, Tokyo University created its social psychology department in 1973. In 1984, a collection of research papers was published to celebrate its 10th anniversary (Mizuhara & Tsujimura, 1984). These research papers include both theoretical arguments and original studies such as surveys. Among them is a study of persuasive communication based on the data gathered by Hovland and others (Hovland et al., 1953), reported by Mizuhara (1984) and Yamaguchi (1984). Also included are a study of teacher-student communication (Furuhata, 1984); an image study (Iwao, 1984); a study of communication gaps and communication culture (Akuto, 1984); an innovation process study that tried to bridge sociology and psychology (Tsujimura, 1976); an investigation into the influence of political campaigns on TV (Tsujimura, 1979; Tsujimura & Inaki, 1977); a look at the influence of best-sellers (Tsujimura & Inaki, 1983); and a description of the communication gaps between Japan and Korea (Tsujimura & Kim, 1980; Tsujimura, Kim, & Ikuta, 1982).

Uncertainty reduction theory (Berger & Calabrese, 1975) and social penetration theory (Altman & Taylor, 1973) have been tested against Japanese culture by Gudykunst and Nishida (Gudykunst & Nishida, 1984, 1990; Nishida, 1992; Nishida & Gudykunst, 1986) over the past 7 years. The results of the cross-cultural research we have conducted are consistent with uncertainty reduction theory (Berger & Calabrese, 1975) and social penetration theory (Altman & Taylor, 1973). The cross-cultural similarities and differences that have emerged in our studies are compatible with Triandis's (1988) conceptualization of individualism-collectivism, Hofstede's (1980) dimensions of cultural variability, and Hall's (1976) low- to high-context continuum. Most of our findings are also compatible with research conducted by other scholars who have not theoretically explained the cultural differences observed in their studies (e.g., Barnlund, 1975, 1989). These results have been reported in major journals in the areas of communication and cross-cultural psychology (Gudykunst et al., 1992; Gudykunst & Nishida, 1983, 1984, 1986, 1989, 1990; Gudykunst, Nishida, & Chua, 1987; Gudykunst, Nishida, & Schmidt, 1989; Gudykunst, Yang, & Nishida, 1985, 1987; Gudykunst, Yoon, & Nishida, 1987).

During the 1970s, the study of communication, particularly of intercultural communication, attracted the attention of both students and the general public. The first large-scale Japan-U.S. Intercultural Communication Workshop was held in Nihonmatsu, Japan, in 1974. The Japan-U.S. Intercultural Communication Workshop was the result of a 2-year planning effort by a joint U.S. and Japanese steering committee. The workshop was cosponsored by The Intercultural Communication Network of the Regional Council for International Education in the United States and The International House of Japan, Inc. This workshop brought together scholars and practitioners from the two countries for an 8-day program (Gudykunst & Nishida, 1981).

As for publications, although most of them were comparative in nature, Barnlund's self-disclosure study (1975), Knapp's nonverbal communication (1979), and Condon's intercultural communication (Condon & Yousef, 1975) were translated into Japanese. In addition, books on communication in a business context and on culture shock were published in Japan at about the same time. In the 1980s, more books on intercultural communication, both Japanese originals and translations, appeared on the Japanese market (Kondo, 1981; Nishida, 1989a; Samovar, Porter, & Jain, 1983; Sitaram, 1985).

Nonverbal communication studies have also been conducted in Japan. Studies that have been well received in Japan include Hall's (1959, 1966, 1976, 1983) studies of distance, space, and high- and low-context communication or cultures; Birdwhistell's (1970) system of nonverbal postures; and Argyle's (1975) study of gestures and nonverbal messages. We also find Japanese studies based on these theories of nonverbal communication. For example, Inoue (1982) contends that the above mentioned studies are "scientific" in approach and that a humanistic approach based on rules and a historical perspective should be used in research on nonverbal communication. Tsujimura (1980) investigated walking speed across cultures and found that the people of Osaka were the fastest walkers. Mehrabian's work on implicit messages (1986) was also translated into Japanese. His framework for measuring implicit communication has attracted attention from scholars in Japan.

What all of these studies in the areas of communication theories, sociology, psychology, social psychology, and intercultural and nonverbal communication have in common is that they each evolved from the starting point of a theory that was originally put forward by North American scholars and then introduced into Japan. Because of this historical trend over the past 20 years, many concepts have been used to explain interpersonal communication under the assumption that they—as well as the conceptualization of communication they have been derived from—are universal. It is rather therefore natural that Japanese take this for granted. Whether or not such North American theories can apply to other cultural concepts, such as Japan, is not addressed in the theories themselves.

There are nevertheless some differences among the studies reported above. Relatively old theoretical arguments were introduced to Japan without determining, for example, whether they were valid across cultures. On the other hand, more recent research projects have clearly addressed this issue. Taking cultural factors into account in the discussion of development of communication theory is important and necessary.

It is safe to say that the study of intercultural and nonverbal communication as it has been introduced into Japan is comparative and descriptive in nature. For this reason, descriptions of intercultural and nonverbal communication tend to be partial and brief. Therefore, I must say that the Japanese study of nonverbal communication is quite limited and in its beginning stage.

In the next section, I will examine Japanese theories of communication that developed independently of the work being done outside of Japan.

The Japanese Perspectives

The Japanese communication studies covered in the previous section all rely on North American theoretical perspectives. Here I will examine work by Japanese scholars that reflects a uniquely Japanese cultural perspective. In this section, I will present Japanese views on the communication process as well as studies on Japanese attitudes toward nature, interpersonal relationships, communication, and communicative style.

Communication Process

Referring to communication models, Inoue (1982) argues that a two-person model functions only in the abstract. Human relations occur only when we assume the third person in a real sense. He suggests that in order to understand Japanese communication behaviors better, an appropriate model for the analysis of Japanese behaviors would be the three-person structure, including the *seken* (the world) as the third person.

Inoue (1982) defines the *seken* (the world) as a kind of reference group. Of course, the *seken* is not exactly a reference group in a strict sense. The concept of a reference group, however, helps to clarify the nature of the *seken*. Reference groups can be differentiated from other groups using the concepts of *uchi* (in) and *soto* (out). The innermost group will be the *miuchi* (family) group or the *nakamauchi* (friends) group, and the outermost group will be *tanin* or *yosonohito* (strangers). Thus, the Japanese use the *miuchi* and *tanin* reference groups as standards of behavior. Inoue argues that reference groups or *seken* should be included in communication models as they apply to Japanese.

Stewart (1971) points out three characteristics of American culture. First, North Americans tend to make twofold judgments. Second, of two possibilities, one is usually valued more than the other. Third, North Americans tend not to describe or judge something in terms of itself or in its own context. These thought patterns may influence North Americans' perception and may create problems in understanding Japanese culture.

A dichotomy often used to understand and compare cultures is individualism-collectivism. In defining the terms *individualism* and *collectivism,* many have argued over the meanings of "individualistic" and "collectivistic" culture. One view, commonly held in the United States, contends that individualistic cultures emphasize the goals of the individual, whereas collectivistic cultures stress group goals over individual goals. According to this view, individuals in individualistic cultures assume responsibility for themselves and their immediate family only. In collectivistic cultures, on the other hand, individuals belong to ingroups that look after them in exchange for the individuals' loyalty to the group (Hofstede, 1980).

Although this value orientation has been frequently postulated (Gudykunst & Nishida, 1986; Hofstede, 1980; Kluckhohn & Strodtbeck, 1961; Triandis, 1988; Yamaguchi, 1984), one problem with this dichotomy as it applies to Japan, according to some Japanese scholars, is its framework; another is the way in which collectivism has been defined.

First, in the dichotomy A (individualism) and Non-A (collectivism), A's understanding could be very accurate but Non-A's would not be if what Stewart (1971) stated is true. For instance, the North American preference for making twofold judgments is reflected in the well-received intercultural training method developed by Stewart (1966). The same structure is found in the *Bafa Bafa* simulation game (Shirts, 1973). The creation of this kind of training is based on the dichotomous categorization of cultures by which North Americans, according to Stewart (1971), feel comfortable understanding other cultures.

Second, although the terms *individualistic* and *collectivistic* may not be heavily value-laden in the United States, there has been some disagreement about this in Japan. Some Japanese (e.g, Hamaguchi, 1982) object to the use of the translation of the term *collectivism, zentai-shugi,* because it is often used in Japanese to refer to dictatorial political systems. Rather, they use terms like *relationalism (aidagara-shugi;* Kumon, 1982; Watsuji, 1934; Yamane, 1987) and *contextualism (kanjin-shugi;* Hamaguchi, 1982). In their interpretation, like individuals in individualistic society, members of a contextualistic society share *aidagara* (interpersonal context), valuing things between people, including relationships and situations.

The objections of these researchers, however, go beyond the problem of labeling. Hamaguchi (1982) contends that the concept of collectivistism does not help us to understand Japanese culture. For example, when we examine Japanese culture using the concept individualism, we will characterize it as nonindividualistic and conclude that it is a collectivistic culture. Yet what we are actually seeing is the inevitable result of the application of a framework that is valid only in the context of individualistic cultures. What is needed is a theoretical framework for understanding Japanese culture on its own terms.

Hamaguchi (1982) claims that such a uniquely Japanese view must be developed in order to explain Japanese culture properly. As the basis for such a new perspective, he proposes the adoption of the Japanese concept *kyodo-dantai-shugi* (corporativism) (Wagatsuma, 1982, calls this "joint autonomy"). According to Hamaguchi, Japanese culture is characterized by collective independence rather than individual independence within organizations. Collective independence does not conform to the dichotomy of individualism and collectivism. Rather, it places the independent individual within the organized group. Hamaguchi proposes this notion of collective independence as the starting point for beginning to understand Japanese society and culture. That is the basis upon which we have to construct a theory to explain Japanese human relations.

From a different angle, acceptance of the group model (e.g., Hamaguchi's approach) has led scholars to overlook the Japanese notion of "personhood" (Befu, 1980a, 1980b). Befu contends that the distinction between *tatemae* (the principle by which a person is bound outwardly) and *honne* (a person's "real" attitude) must be taken into consideration in explaining Japanese personhood.

He states that the group model (collectivism) can explain public matters, but not private matters (also in Araki, 1973). In addition, Befu suggests that Japanese interpersonal relationships can be explained from an exchange theory perspective. Social exchange theory, he maintains, has offered insight into individual and collective behavior in interpersonal relations. This theory could help to develop an integrated model of interpersonal relations in Japan.

Further, Hamaguchi (1982) insists that many evaluations of Japanese culture, such as Benedict's (1946) "culture of shame," Nakane's (1970) "vertical society," and Doi's (1973) "dependence," are all filtered through North American views and thus negatively evaluate the Japanese as "nonindependent" and "nonreasoning," and Japanese society as a "peculiar culture" and an "undeveloped society." He argues that neither of the Western-based characterizations—individualistic or collectivistic—apply to the Japanese situation. Wagatsuma (1982) points out that Doi and Nakane do not describe the Japanese and Japanese society objectively: rather, he characterizes their descriptions as both negative and critical. Wagatsuma emphasizes that Doi's and Nakane's descriptions are not objective because their arguments are not scientifically based. Wagatsuma goes on to argue that objective descriptions regarding Japanese behaviors and human relations are needed in order to characterize Japanese culture accurately.

Japanese Attitudes

The topics covered in this section involve Japanese attitudes toward nature, interpersonal relationships, communication, and communication style.

Attitudes Toward Nature. Regarding the attitude of Japanese toward nature, Matsumura (1984) points out that Japanese value harmonious relations with nature and with other people, and that this orientation is reflected in the way Japanese handle verbal and nonverbal communication. Matsumura contends that four attitudes characterize the Japanese orientation toward nature: (a) The Japanese believe that nature should be understood sensationally; (b) the Japanese identify themselves with nature (e.g., Doi's *amae*); (c) they believe that nature should be understood holistically; and (d) the Japanese are optimistic about nature. Matsumura contends that these attitudes apply to the Japanese approach to communication as well, and he therefore characterizes Japanese communication as harmonious.

Regarding Japanese holistic attitudes toward communication, Matsumura (1984) emphasizes that Japanese pay attention not only to verbal communication but also to nonverbal behaviors such as physical touching, interpersonal distance, posture, appearance, facial expressions, gestures, eye contact, the situation in which communication takes place, and the human relations in a given communicative situation. Because these elements of communication are also recognized in the United States, I assume that Matsumura suggested that these nonverbals play an important part in Japanese communication because their communication styles among Japanese, for instance, are not argumentative.

Being not argumentative is highly valued among Japanese. Because of a feeling of "oneness" among Japanese as a result of geographical factors and the placing of much confidence in nature, Japanese tend to reinforce existing information and to avoid new or conflicting messages. In addition, they are willing to abandon personal opinions when conflict arises. On the other hand, according to Matsumura (1984), there are risks in the Japanese style of communication. These are dysfunction in communication with outgroup members, failure to reach a true solution to a problem because disputes tend to be covered up rather than identified, and inhibition of the development of communication skills.

Attitudes Toward Interpersonal Relationships. According to Suzuki (1980), Japanese consider human relations extremely important. Losing or damaging relations with others is one of a Japanese person's greatest fears. Suzuki argues that when Doi (1973) identifies a Japanese tendency toward dependence and when Benedict (1946) describes a "culture of shame," what they are really talking about is this fundamental concept, "something between people" (human relations). For many Japanese, the role of interpersonal relations in their lives is akin to the role of religion in the lives of many North Americans.

Based on Nakane's (1970) vertical society, Ichikawa (1980) lists some characteristics of Japanese human relations. First, value is placed on *ba* (who you are in relation to the people involved). Second, group membership is enforced. Emotional participation, *marugakae* (completely enveloped), one-to-one relationships, and total involvement in the group are the norm. Third, intragroup communication is effective, but intergroup communication is not. There is a clear distinction between ingroup and outgroup, and communication is local and tangible. Fourth, a strong seniority system is based on birth date and one's length of service. In this respect, equal ability among people is assumed.

Observing social occasions, Ohtsubo (1984) reports on some of the rules for interactions in Japanese society. In forming groups, for example, company relations (e.g., boss, subordinate, colleague), degree of intimacy, and sex (e.g., same) are determining factors in social gatherings. Conversational topics among people with company relations may become intimate even at large parties because of the intimacy level of the people involved. Style of speech is determined by whether the speech partner is a member of the ingroup, an outgroup, or other groups (e.g., strangers).

Attitudes Toward Communication. Commenting on the pragmatic aspects of language, Kindaichi (1975) lists some of the characteristics of Japanese linguistic expressions. First, there is a tendency to place value on silence, on not speaking, on not writing, in language use. Second, included among these restrictions is one that has reason to be particularly avoided, especially among men: Men who speak a lot tend to be considered "light." Third, speaking and writing, when necessary, are kept to a minimum. There is a saying that talking too much and writing too much ruin one's chances of success (*Iwanuha iunimasaru*). Fourth, in contrast with the above mentioned characteristics, Japanese enjoy talking and writing among intimates. Thus these restrictions on language use apply primarily to public situations. Fifth, defending oneself verbally is to be avoided at all cost. Sixth, arguments are avoided. Sympathy is accorded to those who are defeated in arguments. Seventh, indirect expressions are preferred. Speech is ambiguous from beginning to end. Most of the claims summarized by Kindaichi above indicate that Japanese traditionally have a negative attitude toward verbal communication and often abandon it.

In considering both linguistic and paralinguistic variables in Japanese language communication, Toyama (1976) has formulated the following guidelines. First, use of "I" is not stable. More than half a dozen forms of the first-person singular pronoun are commonly used in present-day Japan. Second, if we call speech activities that are engaged in for the formation and maintenance of human relations "alpha code" and speech activities in which information and ideas are exchanged "beta code," most of Japanese daily activities will involve the former.

This attitude toward language use reflects Japanese attitudes toward human relations. Japanese change first-person pronouns depending on the person to whom they are speaking. The first-person pronoun used in a given situation reveals a relationship between the people involved. It is often the case that they have known each other since they were children.

Recently, Tsujimura (1987) discussed the tendency for the Japanese to remain taciturn. He pointed out three social causes for this phenomenon: "the experience of oppression during the feudal era, the high level of racial and linguistic homogeneity, and the small ratio of positions per person in the behavioral settings of Japanese society" (p. 126). Japanese taciturnity also is influenced by the communication concept of *ishindenshin* (communication of thoughts from one mind to another without using language. Putting it differently, this can be attained by the mechanism of *sasshi,* which is described below) in interpersonal communication.

Japanese Language Styles

In this section some language styles unique to the Japanese culture are selected for discussion. They are (a) the localized, self-controlled, and situation-oriented styles; (b) the chain of monologues; and (c) indirectness.

The Localized, Self-Controlled, and Situation-Oriented Styles. Based on his review of Barnlund (1975) and Benedict (1946) and an examination of Japanese sayings, Shimura (1982) identified three communication styles prevalent among Japanese, (a) *Amae-gata* (localized style), (b) *Jiko-yokusei-gata* (self-controlled style), and (c) *Johkyo-siko-gata* (situation-oriented style). *Amae-gata,* according to Shimura, is the result of Japanese homogeneity of race, language, habit, and of geographic isolation. As a result of this, however, communication with other groups from outside Japan can be difficult. The second type of communication, the self-controlled style, is identified in Barnlund's comparison of Japanese and U.S. levels of self-disclosure in communication, in which he found that North Americans disclose more than Japanese on all topics in initial interactions. The third style, which Shimura identified as situation-oriented, reflects the fact that Japanese self-references change according to the interlocutor with whom they are communicating—this is, Japanese use several forms to say "I."

The Chain of Monologues. Nakano (1982) describes a typical traditional Japanese town meeting. Attending members state their opinions on the issue but there is no exchange of ideas. Therefore, no arguments or direct clashes occur among the members, although some conflicting ideas may be expressed. This is how the first meeting will end. A few days later, there will be another meeting. Again, all participants express their opinions. Still, no direct exchange of ideas takes place. This time, disagreement among members decreases. As additional meetings proceed, conflicts decrease as compromises are made. Eventually, a conclusion is reached without any direct confrontation among members.

Nakano (1982) thus demonstrates that dialogue does not occur among the members of these town meetings. Rather, there is a chain of monologues in which individuals express their ideas, points of view, and positions on an issue. Although these ideas and views are adjusted in subsequent meetings, these adjustments are in fact made between meetings by individual members as a result of what they have heard of other members' opinions and views in previous meetings. Because this is an internal process within each individual, rather than something that happens in the course of any single meeting, we cannot observe it occurring.

Such a lack of dialogue, however, results in relatively undeveloped rhetorical skills among Japanese. On the other hand, each individual has the opportunity to present his or her opinion equally to other members of the group. This style of communication is characteristic of a feudalistic vertical society, such as Japan's prior to the Meiji era. Nakano (1982), however, reports that he witnessed such chains of monologues in farming families before and during the Second World War. And this style can still be found in conversations among family members or friends, in informal conversations in coffee shops or drinking places, or in discussions in official places.

Indirectness. Tsujimura (1987) describes the Japanese style of communication as indirect. He explains that Japanese enjoy the traditional games, such as the exchange of *Waka* (poems) and the card game of one hundred poems where "one's love or human relationships" (p. 126) are expressed indirectly. Okabe (1987), using speech act theory, stated that there are many expressions in the present-day Japanese language that can be classified as indirect speech acts.

Higuchi (1992) points out that Japanese tend to keep the words they use to a minimum and to leave much of what they wish to communicate implied rather than explicitly stated. Understanding is often left up to the listener's *sasshi* (guessing what someone means) ability. The concept of *sasshi* is defined as conjecture, surmise, or guessing what someone means. In its verb form (*sassuru*), its meaning is expanded to mean to imagine, to suppose, to empathize with, or to make allowances for others (Nishida, 1977).

Japanese Nonverbal Styles

In this section, Japanese nonverbal styles are covered. Included are pauses and silences in speech, as well as gestures and bodily movements.

Pauses and Silences in Japanese Speech. Among Japanese, emotional messages and other things that are difficult to express verbally (such negative things as criticism, self-defense, or refusal), often are communicated with nonverbal signals. These nonverbal signs include faint eye movements and facial expressions, moderate bodily movements, and pauses or silences (Higuchi, 1992). From these nonverbals, listeners infer what is meant (again, a function of their *sasshi*). For example, when a person who is requested to do something wishes to refuse the request, he or she will pause and not respond within an appropriate time period. This sends a negative message to the person who made the request, who will then be ready to receive the explicit message or refusal, when it eventually comes.

Lebra (1987) presented four possible interpretations of the significance of silence in Japan: truthfulness, social discretion, embarrassment, and defiance. With respect to truthfulness, a person who speaks little is trusted more than a person who speaks a lot. Truthfulness emerges from silence, not words, in Japan. Silence also allows Japanese to be socially discreet. "Social discretion" here means silence that is considered necessary to gain social acceptance. Silence also saves Japanese people from being embarrassed by not disclosing their opinions or expressing their emotions. Silence is also used to express estrangement or defiance.

Gestures. Gestures and bodily movements also play an important role in Japanese nonverbal communication. There are gestures linked to speech, conventional signs (e.g., head-nod, clapping), movements expressing emotional states, and movements used in ritual. Among these gestures are movements unique to Japanese culture, which maintain and control the flow of conversation, called *aizuchi* (gestures used with words of agreement during conversations). For example, Nomura (1980) reports that Japanese are expected to chime in, echo words, or say something every 2 to 3 seconds in telephone conversations. If more than 4 or 5 seconds elapse without such affirmation, a speaker will say "hello" to confirm whether the listener is still on the line.

There is also the matter of the Japanese "social smile." This pattern of smiles or grinning during conversations is often understood as expressing an emotional state, although they are actually gestures of acknowledgment or movements for self-control (Nomura, 1980).

Concerning eye contact, Inoue (1982) summarizes the key ideas of cultural anthropologist Kunio Yanagida, the first Japanese scholar to identify the importance of nonverbal studies (*shigusa*, to use his term). First, according to Yanagida, nonverbals, including eye contact, play an important role in Japanese interpersonal communication. He was the first scholar to recognize the importance of nonverbals in interpersonal communication. Second, understanding Japanese eye contact means understanding Japanese culture. It may even be more important than understanding the language. Third, changes over historical time can be seen in the way that gestures and eye contact have been used.

Conclusion

As the first section of this chapter shows, much of the communication research that has been carried out in Japan has been heavily influenced by theories first developed and promulgated in North America. More recently, however, many Japanese researchers have begun to question the appropriateness of applying such theories to the Japanese communicative context. In the second section, I have presented the work of some of the Japanese communication theorists who have taken the position that only through the development of an independent, "Japanese" theoretical framework can communicative behaviors in Japan be accurately studied and explained.

As pointed out in the second section, the three-person structure for the analysis of Japanese communication is an alternative to the two-person structure, which seems most effective in describing individualistic cultures. In this light, Inoue's (1982) discussion of the reference group as the third person deserves more attention.

It is important to note, however, that the dichotomous categorization of cultures may not be a prejudice unique to U.S. researchers. Japanese researchers, too, are vulnerable to this temptation. Hamaguchi (1982) claims at one point, for example, that we have to create a measure that is suited to the analysis of Japanese behaviors and then use that structure for analyzing other cultures as well. Such an approach would result in the same problems Japanese researchers have faced.

More data are needed for developing a culture-free perspective that describes communication variables across cultures. Some of the perspectives used in this field are characterized variously as "views" or "what it should be" (e.g., Nakane, 1970) or as merely "guessing" (e.g., Toyama, 1976). The immature state of the field is demonstrated by the fact that full-fledged communication studies have just started in Japan. For the future of this field, cooperative gathering of data across cultures is recommended.

As one example of such research, Gudykunst and I (1986) have conducted a series of cross-cultural studies of communication in interpersonal relationships in Japan and the United States over the past several years. We developed a two-dimensional measure of attributional confidence with descriptions of communication in low- and high-context cultures.

Notes

1. These are the same theories that have informed American communication studies in recent years. For instance, "North American" theories identified by Littlejohn (1992) are familiar to Japanese academics. A review of these North American theories can be found in H. Nishida (1989b).

2. Although these arguments are not influenced directly by North American theories, communication-oriented research received considerable attention in Japan in the 1970s. That was when the study of intercultural communication was introduced to Japan by various media (e.g., Condon & Yousef, 1975, on NHK programs). Since then, research in the communication area has constantly appeared in books and journals.

References

Akuto, H. (1984). *Komyunikehshon bunka no nichibei hikaku* (A comparison of U.S.-Japan communication cultures). In T. Mizuhara & A. Tsujimura (Eds.), *Komyunikehshon no shakai sinrigaku* (Communication in social psychology) (pp. 209-226). Tokyo: Tokyo University Press.

Akutsu, Y. (1976). *Komyunikehshon no gainen, moderu, ruikei* (Communication concepts, models, & types) In Y. Akutsu (Ed.), *Gendai no esupuri 110* (Modern esprit 110) (pp. 5-20). Tokyo: Shibundo.

Altman, I., & Taylor, D. (1973). *Social penetration: The development of interpersonal relationships.* New York: Holt, Rinehart & Winston.

Araki, H. (1973). *Nihonjinno koudouyoushiki* (Japanese behavioral patterns). Tokyo: Kohdansha.

Argyle, M. (1975). *Bodily communication.* London: Methuen.

Barnlund, D. (1975). *The public and private self in Japan and the United States.* Tokyo: Simul Press. (Original work published 1973, in Japanese)

Barnlund, D. (1989). *Communicative styles of Japanese and Americans: Images and realities.* Belmont, CA: Wadsworth.

Befu, H. (1980a). A critique of the group model of Japanese society. *Social Analysis, 5/6,* 29-43.

Befu, H. (1980b). The group model of Japanese society and an alternative. *Rice University Studies, 66,* 169-187.

Benedict, R. (1946). *The chrysanthemum and the sword: Patterns of Japanese culture.* Boston: Houghton Mifflin.

Berger, C., & Calabrese, R. (1975). Some explorations in initial interaction and beyond: Toward a developmental theory of interpersonal communication. *Human Communication Research, 1,* 99-112.

Berlo, D. (1960). *The process of communication.* New York: Holt, Rinehart & Winston.

Birdwhistell, R. L. (1970). *Kinesics and context.* Philadelphia: University of Pennsylvania Press.

Bormann, E. G. (1980). *Communication theory.* New York: Holt, Rinehart & Winston.

Condon, J. C., & Yousef, F. S. (1975). *An introduction to intercultural communication.* Indianapolis, IN: Bobbs-Merrill.

Cooley, C. H. (1953). The significance of communication. In B. Berelson & M. Janowitz (Eds.), *Reader in public opinion and communication* (pp. 145-153). New York: Free Press.

Doi, T. (1973). *The anatomy of dependence.* Tokyo: Kohansha.

Furuhata, K. (1984). *Kyoshi-seito kan no komyunikehshon no ni, san no mondai* (Some problems in teacher-student communication). In T. Mizuhara & A. Tsujimura (Eds.), *Komyunikehshon no shakai sinrigaku* (Communication in social psychology) (pp. 61-78). Tokyo: Tokyo University Press.

Gudykunst, W. B., Gao, G., Schmidt, K. L., Nishida, T., Bond, M. H., Leung, K., Wang, G., & Barraclough, R. (1992). The influence of individualism-collectivism on communication in ingroup and outgroup relationships. *Journal of Cross-Cultural Psychology, 23,* 196-213.

Gudykunst, W. B., & Nishida, T. (1981). The intercultural communication workshop: Foundations, development, and affects. In T. Nishida & W. B. Gudykunst (Eds.) *Readings in intercultural communication* (pp. 107-135). Tokyo: Geirinshobo.

Gudykunst, W. B., & Nishida, T. (1983). Social penetration in Japanese and American close friendships. In R. Bostrom (Ed.), *Communication yearbook 7.* Beverly Hills, CA: Sage.

Gudykunst, W. B., & Nishida, T. (1984). Individual and cultural influences on uncertainty. *Communication Monographs, 51,* 23-36.

Gudykunst, W. B., & Nishida, T. (1986). Attributional confidence in low- and high-context cultures. *Human Communication Research, 12,* 525-549.

Gudykunst, W. B., & Nishida, T. (1989). Theoretical perspectives for studying intercultural communication. In M. K. Asante & W. B. Gudykunst (Eds.), *Handbook of international and intercultural communication.* Newbury Park, CA: Sage.

Gudykunst, W. B., & Nishida, T. (1990). Communication in interpersonal relationships in Japan and the United States: Overview of a research program. *The Bulletin of the Institute for Communications Research* [Keio University], pp. 1-49.

Gudykunst, W. B., Nishida, T., & Chua, E. (1987). Perceptions of social penetration in Japanese-North American dyads. *International Journal of Intercultural Relations, 11,* 171-190.

Gudykunst, W. B., Nishida, T., & Schmidt, K. (1989). Cultural, relational, and personality influences on uncertainty reduction processes. *Western Journal of Speech Communication, 53,* 13-29.

Gudykunst, W. B., Yang, S. M., & Nishida, T. (1985). A cross-cultural test of uncertainty reduction theory: Comparisons of acquaintance, friend, and dating relationships in Japan, Korea, and the United States. *Human Communication Research, 11,* 407-454.

Gudykunst, W. B., Yang, S. M., & Nishida, T. (1987). Cultural differences in self-consciousness and self-monitoring. *Communication Research, 14,* 7-36.

Gudykunst, W. B., Yoon, Y. C., & Nishida, T. (1987). The influence of individualism-collectivism on perceptions of communication in ingroup-outgroup relationships. *Communication Monographs, 54,* 295-306.

Hall, E. T. (1959). *The silent language.* Garden City, NY: Doubleday.

Hall, E. T. (1966). *The hidden dimension.* Garden City, NY: Doubleday.

Hall, E. T. (1976). *Beyond culture.* Garden City, NY: Doubleday.

Hall, E. T. (1983). *The dance of life.* Garden City, NY: Doubleday.

Hamaguchi, E. (1982). *Nihonteki shuhdanshugi towa nanika* (What is Japanese "groupism"?). In E. Hamaguchi & S. Kumon (Eds.), *Nihonteki shuhdanshugi* (Japanese "groupism") (pp. 1-26). Tokyo: Yuhhikaku Sensho.

Hartley, E. I., & Hartley, R. E. (1952). *Fundamentals of social psychology.* New York: Knopf.

Higuchi, K. (1992). *Nihonjin no ningen kankei* (Japanese human relations). Tokyo: Tankohsha.

Hofstede, G. (1980). *Culture's consequences: International differences in work-related values.* Beverly Hills, CA: Sage.

Hovland, C. I., Janis, I. L., & Kelley, H. H. (1953). *Communication and persuasion.* New Haven, CT: Yale University Press.

Ichikawa, K. (1980). *Tate to yoko* (Vertical and horizontal social structure). In H. Minami (Ed.), *Nihonjin no ningen kankei jiten* (Japanese human relations) (pp. 47-61). Tokyo: Kohdansha.

Inoue, C. (1982). *Manazashi no ningen kankei* (Nonverbals in Japanese human relations). Tokyo: Kohdansha.

Iwao, S. (1984). *Kokusai komyunikehshon to imehji* (International communication and image). In T. Mizuhara & A. Tsujimura (Eds.), *Komyunikehshon no shakai sinrigaku* (Communication in social psychology) (pp. 191-208). Tokyo: Tokyo University Press.

Kindaichi, H. (1975). *Nihonjin no gengo hyohgen* (Japanese verbal expressions). Tokyo: Kohdansha.

Kluckhohn, F., & Strodtbeck, F. (1961). *Variations in value orientations.* New York: Row, Peterson.

Knapp, M. L. (1979). *Ningen kankei niokeru higengo joho dentatsu* (Nonverbal communication in human interaction). Tokyo: Tokai University Press. (English version: *Nonverbal communication in human interaction.* New York: Holt, Rinehart & Winston, 1972).

Kondo, H. (1981). *Karucha shokku no sinri* (The psychology of culture shock). Tokyo: Sogensha.

Kumon, S. (1982). *Nihonshakai no soshikika genri* (Organizing principles in Japanese society). In E. Hamaguchi & S. Kumon (Eds.), *Nihonteki shuhdanshugi* (Japanese "groupism") (pp. 75-101). Tokyo: Yuhhikaku Sensho.

Lebra, T. S. (1987). The cultural significance of silence in Japanese communication. *Multilingua, 6,* 343-357.

Littlejohn, S. W. (1992). *Theories of human communication* (4th ed.). Belmont, CA: Wadsworth.

Matsumura, T. (1984). *Nihonteki komyunikehshon to nihon no fuhdo* (Japanese communication and climate). In T. Mizuhara & A. Tsujimura (Eds.), *Komyunikehshon no shakai sinrigaku* (Communication in social psychology) (pp. 171-189). Tokyo: Tokyo University Press.

Mehrabian, A. (1986). *Higengo komyunikehshon* (Silent messages). Tokyo: Seibunsha. (English version: *Silent messages* [2nd ed.]. Belmont, CA: Wadsworth, 1981)

Mizuhara, T. (1984). *Settokuteki komyunikehshon to ninchi hannou* (Persuasive communication and cognitive response). In T. Mizuhara & A. Tsujimura (Eds.), *Komyunikehshon no shakai sinrigaku* (Communication in social psychology) (pp. 13-28). Tokyo: Tokyo University Press.

Mizuhara, T., & Tsujimura, A. (Eds.). (1984). *Komyunikehshon no shakai sinrigaku* (Communication in social psychology). Tokyo: Tokyo University Press.

Nakane, C. (1970). *Japanese society.* Berkeley, CA: University of California Press.

Nakanishi, M. (1986). Perceptions of self-disclosure in initial interactions: A Japanese sample. *Human Communication Research, 13,* 167-190.

Nakano, O. (1982). *Nihongata sosiki niokeru komyunikehshon to sikettei* (Communication and decision making in Japanese organizations). In E. Hamaguchi & S. Kumon (Eds.), *Nihonteki shuhdanshugi* (Japanese "groupism") (pp. 143-168). Tokyo: Yuhhikaku Sensho.

Nishida, H. (1989a). *Jitsurei de miru nichibei komyunikehshon gyappu* (The communication gap between Japanese and Americans). Tokyo: Taishukan.

Nishida, H. (1989b). *Komyunikehshon riron no hensen* (A history of communication theories). In K. Watanabe & Y. Kohama (Eds.), *Kokusai kankei no siza tenkan* (New directions in international relations) (pp. 121-191). Tokyo: Hokuju Shuppan.

Nishida, T. (1977). An analysis of a cultural concept affecting Japanese interpersonal communication. *Communication, 6,* 69-80.

Nishida, T. (1990). *Taijin kankei riron no ibunkateki kensho* (Theoretical analyses in intercultural human relationships). *Nihon University Studies on International Relations, 10,* 207-219.

Nishida, T. (1992). *Kokusai koudou no tameno rironteki pahsupekutebu* (Theoretical perspectives on studies in intercultural communication). *Nihon University Studies on International Relations, 13,* 9-30.

Nishida, T., & Gudykunst, W. B. (1986). *Fukakujitusei gensho riron ni kansuru kojinnteki oyobi bunkateki eikyo* (Individual and cultural influences on uncertainty reduction). *Nihon University Studies on International Relations, 7,* 295-308.

Nomura, M. (1980). *Miburi, sigusa, hyojo* (Nonverbals). In H. Minami (Ed.), *Nihonjin no ningen kankei jiten* (Japanese human relations) (pp. 332-345). Tokyo: Kohdansha.

Ohtsubo, K. (1984). *Nihonjin no komyunikehshon* (Japanese communication). In Nagoya University (Ed.), *Gendai no komyunikehshon* (Modern communication) (pp. 89-104). Aichi, Japan: Nagoya University Press.

Okabe, K. (1987). Indirect speech acts of the Japanese. In D. Kincaid (Ed.), *Communication theory: Eastern and Western perspectives* (pp. 126-136). San Diego, CA: Academic Press.

Osgood, C. E. (1952). The nature and measurement of meaning. *Psychological Bulletin, 49,* 197-237.

Samovar, L. A., Porter, R. E., & Jain, N. C. (1983). *Ibunkakan komyunikehshon nyumon* (Understanding intercultural communication). Tokyo: Seibunsha. (English version: *Understanding intercultural communication.* Belmont, CA: Wadsworth, 1983.)

Schramm, W. L. (1954). How communication works. In W. L. Schramm (Ed.), *The process and effects of mass communication* (pp. 1-9). Urbana: University of Illinois Press.

Shannon, C. E., & Weaver, W. (1949). *The mathematical theory of communication.* Urbana: University of Illinois Press.

Shimura, Y. (1982). *Nichibei hikaku ni miru nihongata komyunikehshon no kousatu* (A study of the Japanese communication style in comparison with the U.S. style). *Kwansai Foreign Language University Annual, 36,* 75-87.

Shirts, R. G. (1973). *Bafa bafa.* Del Mar, CA: Simile.

Sitaram, K. S. (1985). *Ibunkakan komyunikehshon* (Intercultural communication). Tokyo: Tokyo Sogensha. (English version: *Foundations of intercultural communication.* Columbus, OH: Charles E. Merrill, 1976).

Stewart, E. (1966). The simulation of cultural differences. *Journal of Communication, 16,* 291-304.

Stewart, E. C. (1971). *American cultural patterns: A cross-cultural perspective.* Washington DC: Society for Intercultural Education, Training and Research.

Suzuki, H. (1980). *Douteki fuudoron ni yoru nihonjin no ningen kankei no kousatsu* (A study of Japanese human relations from the dynamic climate perspective). In H. Minami (Ed.), *Nihonjin no ningen kankei jiten* (Japanese human relations) (pp. 32-42). Tokyo: Kohdansha.

Takeuchi, I. (1973). *Shakaiteki komyunikehshon* (Social communication). In Tokyo University (Ed.), *Gendai no shakai to komyunikehshon* (Modern society and communication) (pp. 3-39). Tokyo: Tokyo University Press.

Takeuchi, I. (1990). *Masu komyunikehshon no riron* (Social theories of mass communication). Tokyo: Tokyo University Press.

Toyama, S. (1976). *Nihongo no kosei* (The characteristics of Japanese language). Tokyo: Chuo-koronsha.

Triandis, H. C. (1988). Collectivism vs. individualism: A reconceptualization of a basic concept in cross-cultural psychology. In G. Verma & C. Bagley (Eds.), *Cross-cultural studies of personality, attitudes, and cognition* (pp. 60-95). London: Macmillan.

Tsujimura, A. (1976). *Denpa fukyu katei no shakaisinrigaku kenkyu* (A social psychological study of the communication process). *Tokyo University Mass Communication Study, 24*, 11-21.

Tsujimura, A. (1979). *Terebi seiken housou no kohka ni kansuru kenkyu* (A study on influences of televised political campaigns). *Tokyo University Mass Communication Study, 6*, 1-11.

Tsujimura, A. (1980). *Kohsokushakai to ningen* (High speed society and human beings). Tokyo: Kanki Press.

Tsujimura, A. (1987). Some characteristics of the Japanese way of communication. In D. Kincaid (Ed.), *Communication theory: Eastern and Western perspectives* (pp. 115-126). San Diego, CA: Academic Press.

Tsujimura, A., & Inaki, T. (1977). *Terebi seiken housou no kohka* (The influences of televised political campaigns on Japanese society). In N. Soma (Ed.), *Kokusei senkyo to seitou seiji* (National elections and party politics). Tokyo: Seiji Kohho Center.

Tsujimura, A., & Inaki, T. (1983). *Besutoserah no eikyo ni kansuru jikkenteki kenkyu* (An experimental study of the influence of bestsellers). *Tokyo University Mass Communication Study, 31*, 21-30.

Tsujimura, A., & Kim, K. (1980, April). *Nikkan komyunikehshon gyappu* (The Japan-Korea communication gap). *Shokun.*

Tsujimura, A., Kim, K., & Ikuta, M. (1982). *Nihon to Kankoku no bunka masatsu* (Cultural conflicts between Japan and Korea). Tokyo: Idemitsu Press.

Wagatsuma, H. (1982). *Nihonteki shudan shugi no kokusaika ha kanouka* (Can Japanese "groupism" be international?). In E. Hamaguchi & S. Kumon (Eds.), *Nihonteki shuhdanshugi* (Japanese "groupism") (pp. 195-226). Tokyo: Yuhhikaku Sensho.

Watsuji, T. (1934). *Ningen no gaku to siteno rinrigaku* (Ethics as a study of human beings). Tokyo: Iwanami.

Wesley, C. E., & MacLean, M. S. (1957). A conceptual model for communication research. *Journalism Quarterly, 34*, 31-38.

Yamaguchi, S. (1984). *Saikinno settokuteki komyunikehshon kenkyu* (Recent studies on persuasive communication). In T. Mizuhara & A. Tsujimura (Eds.), *Komyunikehshon no shakai sinrigaku* (Communication in social psychology) (pp. 29-42). Tokyo: Tokyo University Press.

Yamane, I. (1987). *"Koibito" toiu aidagara wo imisuru sho koui no kigougakuteki bunseki* (A semiological analysis on conducts meaning the aidagara of lover-sweetheart relation). *Research in Social Psychology, 2*(2), 29-34.

6

Interpersonal Relationships in Korea

Tae-Seop Lim
Soo-Hyang Choi

Traditionally, Koreans have valued social relationships more than anything else. Koreans often forego their own personal interests and the welfare of the groups they belong to for the sake of their interpersonal relationships. They will relinquish their turns to their friends and be willing to use both private and public power to benefit those whom they know well and like (Yum, 1988). Because Koreans emphasize social relationships, the abilities to maintain good interpersonal relationships are also valued. Persons are judged based upon their abilities to maintain successful relationships. Having good relationships with others is considered to reflect one's character as well as competence. Naturally, Koreans tend to have the desire to maintain good interpersonal relationships.

In order to develop and maintain good relationships, Koreans spend an enormous amount of time and energy in dealing with the needs of the other and projecting their images as desirable relational partners. Thus the matters they are concerned with and the communication strategies they employ in social interactions are very sophisticated and unique. In order to understand the nature of interpersonal relationships in Korea, therefore, it is necessary to explore these more or less unique aspects of Koreans' social behavior. The purpose of this chapter is to discuss three of the most fundamental concepts that affect the social behavior of Korean people: *Che-Myon, Jung,* and *Noon-Chi.*

Che-myon is one of many terms that Koreans use to represent what is similar to but much more complex than the Western (Goffman, 1967) or Chinese (Ho, 1975; Hu, 1944) concept of "face." *Jung* is a kind of psychological bond that connects two persons in a relationship, but it is much more comprehensive and diverse than its Western counterpart, "love" or "emotional attachment." *Noon-chi,* which may be roughly translated as "mind-reading" or "reading the situation," is a key element that constitutes what can be called "tacit communication."

Che-Myon and Other Concepts of Face

Face pervades every aspect of Koreans' daily social interaction (Choi & Choi, 1991). Behind all kinds of decision making is usually one's desire to elevate or maintain face. Koreans think of face when they interact with others; when they appear in public; when they select their associates; when they buy food, clothing, housing, and automobiles; when they choose their schools and occupation; that is, whenever they do something that might attract others' attention.

The pervasiveness of face in Koreans' everyday lives is reflected in the multiplicity of face-related notions. *Myon-mok, ul-gool, nott, mo-yang-sae, che-mo,* and *che-myon* are some of the commonly used words that refer to face (Choi & Choi, 1991). Of these terms, *che-myon* is the most general and commonly used. Etymologically, *che-myon* is a compound word of Chinese origin. The first part, *che,* stands for "body" and the second part, *myon,* for "face." Together, however, *che-myon* refers to something that is similar to what Westerners call face.

Che-Myon and the Western Concept of Face

Although *che-myon* shares certain commonalities with the Western concept of face, which is delineated by Goffman (1967), they are different in many respects. Following Goffman, face is the image of self, delineated in terms of positive social values, that persons claim for themselves in social encounters. Goffman's notion of face, in other words, has three properties: "the image of self," "claimed and reinforced through social interaction," and "composed of positive social values." *Che-myon* also has three properties. However, the

Korean concept of face is different from its Western counterpart in the exact natures of these properties. First, *che-myon,* like face, is the image of self. However, while the Western concept of face is mostly the image of personal or psychological self, *che-myon* is the image of sociological self more than that of personal self (Choi & Choi, 1991). Second, like face, certain aspects of *che-myon* are claimed and reinforced through social interactions. However, the greater part of *che-myon* is given by society, and individuals protect it by meeting the expectations of the society. Finally, *che-myon,* like face, consists of positive social values. But, while the positiveness of Western face is conceived of as a continuum, that of *che-myon* is sometimes understood as a pass-fail dichotomy. In short, *che-myon* is a double-faced concept. On the one hand, it is the image of personal self that is claimed and negotiated through social interactions. On the other hand, it is the image of sociological self that is defined by the society and must be protected by passing the normative standards of positiveness of relevant social values. When Koreans refer to *che-myon,* therefore, they at times mean the personalized image of a person that is negotiable, and at other times mean the normative image of a person that is defined socially.

Personalized *Che-Myon*

Personalized *che-myon* is very similar to the Western concept of face. Face, according to Goffman (1967), is individualized and negotiated through social interactions. First, face is the property of a person as an individual rather than as a member of a group. The social worth that persons claim for themselves in the current interaction is largely dependent upon the result of their past interactions with others, and by the same token, the result of the current interaction will affect the face they put on in the future (Goffman, 1967). As persons have different interactional experiences, their claims of face will be different from person to person dependent upon their previous experiences of their claims being accepted or rejected.

Second, the face of a person is negotiated through interactions with others. When engaged in social interactions, persons claim for themselves certain amounts of social worth by taking "lines," that is, patterns of verbal and nonverbal acts by which they express their views of the situation and their evaluations of the participants, especially themselves (Goffman, 1967). When others assume that a person has taken a line, they may issue their own lines to express their evaluations of the person and/or themselves. When exchanged lines are in harmony, the projected face is sustained. When they are in discord, participants should start the process of negotiating each other's face, that is, the "corrective process," in order to keep the interaction functioning. The facework strategies Westerners employ to support and negotiate each other's individualized face is well explained in Lim and Bowers (1991) and Lim (1988, 1989, 1990, 1991).

Che-myon is sometimes perceived as personalized and interactional. In this case, all ordinary adults are viewed as functioning autonomous units and endowed with their own *che-myon*. The personalized *che-myon* of individuals is not determined by absolute standards but by the person's relative position in the given relationship. Thus the same person may put on very different natures of personalized *che-myon* in different relationships. Like face, the claim of personalized *che-myon* is based on such relational factors as power differences and relational intimacy. Persons of higher relational power or interpersonal authority normally claim more *che-myon*. Subordinates should therefore be very careful not to impose on and/or criticize their superiors, but superiors are relatively free to commit these face-threatening acts. Superiors in Korea often say to their subordinates, "Fella! You don't want to mention your *che-myon* in front of me."

The way intimacy affects *che-myon* is the same as the way it influences face wants in Western society (Lim & Bowers, 1991). For insignificant matters that will not affect the state of the relationship, persons claim less *che-myon* as the relationship becomes closer. Koreans often say to their close friends, "Listen! We're friends. You don't want to be concerned with *che-myon* over such a trivial matter." However, when the matters at hand may be consequential to the given relationship, Koreans become more sensitive to *che-myon* as the relationship becomes closer. Koreans often do not care about *che-myon* in front of strangers. As the *yi-mok* (ears and eyes) that scrutinize them become more familiar, however, Koreans act more carefully not to damage their *che-myon*. Married couples may quarrel in front of strangers, but not in the presence of their friends. Koreans often say, "He's a good friend of mine. When you are with him, behave yourself so that you would not hurt my *che-myon* toward him."

Personalized *che-myon*, like face, is very dynamic and transitional. It is promoted or damaged easily, depending on how participants deal with everyday face-threatening acts. If one criticizes the other on a particular performance or imposes on the other, the relevant *che-myon* of the other, that is, the image that the other is competent and self-governing, is damaged. Yet in the same interaction one can compliment other performances of the other or seek advice or guidance from the other on some other matters, which may help the other recover the damaged *che-myon.*

Because this personalized *che-myon* is easily threatened or damaged in any kind of social interaction, Koreans, like Westerners, use various types of face-work. Following Lim and Bowers (1991), North Americans use three different types of facework: solidarity, approbation, and tact. Solidarity is purported to support the image that one is accepted and appreciated by others. Approbation is intended to support the image that one is competent in whatever one is supposed to handle. Tact is aimed at supporting the image that one is autonomous by mitigating the imposition that restricts the other's freedom of action. In social interactions, Koreans also use solidarity, approbation, and tact to mitigate the threats to each other's personalized *che-myon.* They often use informal or intimate language, and emphasize the need for cooperation, similarities, shared fate, and mutual trust to promote solidarity. They usually ignore or understate negative aspects of the other, and notice and exaggerate positive aspects of the other to support the other's *che-myon* of competence. They often ask for suggestions and directions, avoid explicit directives, and use pleas and conventional indirectness to protect the other's *che-myon* of autonomy.

Normative *Che-Myon*

The normative aspect of *che-myon* is the social worth of a person, not as an individual but as an occupant of a social position. In other words, sociological or normative *che-myon* is the socially expected quality of a person in association with his or her particular social position or status (Choi & Choi, 1991). Individuals have little to do with the specific contents of these social qualities. They are assigned their social worth by implicit but "somewhat fixed symbolic value systems" of the society (Choi & Choi, 1991). Several characteristics distinguish normative *che-myon* from interactional *che-myon* or its Western counterpart, face.

First, different from personalized *che-myon,* normative *che-myon* is stipulated by somewhat absolute social standards, and thus applied consistently to different situations and relationships. Professors, for example, are expected to sustain certain social values by behaving, speaking, dressing, and leading life in a "professorly" fashion. These expectations, which are effective for all professors regardless of their idiosyncracies, are constant across the different relationships they are involved in, different activities they are engaged in, and different circumstances they are under.

Second, all distinct social positions in the Korean society are given their own normative *che-myon,* but when a social position is more important and socially respected, it is given higher normative *che-myon.* In other words, persons of higher social positions are expected to have greater amounts of social worth. Furthermore, this expectation is very generalized; that is, a person of a higher social position is expected to be better than a person of a lower social position in almost every respect of social desirability: integrity and personality, authority, possessions, performance, associations, appearance, general conduct, and so on.

Third, different from personalized *che-myon* or the Western concept of face, normative *che-myon* is not individually negotiable. One cannot claim more normative *che-myon* than is extended to oneself or enhance one's own normative *che-myon* by making a series of good showings. The only way to enhance the normative *che-myon* of a person is for all occupants of the social position that the person holds to make good showings so that the society might reevaluate the amount of *che-myon* allowable to the position. In this sense, normative *che-myon* is a very collective concept.

Fourth, normative *che-myon* is quite static. When one's social position is known to others, that is, when normative *che-myon* is assigned to one, all one can do is to maintain it or fail to maintain it. One maintains or defends normative *che-myon* if one is able to meet all social expectations pertinent to a person of one's position. If not, one fails to maintain or damages the normative *che-myon.* What is important about this aspect of *che-myon* is not the extent to which one maintains or damages it, but whether one succeeds or fails to maintain it. The process of enacting normative *che-myon,* therefore, is often understood as a pass-fail dichotomy.

Fifth, different from personalized *che-myon,* which is negotiated through interaction in speaker-addressee relationships, normative *che-myon* usually is appraised in actor-observer relationships. What is important to the maintenance of personalized *che-myon* are the opinions of the addressee or interactional partner. What is crucial to the maintenance of normative *che-myon,* however, are the opinions of others in general, that is, all potential observers. Thus, persons need to be careful not to damage their *che-myon* as long as there is a possibility that what is going on may be seen or heard of, later if not immediately, by others who may know their social positions. "Watch the *yi-mok* (ears and eyes) of others," therefore, normally means in Korea, "Be careful not to damage your *che-myon.*"

Because the threats to normative *che-myon* come from a variety of observers, Koreans tend to go through a great deal of consideration when they make a decision about something that can be observed by many people over a long range of time. For example, fixed or semi-fixed features such as house, automobile, and furniture, and actions that require long-term commitment such as engagement, marriage, and selecting schools and jobs usually attract endless attention from all kinds of observers. To protect and sometimes to overprotect *che-myon,* Koreans often buy houses and cars they can hardly afford, and put pressure on their children to marry someone whom they do not love and to be admitted to schools and occupations for which they are not qualified.

Sixth, maintaining or protecting *che-myon* is often one of the main objectives of social interaction for Koreans. Goffman (1967) argues that maintenance of face is a condition of interaction, whereas gaining face is one of the objectives. Gaining (or "hoisting," in the Korean expression) *che-myon* is of course an important objective of Koreans' lives. However, it is not likely to be an objective of a single interaction because, as mentioned earlier, normative *che-myon* is not negotiated through interaction. To hoist normative *che-myon,* persons need to raise their social positions or status.

However, normative *che-myon* is readily damaged when persons do not meet social expectations, that is, when they do not make the good showings expected of them. To maintain *che-myon,* in other words, Koreans need to be involved in the activities that are designed to fulfill their face-related social expectations. Maintenance of *che-myon* is the major, if not the only, objective of these activities, which Koreans appropriately call "*che-myon* maintenance activities." *Che-myon* maintenance activities are different depending on the social position of the person. Activities that are common to all Koreans include visiting others and giving gifts, regularly inviting and entertaining others, and helping others pay for weddings or funerals.

Finally, *che-myon* is what Koreans value dearly. Westerners value face, too. When they gain face, they "feel good," and when they lose it, they "feel bad" or "feel hurt" (Goffman, 1967). Koreans' emotional attachment to *che-myon* is much stronger. When they hoist their *che-myon,* they do not simply feel good, but feel as though they were much better persons than before. They think that they have actually become more socially desirable. If they lose *che-myon,* that is, if they fail to meet social expectations, they "cannot lift their face to others because of shame." Shame is a powerful feeling that prevents a person from interacting with others with dignity. A person with damaged *che-myon,* therefore, is not able to function properly in the society.

Other Korean Concepts of Face

Ul-gool and *nott* are two different terms that refer to the same thing, face, and they are mutually interchangeable. Three characteristics distinguish *ul-gool* and *nott* from *che-myon:* informality, concreteness, and negativity. First, *ul-gool* and *nott* are used in informal situations. When persons refer to their own face or the face of their equals and subordinates, they may use *ul-gool* or *nott* instead of *che-myon. Ul-gool* and *nott* may not be used to refer to the face of superiors and equals who are not close to one. *Che-mo,* which is an honorific, or *che-myon* is usually used to refer to the face of superiors or distant equals.

Second, though *che-myon* is abstract, *ul-gool* and *nott* are concrete. Specifically, *che-myon* does not imply the physical face, but *ul-gool* and *nott,* like the English word *face,* refer to the physical and concrete face. When they are used to mean *che-myon,* they are used metaphorically. Third, *ul-gool* and *nott* are usually used when face is lost or barely saved. "With what *ul-gool/nott* can I face him," "I can lift my *ul-gool/nott,"* and *"Ul-gool/nott* is ashamed," are some examples of the expressions about *ul-gool* and *nott.* The term *che-myon* is used much more broadly. It includes positive cases such as promoting and supporting face as well as negative cases such as losing and damaging face. Some examples of the expressions involving *che-myon* are "to damage *che-myon,"* "to lose *che-myon,"* "to salvage *che-myon,"* "to maintain *che-myon,"* and "to hoist *che-myon."*

Che-mo, myon-mok, and *mo-yang-sae* are not used as often and as widely as *che-myon, ul-gool,* and *nott.* As mentioned before, *che-mo* is used to refer to the *che-myon* of superiors or someone to whom one needs to show reverence. Contrary to *che-mo, myon-mok* is used to abase the face of oneself or someone else. It usually is employed when a person makes a shameful mistake. The expression "I have no *myon-mok* to face you" implies that the speaker is too ashamed to face the addressee.

Mo-yang-sae objectifies and neutralizes the very subjective and emotional concept of face. It literally means "appearance." Thus, different from the other concepts of Korean face, *mo-yang-sae* is not gained, saved, or lost; rather, it is good or bad, as in "the *mo-yang-sae* is good" or "the *mo-yang-sae* is bad." Koreans use the term *mo-yang-sae* instead of *che-myon* when they need to treat their face as if it were a separate object. Strong emotion is usually attached to face (Goffman, 1967). Thus persons react sensitively to anything that has the potential to change the current state of their face. Particularly when they judge that their face has been lost or promoted, the reaction can be very emotional.

Being emotional is not desirable in the Korean culture, as well as in many other cultures. Thus despite a loss or gain of face, persons need to show composure by objectifying and neutralizing their face, that is, by using the term *mo-yang-sae* instead of *che-myon.* "The *mo-yang-sae* is not good" is much more poised than "oh, I lost my *che-myon.*"

Noon-Chi

Noon-chi is a type of communicative strategy that is used when one needs to figure out the intention, desire, mood, and attitude of another person without resorting to the exchange of explicit verbal messages (Choi & Choi, 1990a). In Western terms, it is an element of communicative proficiency that enables communicators to interpret indirect or ambiguous messages.

The Korean culture is a high-context culture (Hall, 1976). People depend upon the context of interaction more than the message itself in order to communicate their meanings. Koreans believe that meanings are not universal but particular; that is, the meaning of a message can be shared only by those who share the knowledge of the particular context (Bernstein, 1970; Yum, 1988). Because Koreans believe that meanings can be communicated through the context as effectively as, if not more effectively than, the message, they prefer not to express their meanings explicitly when the meanings have the potential to make the situation unpleasant or awkward. Especially when the personalized or normative *che-myon* of one or the other is possibly at risk, Koreans tend to adopt the "don't do the face-threatening act" strategy (Brown & Levinson, 1978, 1987) and avoid expressing their intentions, desires, moods, and attitudes. Because meanings often are not verbalized, the skill of capturing the intended meanings of others, that is, *noon-chi,* is required of everybody to communicate competently.

As a matter of fact, Westerners use *noon-chi,* too. For example, an elderly father who is asked by one of his grown-up daughters what he wants for his birthday present, may say, "Oh, I don't want anything. I have everything I need." However, the daughter may interpret it as, "I don't want to say what I want. You figure it out" (Craig & Tracy, 1983). Westerners call this process of figuring out the real meaning "to read between the lines."

Grice (1975, 1978, 1981) explains this process very well in his implicature theory. He argues that communicators who want to express their meanings explicitly usually follow the four maxims of conversation: the maxims of quality, quantity, relevance, and manner. However, when communicators want to mean more than or other than what they say, they "flout" or purposefully violate these maxims. They flout the quality maxim by telling what is not truthful, the quantity maxim by giving more or less information than is required, the relevancy maxim by not being topical, and the manner maxim by being ambiguous or not precise. When a speaker flouts maxims, the addressee assumes that the speaker is still cooperating and tries to figure out the real meaning. When the speaker flouts maxims and the addressee interprets this, they share a mutual assumption that the speaker knows that the addressee knows that the speaker said A to mean B.

One of the major differences between the operation of *noon-chi* and the process of generating implicature or reading between the lines is that, to those who have to use *noon-chi* to figure out the other's intended meaning, the mutual assumption that saying or doing A in the given context means B is not available. Koreans who decide not to express their meanings explicitly do not necessarily want the other to figure out their meanings, or do not necessarily assume that the other will be able to figure out their intentions. In addition, the parties who have to use *noon-chi* to figure out the intention of the other do not necessarily have concrete clues about the intention. They have to go through the *noon-chi* operation, which makes use of all kinds of world knowledge, the knowledge of the other, the knowledge of the context, the history of their interactions, and verbal and nonverbal messages, if any. The process of operating *noon-chi,* in other words, is not routine but highly arbitrary. Thus the interpretations generated by *noon-chi* mostly represent the perspective of the operator of *noon-chi,* that is, the hearer or observer. The interpretations sometimes are very different from what the other really intended.

Noon-chi often performs a face-protecting function. When one operates *noon-chi,* the other does not have to go on record with a potentially face-threatening act. For example, making a request often threatens the *che-myon* of the requester as well as that of the requestee, because it signals the lack of the requester's ability to deal with the situation alone. When the request becomes a plea or begging, it obviously damages the *che-myon* of the requester. Koreans therefore tend to avoid making requests that may potentially damage the *che-myon* of either person. If the other operates *noon-chi* and volunteers to help with the unspoken but detected need, no one loses *che-myon.*

This is also true for the act of criticism. Koreans believe that criticism threatens not only the *che-myon* of the criticized person but also the *che-myon* of the criticizing person because it reflects a lack of tolerance or generosity on the part of the criticizing person. Koreans, therefore, are very careful not to make negative comments about others' possessions or performances, even when they do not like them. If wrongdoers operate *noon-chi* and correct the problems voluntarily, both parties can maintain their *che-myon*.

Noon-chi is an element of communicative competence. The ability to use *noon-chi* is different from person to person, and usually persons of more experience use *noon-chi* better. Persons who do not have the proper abilities to use *noon-chi* often threaten the other's *che-myon* by forcing the other to say explicitly something that may lower the other's and/or their own respectability. They are condemned for "not having proper *noon-chi*" or "lacking *noon-chi.*" Persons who are equipped with the abilities to operate *noon-chi* are always able to prevent any incident that may cause embarrassment. They are liked by others for "having swift *noon-chi.*"

To have "swift *noon-chi*" is an important virtue in subordinates. Superiors may sometimes force subordinates to express their intentions explicitly without causing great embarrassment on either side. Yet when subordinates force superiors, who are endowed with more normative *che-myon,* to express their intentions, needs, mood, or attitudes verbally, superiors are likely to lose *che-myon.* Subordinates, therefore, are normally prohibited from asking what superiors want, think, or intend to do. They have to figure out superiors' intentions, needs, and moods, and respond appropriately. Thus, in order to be liked by superiors, subordinates have to keep their *noon-chi* at the alert, and analyze constantly what superiors want and how superiors feel. Some subordinates become extremely sensitive and react nervously to every cue sent by superiors. They are at the stage of "seeing *noon-chi.*"

Jung and Love

Interpersonal relationships in Western society are built on the psychological basis that is called love. The psychological basis of interpersonal relationships in Korea is twofold. One is love (or *sah-rang* in Korean), and the other is *jung.* Love, as in Western society, is a feeling of affection for or attachment to an object or objects. It is purely affective. *Jung* is a much broader concept than love. In addition to the affective aspect of love, *jung* comprises the forces of inertia of a relationship. *Jung* is what ties two or more persons together, what keeps a relationship going. This aspect of *jung,* that is, the force of inertia of a relationship, is very different from the Western concept of commitment.

Whereas commitment is conscious and obligatory, *jung* is unconscious and voluntary.

Choi and Choi (1990b), in an attempt to examine the ways in which Koreans conceive *jung,* identified four properties of *jung:* duration, togetherness, warmth, and solidarity. First, *jung* grows gradually through a long history of a relationship. Persons in a new relationship may have strong love for each other, but they normally do not have strong *jung* toward each other. Jung requires a long history of interaction, mutual experiences, and mutual interdependence. For example, a mother normally has strong love for her newborn baby, but their mutual *jung* is not very "deep" yet. As she goes through years of "laughing and tears" with the baby, their *jung* becomes deep. As a relationship grows older, love may grow thinner, but *jung* usually grows "deeper."

Because *jung* takes a long time to become established, it does not easily fade away. Sometimes love turns into hatred, which facilitates the dissolution of love. *Jung,* however, does not turn into any negative feeling. Thus once a relationship with deep *jung* is lost, the involved person or persons go through serious emotional distress. Koreans use the expression "lamenting over *jung"* to depict this sorrow. Lamenting over *jung* has been one of the most popular themes of various Korean art forms including music, poetry, and fiction.

Second, *jung* evolves when two or more persons, whether they like each other or not, live through their lives together. This property of *jung,* in other words, emphasizes the proximity between persons. When persons see each other all the time, regardless of the nature of their relationship, they tend to have *jung* for each other. Koreans say that neighbors are cousins, which expresses the importance of *jung* among people who are spatially close to each other. *Jung* is deep for those who live together or go through good and bad times together.

Although *jung* requires frequent contacts to become deep, the contacts do not necessarily have to be rewarding. Koreans think that *jung* can be established between rivals who have to meet each other frequently. For example, two tennis stars who play against each other all the time may act like they hate each other. But, *jung* may unknowingly grow between them, and they may feel that they somehow are bonded together. Koreans call this kind of *jung* "bitterness-based *jung,"* whose origin is bitter but whose end is sweet.

Third, *jung* is warm, caring, and understanding. Those who are engaged in a relationship with "deep *jung"* accept and understand each other. This aspect of *jung* is very similar to the "caring" aspect of love (Kelley, 1979). The only difference between these two aspects is that although the act of caring based on love may be enthusiastic and animated, the act of "giving *jung*" is always poised and reticent. Love may be brisk and unsteady, but *jung* is slow and sure. Love may be intense, but *jung* is lasting. Those who share *jung* simply accept, understand, appreciate, and help each other.

Because of its "warmness" aspect, *jung* is often used to describe the personality of a person. Choi and Choi (1990b) identify four characteristics of a person with "bountiful *jung*": altruistic, empathetic, tender, and innocent. Persons with "lots of *jung*," in other words, understand and care for others and are emotionally vulnerable and naive. In contrast, those who "lack *jung*" or "have no *jung*" for others are self-centered, insensitive, unemotional, and ingenious. *Jung,* different from love, is almost always reciprocal. Only those who give out *jung* to others receive *jung* from others. In other words, people give their *jung* to those who have lots of *jung* for others, but not many people give *jung* to those who have no *jung* for others.

Finally, persons who share deep *jung* with each other are high in solidarity. Deep *jung* usually eradicates the individual differences and emphasizes the similarities and shared fates. Sometimes persons sharing deep *jung* perceive themselves as one unit rather than as separate individuals.

Whereas love is a volatile emotion and makes a relationship intense, *jung* is a very solid emotion and makes a relationship stable. Love changes very easily, depending on the outcome of the relationship (Thibaut & Kelley, 1959). When persons find their relationship rewarding, their love stays the same or becomes strong, but when they think their relationship is not working, their love may deteriorate. *Jung* is not really dependent upon the outcome of the relationship. Even when persons do not find their relationship rewarding, their *jung* toward each other does not significantly deteriorate as long as they maintain the normal frequency of contact. Old relationships in Korea, therefore, do not dissolve easily. When Koreans realize that they do not love each other any longer, they usually find mutual *jung* that is too profound to be thrown away. In short, *jung* is a warm and caring feeling that grows over time as persons in a relationship make repeated contacts with each other, which makes the relationship strongly bonded.

Summary and Conclusion

This chapter delineated three concepts essential to the understanding of interpersonal behavior and interpersonal relationships in Korea: *che-myon, noon-chi,* and *jung. Che-myon* is what enables a person to face others with dignity. Part of *che-myon,* like the Western concept of face, is personalized and negotiated through interaction. The aspect of *che-myon* that Koreans are really sensitive to, however, is sociological and normative *che-myon.* This is extended to one in relation to the social position one holds.

Noon-chi is what makes tacit communication possible. It is a strategy that enables one to figure out the intention, desire, mood, and attitude of the other without exchanging explicit verbal messages. It is similar to the Western notion of "reading between the lines," but is much more complicated than its Western counterpart. *Noon-chi* sometimes reads something out of nothing; that is, it reads the mind of the other even before the other knows his or her own mind. *Noon-chi* is often used to protect each other's *che-myon.* When one needs to perform a certain face-threatening act, if the other figures out one's needs before one expresses them and reacts appropriately, then both parties do not have to endanger their *che-myon.*

The psychological basis of close relationships in Korea is twofold. On the one hand, a close relationship needs love between partners. Love is what makes a relationship intense and intimate. On the other hand, a relationship needs mutual *jung* to be solid. *Jung* is a type of emotional attachment that grows over time as persons in a relationship make repeated contacts with each other. It functions to make a relationship strongly bonded. As a relationship grows old, love often fades away, but *jung* usually grows deep. Thus many persons in long-lasting relationships maintain their relationships not because of love, but of *jung.*

References

Bernstein, B. (1970). A sociolinguistic approach to socialization: With some reference to educability. In F. Williams (Ed.), *Language and poverty: Perspectives on a theme* (pp. 25-61). Chicago: Markham.

Brown, P., & Levinson, S. (1978). Universals in language usage: Politeness phenomena. In E. Goody (Ed.), *Questions and politeness: Strategies in social interaction* (pp. 56-89). Cambridge, UK: Cambridge University Press.

Brown, P., & Levinson, S. (1987). *Politeness: Some universals in language use.* Cambridge, UK: Cambridge University Press.

Choi, S., & Choi, S. C. (1991). *Che-Myon: Koreans' social face.* Unpublished manuscript, Chung-Ang University, Seoul, Korea.

Choi, S. C., & Choi, S. (1990a). *The conceptualization of Korean tact, noon-chi.* Paper presented at the 10th International Association of Cross Cultural Psychological Congress, Nara, Japan.

Choi, S. C., & Choi, S. (1990b). *Psychological structure of Jung (Cheong).* Paper presented at the annual meeting of the Korean Psychological Association, Pusan, Korea.

Craig, R. T., & Tracy, K. (1983). Appendix: The B-K conversation. In R. T. Craig & K. Tracy (Eds.). *Conversational coherence: Form, structure, and strategy* (pp. 299-320). Beverly Hills, CA: Sage.

Goffman, E. (1967). *Interaction ritual: Essays on face-to-face behavior.* Garden City, NY: Doubleday/Anchor.

Grice, H. P. (1975). Logic and conversation. In P. Cole & J. L. Morgan (Eds.), *Syntax and semantics: Vol. 3. Speech acts* (pp. 41-58). New York: Academic Press.

Grice, H. P. (1978). Further notes on logic and conversation. In P. Cole (Ed.), *Syntax and semantics: Vol. 9. Pragmatics* (pp. 113-128). New York: Academic Press.

Grice, H. P. (1981). Presupposition and conversational implicature. In P. Cole (Ed.), *Radical pragmatics* (pp. 183-198). New York: Academic Press.

Hall, E. T. (1976). *Beyond culture.* Garden City, NY: Doubleday.

Ho, D. Y. (1975). On the concept of face. *American Journal of Sociology, 81,* 867-884.

Hu, H. C. (1944). The Chinese concepts of face. *American Anthropologist, 46,* 45-64.

Kelley, H. H. (1979). *Personal relationships: The structures and processes.* Hillsdale, NJ: Lawrence Erlbaum.

Lim, T. (1988). *A new model of politeness in discourse.* Paper presented at the annual meeting of the Speech Communication Association, New Orleans.

Lim, T. (1989). *Positive and negative politeness in performing face-threatening acts.* Paper presented at the annual meeting of the International Communication Association, San Francisco.

Lim, T. (1990). Politeness behavior in social influence situations. In J. Dillard (Ed.), *Seeking compliance: The production of interpersonal influence messages* (pp. 75-86). Scottsdale, AZ: Gorsuch-Scarisbrick.

Lim, T. (1991). *Face renegotiation: The effects of confrontations on facework shifts.* Paper presented at the annual meeting of the Speech Communication Association, Atlanta.

Lim, T., & Bowers, J. W. (1991). Face-work: Solidarity, approbation, and tact. *Human Communication Research, 17,* 415-450.

Thibaut, J. W., & Kelley, H. H. (1959). *The social psychology of groups.* New York: John Wiley.

Yum, J. O. (1988). The impact of Confucianism on interpersonal relationships and communication patterns in East Asia. *Communication Monographs, 55,* 374-388.

Respeto:
A Mexican Base for
Interpersonal Relationships

Wintilo Garcia

Mexican communication reflects both Indigenous and European cultures. The combination of these traditions is reflected in the Spanish language. Here, norms, rules, and beliefs are monitored in myriad communicative and behavioral rituals. For Mexicans, the Spanish language serves as a source of identification and guidance. Discourse thus reflects a tradition in which message exchange validates and supports the overall culture.

Much of the theoretical research bases used to study Mexican communication are Eurocentric. Although these perspectives are valid within the United States, they ignore communication nuances specific to México's culture. In effect, these Eurocentric perspectives are not able to capture the entire Mexican communication experience because the standards that underlie these perspectives cannot tap salient aspects inherent in the Mexican communication tradition. This inability is by no means an assumption of inferiority but rather an assumption of cultural and linguistic difference.

Many communication concepts are vital to the understanding of Mexican communication patterns: One is the relational undertones that accompany discourse (Ross, 1988; Whitaker & Prieto, 1989). For example, the word *simpatico* connotes qualities of "kindness," "cuteness," and an overall sense of being "mild-mannered." From a relational perspective, *simpatico* implies an immediacy component. That is, a person who is referred to as *simpatico* is perceived to be approachable and personable. Although there is no literal English translation, *simpatico* is a term readily understood by native Spanish-speakers. Other terms specific to the Mexican communication system are unrecognizable to people from other cultures. This phenomenon is apparent only to those individuals who live, or have lived, in México. Thus the Mexican's use of the Spanish language conveys a mixture of messages describing and prescribing cultural norms and rules.

In this chapter, México's communication tradition is investigated. First, a definition of *communication* is conceptualized by combining historical and folkloric aspects. This conceptualization results in a México-centric perspective. Second, the relational concept of *respeto* is explored. This concept is an important building block for interpersonal transactions. Third, the Mexican use of the Spanish language is examined for culture-specific messages in the relational arena. These messages are common to the native speaker and ambiguous to a nonnative speaker. Finally, future research directions are suggested.

Conceptualization of Mexican Communication

History

Historically, class affiliation has been associated with power. That is, perceived "class" has reflected perceived power (Dolson, 1985). In this definition, perceived power does not refer to physical aggression or physical force. Instead, the association of class and power refers to the ability to construct transactional boundaries based on group affiliation. This sense of class can be traced to the Greco-Roman era. For example, intellectual ability was highly valued by the ancient Greeks (Grant, 1987). As a result of this ability, they considered themselves members of an elite group. On the other hand, Greeks considered

Romans to be barbarians with no intellectual tendencies. Consequently, Greeks considered themselves members of a "high" class group while categorizing Romans as "lower" class members. Thus a group difference was established where perceived class functioned as a factor of identification. According to Grant (1987), this factor limited transactions among Greeks and Romans. Although this class difference stems from antiquity, the consequences are evident in the present day.

From its European conception, México took the form of a class society. Historically, these social boundaries kept the physically weak, the ill-educated, the poor, and the racially and ethnically diverse from participating in an exclusive, though transplanted, European society (Adler, 1979; Benítez, 1965; Lowenthal, 1987). Ironically, these "excluded" members, or members of the lower classes, developed a system similar to the one that excluded them. That is, the excluded members developed a sense of discrimination toward other excluded individuals. For example, lower class members who were considered to possess a mixed background (a combination of Spanish and Indigenous background) were also considered members of a higher class within the low class group. Those people who possessed only an Indigenous background were considered members of a lower class within the low class group. As a result, a class society was established within the lower classes of México (Adler, 1979; Benítez, 1965; Lewis, 1961; Lowenthal, 1987; Paz, 1961). Some may conclude that the lower class members were at fault for perpetuating a discriminatory system. On closer inspection, however, these lower class systems were control mechanisms condoned by the governing powers. This historical base is important because it introduces a basis of México's culture, a base of class distinction.

As self-proclaimed lords of the new world, the wealthy Spaniards imposed structures of religion, government, and race upon the native population. Just as in other Spanish colonies, these structures were mechanisms of control and hierarchy. For example, religion and government functioned as symbiotic entities overseeing the development and control of colonial humanity (Campos, 1969; Lowenthal, 1987). When this religiously grounded governmental system was put into practice, México's Indigenous cultures were severely altered in the name of "god." This alteration devastated unique practices across the entire landscape. For example, many Aztec ceremonies, because of their perceived violence, were terminated by the Spanish. In these cases, many of the Aztec ceremonies consisted of human sacrifice. This fact countered religious principles imposed by the Spanish. Thus the termination of these ceremonies was undertaken in the name of "god." In addition, games unique to México were also terminated as a result of their perceived "pagan" qualities. In this case, a sport similar to modern basketball was terminated as a result of its "ungodly" quality. For México, the points of the compass signal former native civilizations; the Aztecs in the central and eastern parts of the country, the Mayas in the South, and the Yakis and Tarahumara in the North and West (Siméon, 1988). In their place, the Spaniards imposed a system in which religion (Catholicism), race (Spanish-European), and wealth were characteristics of nobility (high class). As a result, the Indigenous inhabitants of México resigned themselves to societal, economic, and ethnic positions of inferiority.

Over time, the union of European and Indigenous peoples produced a *meztiso* race of individuals who, to this day, proclaim both Spanish and Indigenous roots. Yet these ethnic proclamations are not eclectic. In other words, Mexicans still cling to the very practices, such as class distinction, that overwhelmed Indigenous civilizations (Atwood & McAnany, 1986; García Márquez, 1968; Paz, 1961; Phillips-Lathrop, 1984). Although tolerated, these practices are kept from the visitor and displayed to the native through the use of language. In one sense, these practices provide a historical base to study the dynamism of the Mexican culture.

The historical component of the Mexican culture cannot be underestimated. From a communication-history perspective the common factor of class distinction in everyday conversation emerges. This factor is so powerful that Mexicans are consciously aware of their class position when communicating with others (Adler, 1979; Atwood & McAnany, 1986; Delgado, 1994). From this perspective, class is a predominant factor in the unconscious ability or inability to interact with others. For example, those who perceive their class affiliation to be low may decide to shy away from certain people, events, and areas of a town or city. Persons who perceive themselves as members of a lower class do not interact freely with members of a higher class group. This does not mean, however, that low class members avoid all transactions with high class members. It merely indicates that relationship development is not sought from the low class member. In these cases, impersonal transactions are usually the norm. The lower class member usually assumes the role of a subordinate whereas the higher class member assumes a higher status role. In this way, a communicative hierarchy is applied among members of differing classes, thereby affirming the essence of the Mexican culture. In turn, those who perceive their class affiliation to be high possess limitless power to approach people, participate in various events, and wander in and out of lower class areas of towns or cities. Perceived high class is an implicit license to interact freely. For example, a high class individual is able to seek out the friendship of a low class member. In these cases, the high class individual is usually successful. Although this relationship may develop, the perceived class of the individuals remains fixed. Thus the lower class members are unable to progress to a higher class by mere association. These types of relationships illustrate the imposition of hierarchy within a relational system. When this cultural vestige is placed in a context of communication, perceived class reaffirms the historical legacy of hierarchy.

Unlike that of the United States, the majority of México's population observes similar norms and rules (Fairchild & Cozens, 1981). The most common instance in which Mexicans come in contact with people who observe other norms and rules is through tourism. Although these transactions are becoming more frequent as a result of modern travel, they are still considered superficial and insignificant in terms of everyday life. In addition, ethnic diversity is not significant. In México's case, the *meztiso* race (the Spanish-and-Indigenous offspring) significantly outnumbers other peoples. Thus there is little reason to confirm or acknowledge other cultures in México. In such a society, such things as ethnic identity, culture, and language patterns are intuitable. This means that people interact with little uncertainty. Mexicans perceive their communication patterns to be implicit and thus unspoken. Consequently, there is no need to seek out such aspects of one's existence because patterns of communication remain fixed in the overall culture. Indeed, this communicative pattern is not merely a medium of message exchange but rather an extension of a tradition in which culture reflects the lives of the natives. For Mexicans, history and language are symbiotic entities perpetuating a way of life.

In sum, the historical aspect of Mexican communication is an important factor determining class affiliation. Because these class implications are readily understood by the native Mexican, there is no need to elaborate on such messages. As a result, class affiliation becomes an implicit guide with which people construct transactional boundaries.

Folklore

Operating alongside the historical aspect of Mexican culture is the folkloric aspect of Mexican communication. Folklore combines spiritual and surrealistic myths to construct implicit structures of life (Hecht, Sedano, & Ribeau, 1993; Jensen & Hammerback, 1992). This particular aspect emphasizes events and salient beliefs in a manner that confirms the overall values of the Mexican culture. Here, Mexicans transmit culture by reinterpreting events that promote such things as tenacity, passion, love, and death (Sayer, 1990). This cultural transmission is provided in popularly held myths. For example, the Mexican myth of *El Día de los Muertos* (interpreted as *The Day of the Dead*) emphasizes the coexistence of life and death. Upon analyzing this myth, hierarchy and hope emerge. First, the hierarchical structure provides order for those who are living and for those who are dead. Thus a structure delegating power to the living and the dead is divided into "classes." In this case, the living possess powers not available to the dead. In the same vein, the dead possess other powers not available to the living. Second, this mythic celebration elicits hope. Here, the living relatives of the deceased experience a perceived reunion with the deceased. There is an underlying assumption that this "reunion" will occur in the afterlife. Thus there is hope that these two classes will merge into one. Like the historical component, folklore transmits a cultural guide that functions as a divider among people.

Folklore also stresses the long-suffering existence of the Mexican people. Folklore conveys resignation with a sense of hope. For example, history notes that although México is technically a democracy, it actually reflects the equivalent of a fascist regime. The *Partido Revoluccionario Institucional* (PRI—the dominant political party since México's independence) has always enjoyed supreme authority. Consequently, those officials who proclaim allegiance to the party also enjoy great political power. In many cases, however, this unchallenged power has led to widespread corruption (Benítez, 1965; Henry, 1990; Lewis, 1961; Paz, 1961). To this, Mexicans respond with irony. That is, although Mexicans are resigned to dishonesty in their public officials, they vigorously celebrate patriotic occasions by reciting famous oral statements (e.g., *El Grito de Dolores*), exalt former heroes of the Mexican Revolution, and honor the very public officials who are suspected of corruption. This type of exuberance perpetuates the folklore of hope. These celebrations and orations link the European legacies of exclusion with contemporary ones. This ironic response promotes an inherent folklore that confirms México's tie with history. In one sense, irony fits a pattern in which promises of good result in México's legacy of exploitation.

Narratives that transmit folklore are bound by superstitious beliefs. In essence, Spanish Catholicism and native beliefs of omnipotent beings conceived a culture in which folklore and culture are indistinguishable. In other words, these beliefs are converted into rituals that permeate the general culture of México. For example, the narrative of *La Lloróna* (interpreted as *The Weeping Woman*) depicts a woman who goes about crying in the night (Anaya, 1994). According to this narrative, her cries can be heard floating on the air for many miles. In this case, *La Lloróna* stems from a religiously based idea of life and death. In the same vein, the aforementioned mythic celebration called *El Día de los Muertos* (interpreted as *The Day of the Dead*) incorporates surreal narratives of life and death. On this particular day (close to the U.S. day of *Halloween*), Mexicans crowd the country's cemeteries, carrying flowers and even food and drink to the graves of their loved ones. Belief in communion with the dead is widespread. This cultural celebration perpetuates more outlandish narratives in which the main characters assume the personas of the deceased. In these tales, the mixture of religious ideology and black magic considers the relativity of human existence. This belief of communing with the dead implies that the future exists in the past. Consequently, interacting with the past is a way of knowing the future. For this reason, Mexican folklore can transmit norms and rules by combining notions of spirituality or religion.

For Mexicans, folklore symbolizes a common bond reserved for the people who identify with the culture. In this case, folklore is never challenged because it is a traditional aspect of culture and discourse. This does not mean, however, that Mexicans believe mythic tales to be true. Rather, Mexicans widely accept these cultural "truths" to be specific to the culture and not universal elements of human behavior. For this reason, Spanish-speakers who are not natives may find it difficult to identify with a language that is used to transmit more than mere messages. Here, historical narratives, tales of life coexisting with death, and rituals affirming surreal stories confuse the foreign Spanish-speaker (Macías, 1993). In essence, folklore transmits the affective element of the Mexican culture to the native Spanish-speaker.

In sum, Mexican folklore serves to bind historical events, narratives, and rituals in a context reflecting specific values. In this case, the prevalence of folklore highlights México's preoccupation with hope. To assume that folklore is pure myth is to impose a foreign perspective on the Mexican culture. For Mexicans, folklore conveys more than entertainment. Indeed, this aspect of the culture conveys the very values, norms, and rules that are used for daily survival in México.

Combining History and Folklore as a
Base of Mexican Communication

Conceptually, the combination of history and folklore forms a base of com-munication unique to México. In this system, codes that escape the nonnative are readily understood by Mexican native Spanish-speakers. Although this phenomenon can be observed in other cultures, it overwhelms México's Spanish language by consistently implying class and tradition within messages (Macías, 1993). This communication system extends far beyond the boundaries of any group or subgroup in the country. Many of the nuances demonstrated by a native Spanish-speaker are aspects fixed in the culture.

México's history provides a legacy of structure to the culture. From the Spanish occupation, México's culture has developed a hierarchical mechanism of class. This class aspect is inherent in the Mexican communication tradition. Here, class is an implicit guide directing relational boundaries. As a result, class affiliation affects the relational spectrum of the native.

Similarly, the prevalence of folklore in native discourse signals a link to tradition. Folklore serves to revive cultural rituals and beliefs that bring Mexicans together. The nonnative Spanish speaker can misunderstand or misinterpret messages containing traditional cultural values. This use of language assures the continuity of a culture in an ever-changing world. In this manner, values, ideals, and rituals may be passed on to future generations in common everyday conversations.

For Mexicans, asserting class position includes implications of such things as educational level, financial standing, and social influence. In addition, people affiliated with certain classes also posses unique language systems that exclude others. Here, class affiliation through language use is not so much a deterrent to human transaction as it is a form of identification.

México-Centric Perspective

Regional and social language varieties are interwoven to create a "mainstream" Spanish dialect in México. Because Mexicans are so conscious of their "place" or "position" in most situations, they revert to intuitive cultural rules of establishing class hierarchy. Spanish-speaking visitors from other countries can misunderstand messages from native Spanish-speakers. When the aforementioned Mexican communication base is taken into account, then this misunderstanding is reasonable. Indeed, México's communication system perpetuates a culture that clouds its language channel to those who are not able to identify with México's cultural nuances.

Access to México's language culture requires the ability to decipher specific linguistic elements in normal speech (Ross, 1988). Here, class distinction and folklore are evident in the messages of the natives. In this case, for example, Mexican Spanish-speakers implicitly assert their class and folklore in normal conversation as well as in verbal conflict episodes. Although implicit, the involved players jockey in a web of mixed messages in order to assert an ultimate position in the transaction. On closer inspection, these transactions have roots in historical legacies of class position and hierarchy. Yet to the native, these strategies are merely intuitive ways of communicating with others.

The prevalence of these implicit norms does not mean that Mexicans are a hostile people. On the contrary, this nuance is a manifestation of the natives' vibrant culture. Through these transactions, the native Spanish-speaker provides a glimpse of a personal world to those who understand México's language culture.

For México, as for other cultures, the family symbolizes a fundamental system of interaction (Atwood & McAnany, 1986). Because family is such an important element to the Mexican culture, native Spanish-speakers demonstrate a tie to a cultural value (family) while preserving the ever-present language nuance. For instance, the native may describe his or her father as *jefe* (pronounced *heh-feh,* interpreted as the English word *chief*), mother as *jefa* (pronounced *heh-fah,* interpreted as the English *female chief*), husband as *viejo* (pronounced *vee-eh-ho,* interpreted as the English *old man*), wife as *vieja* (pronounced *vee-eh-ha,* interpreted as the English *old woman*), brother as *carnal* (interpreted as the English word *carnal* or *fleshy*), sister as *carnala* (interpreted as the English word *carnal* or *fleshy*), and children as *escuincles* (pronounced *es-queen-kles,* no English interpretation but meaning *brat*), which is a word rooted in the Indigenous language *Náhuatl* (Siméon, 1988). On closer inspection, these monikers construct a hierarchical system within the family. For instance, the first terms, *jefe* and *jefa,* imply the highest positions within a family system. Second, the terms *viejo* and *vieja* connote comfort or confidence and are therefore indicative of equal positions of power. Third, the words *carnal* or *carnala* also imply equal positions because the names connote an origin from the "same flesh." Lastly, although the word *escuincle* is not part of the Spanish language, it nevertheless connotes the lowest position in the system. From a Mexican communication perspective, this mode clearly assumes elements of class correlating to historical legacies in the most fundamental system known to humanity: the family.

Respeto

In the relational arena, class is implied through *respeto*. *Respeto* is literally interpreted as the English word *respect.* Yet this English interpretation overlooks the nature of the Spanish term *respeto*. In essence, *respeto* implies perceived relational status. The notion of *respeto* is similar to Ting-Toomey and Cocroft's (1994) notion of face, in which elements of honor and dignity are incorporated into a culture-specific transactional norm. Implicit in daily conversations, native Spanish-speakers constantly affirm status by manifesting *respeto*. It is this implicit conversational nature that reaffirms the cultural vestige of class distinction.

Relational players are always aware of their hierarchical position in a relationship. In many instances, *respeto* is communicated indirectly by referring to a relational partner as either *tú* or *usted* (both terms are interpreted as the English word *you*). These terms connote perceived status to the involved players (Hecht et al., 1993; Mainous, 1989). Misusing these terms can therefore result in an unintentional verbal attack on another.

Tú and *Usted*

Although mere words are not complete, or sole, indicators of status, they provide a relatively clear picture of the Mexican communication tradition and its effect on interpersonal relationships. The Mexican use of the Spanish words *tú* and *usted* signal the immediacy and status of the relational partners. *Tú* is the informal application of the pronoun *you*. It is common that individuals refer to their friends, family members, or children by this form of the word. The word *usted* is the formal form of the pronoun *you*. Cultural norms and rules require individuals to use this form when addressing new acquaintances, older people, professional (white-collar) people, and people who possess some sort of power. In addition, formal words are also used as weapons to create either harmony or disharmony in a relationship. In these cases, irony plays a significant role. Addressing someone by the "improper" form is disconfirming to the source, the receiver, and the relationship. For example, referring to a known authority figure, such as a professor, by *tú*, implies informality and relatively equal relational status. As a student, using *tú* when addressing a professor discredits the professor's status and power. By not acknowledging this implicit class difference, the student will implicitly be perceived as *irrespetuoso* (pronounced *eer-es-pet-oo-ohsoh;* interpreted as the English *one who lacks respect*). As a result, the relationship is disconfirmed from the lack of class acknowledgment. All of these factors are apparent to the Mexican. Though this may seem simplistic, the use of these words signals an implicit effort to form class boundaries within relational systems.

Tú

As mentioned, the Spanish word *tú* is the informal application of the English word *you*. Yet to assume that the Mexican notion of informality mirrors that of the United States is an error. For the Mexican, *tú* does not possess a static meaning. Rather it is bound to relational systems. Thus *tú* cannot be used in every "informal" relationship. For this reason, the word *tú* possesses two main cultural characteristics that impact the relationship.

In the first characteristic, *tú* connotes a high degree of intimacy and trust, which leads to comfort for the involved players. In one sense, this implication possesses similarities to Gudykunst's (1988) general perspective of anxiety and uncertainty management. That is, when *tú* is used as the main source of address, it connotes low uncertainty and low anxiety for the relational players. When this is the case, there is an implied climate of freedom that dominates the relationship. Furthermore, this climate provides a sense of safety for the involved players. Therefore, relational partners can feel free and safe to express personal needs, opinions, and beliefs without fear of ridicule or banishment. This characteristic is often applied to very intimate friends or relatives. Thus this shared implication of the word *tú* affirms the intimacy and trust of the relationship.

In the second characteristic, *tú* is a status indicator for relational partners. In other words, players use the word *tú* to imply or assert their status in the relationship. Yet these implications depend on the state of the relationship. Because the word *tú* is an informal application, it can connote either equal status or lower status for relational partners. In the first instance *tú* connotes equal status, and this case is similar to the implications noted in the first characteristic. This use of the word, however, implies that the relational partners possess equal status in the relationship as well as a sense of certainty. Here, individuals readily address classmates, co-workers, neighbors, and siblings with this implied meaning. The maintenance of the relationship, in this case, is dependent upon the partners' willingness to be equal. In a different situation, however, *tú* imposes a lower status on a relational partner. For example, a person with some sort of power (high status) is allowed to use the informal application of the word with someone of perceived lower status. When this is done, it implies a complementary relationship. To illustrate, parents readily use the word *tú* when addressing their children and the children often respond with the formal *usted*. Similarly, in a business context, superiors will often address subordinates by the informal *tú* and the subordinates will usually respond with *usted*. These interactions not only reinforce a power relationship but also impose a status of inequality. This implication is prevalent in most complementary relationships in México. The maintenance of the relationship, in this case, is dependent upon the willingness of one partner to assume a high status position and the willingness of the other to assume a low status position. When this is done, families, businesses, schools, hospitals, and any other entities that possess hierarchies function with fluidity.

The use of the word *tú* reinforces a contextual boundary on the relationship. That is, the word *tú* functions as an implicit guide that determines the type of relationship without regard to the setting. In this case, the word *tú* imposes a context on the relational players. That is, the status of the players is fixed and their class is secured by the use of the word *tú*. In one instance, for example, relational partners who hold equal status in an organization may refer to one another by the *tú* form. When they meet outside of the organizational setting, consistent use of the *tú* form reinforces the context of their relationship; a relationship of equal class and status. Here, *respeto* functions as a means to convey equal relational status. The relationship is thus maintained as a result of observing this implicit norm. In another instance, however, organizational supervisors may refer to their subordinates by the *tú* form within the organizational setting. Yet consistent use of the word *tú* by an organizational supervisor outside of the organizational setting also imposes a context of class distinction. In this example, *respeto* is implicitly requested from the supervisor. Fulfilling this request results in an implicit superior-subordinate context. Thus relational players adhere to the organizational rules that govern communication patterns. This behavior may be perceived as a "one-up" tactic by people from other cultures. Yet to Mexicans, this behavior ensures the preservation of salient cultural norms and rules.

In sum, the word *tú* implies relational climates of intimacy and status. For Mexicans, *tú* is an assertion tool. That is, *tú* is used to create a niche within relationships. Unlike the English equivalent, *tú* is grounded in a tradition of history and folklore that condones a hierarchical culture.

Usted

The Spanish word *usted* is the formal application of the English pronoun *you*. The use of this term implies *respeto* in a power distance relationship. In other words, *respeto* is implied by fostering a formal communication climate. For Mexicans, the formal communication climate implies a sense of deference to the person of higher class. Thus *usted* is used to address people who are not perceived to have close relational ties. That is, Mexicans most often use this form of address with people who are not of equal status or part of an intimate group. In these instances, Mexicans can readily be observed addressing store clerks, receptionists, customers, and other fleeting contacts in a formal manner. On closer inspection, however, the word *usted* incorporates elements grounded in class differences.

In some circumstances, the word *usted* implies a power distance element that is more indicative of class maintenance. In this case, *usted* is indicative of real power and subsequent relational distance. The word *usted* signals a complementary relationship in which one individual assumes the high class (high status) position whereas the other assumes the low class (low status) position. The person who is referred by *usted* implicitly holds a higher class (higher status). From this perspective, the high class individual is allowed to disagree with much more frequency and force than people who are members of lower classes. For example, this cultural latitude enables high class persons fervently to refute arguments posed by lower class individuals, interact (almost at will) more frequently with people who belong to a perceived lower class, interrupt private conversations without fear, and generally impose a personal will on the immediate environment. In these cases, the ability to manipulate an environment clearly sets the high class individual apart from the low class members. In these cases, the low class members resign themselves to a position of inferiority. Examples of these relationships include those of parent-child, teacher-student, coach-player, and the organizational superior-subordinate relationship. To the nonnative, a relationship based on *usted* may seem a bit absurd. Yet these types of relationships further support a base of transaction specific to the Mexican culture.

Using *usted* also creates a status difference that is based on implicit worth. In these cases, for example, elders are referred to by *usted* as a result of their age and experience, teachers are referred to by *usted* as a result of their willingness to share knowledge, and physicians are referred to by *usted* as a result of their medical expertise. In such cases, *usted* is symbolic of perceived high class. Here, the term *usted* grants high class to people with tangible resources. It is these resources that are held in high regard. Thus those people who possess these resources automatically possess a perceived higher class. In these instances, those who refer to others by *usted* are implicitly occupying a lower class position. In doing so, people continually construct differences within the bounds of relationships.

Like the *tú* form, *usted* also reinforces a contextual boundary to a relationship. Here, *usted* is used to create greater distance between the interactants by imposing an implicitly formal communication environment. This formal environment impedes the development of an intimate relationship. For example, students who wish to preserve a sense of interpersonal distance between themselves and professors merely need to use the *usted* form when addressing professors. By consistently employing this term, even if it is employed outside of the educational arena, interpersonal distance will be an implied desire. As a result, relational players adhere to the formal norms that govern such an interaction.

In sum, *usted* implies distance in relationships. This distance is not only the result of power differences, but also a function of cultural deference display. For Mexicans, *usted* signals a tradition that has roots in colonial class legacy. Thus *usted* is a vestige of antiquity that lives in modern culture.

When *Usted* Changes to *Tú*

In México, as relationships become more intimate, the form of address changes. This often occurs over time where people who were once referred to by *usted* will later be referred to by *tú*. A change to informal address indicates a change in relational climate. That is, the change in address indicates a change in status for the relational partners. Usually, this transformation is initiated by the person who holds a perceived higher class. This is reasonable because high class individuals are perceived to possess more power in the relationship. In México, the usual request phrase from the high class player is *tuteame* (interpreted as *you tú me*), which implies a desire for relational equality. In order for this request to be fulfilled, relational players must renegotiate the pattern of communication. This is similar to a professor-student relationship. For example, if a student normally addresses professors by the title *Doctor G* and *Doctor T,* it implies a status and class difference. In general, to change this form of address, the professor must initiate the request. Although the change implies a more equal status relationship, it does not imply equal status in terms of area of expertise. In this way, a student may refer to the professors as Bill and Stella, implying a more intimate relationship, while maintaining a sense of *respeto* for them. If the transformation is successful, then what was once a distant, nonintimate relationship, becomes a more intimate one.

In some cases, the change from the formal *usted* to the informal *tú* can indicate defiance. In such a relationship, *respeto* is lost. Here, the established class and status positions within a relationship are challenged. Generally, these incidents are initiated by low class members who refuse to address the high class members by the formal term *usted*. In such cases, two general responses are prevalent for Mexicans. First, if the high class member is not bothered by such behavior, then it is taken as an implicit message of accepting the *tú* form of address. Depending on the context, such as business or politics, this can be perceived as a sign of weakness. Thus accepting the *tú* form from a lower class member implies equal status (and power) to the low status (and -power) member. If the context is not threatening to the high class member, however, then there is no loss. In a second response, the high class member can vehemently challenge the behavior of the low class individual. In a case such as this, the term *tú* is not only perceived as a challenge to established status positions, but also as a sign of *irrespetuosidad* (interpreted as the English *a person who has no sense of respect*). In responding to this challenge, the high class individual can impose boundaries that reaffirm the boundaries of a formal relationship. For example, the high class player can verbally attack the lower class individual by explicitly imposing superiority. In these instances, negative references to the low class member's ethnic background, economic status, educational level, or social circle can reintroduce class boundaries in the relationship. Thus the relational environment requires that class affiliation be recognized. In these cases, the facets of *respeto* empower the high class relational members.

In sum, initiating the move from the formal *usted* to the informal *tú* must be undertaken by the high class individual. When this move is successful, it implies a renegotiation of relational status differences. In these cases, *respeto* becomes a base of equality. When this move is undertaken by the lower status individual, however, it indicates defiance of the relational system. If the high status member is unaffected, then there are no consequences. However, if the high status member protests, the culture imposes sanctions on the low status individual. Here, *respeto* is perceived as a scarce resource. When this occurs, relational players attempt to impose their view of *respeto* on the relational system. In either case, the move from the formal *usted* to the informal *tú* indicates a status shift in the relationship. From this perspective, the Mexican communication base is supported through the nuances of the natives.

When *Tú* Reverts to *Usted*

In some cases, the more intimate, equal, and informal *tú* is replaced by the more formal *usted*. These cases imply a form of dissolution in relationships. Consequently, *respeto* is lost. Thus, addressing an intimate partner by the *usted* form implies a wish for greater distance, less intimacy, and more status. For

Mexicans, this situation is very severe. Not only is it an indication of a relationship in turmoil, but it is also an indication of a class (power and status) struggle.

For the initiator, or source of the message, *usted* signifies a willingness to flee the relationship. In these instances, irony plays a major role. In other words, *usted* is perceived to possess low class qualities because it implies distance and status difference in an intimate relationship. In this case, *usted* is perceived to subvert cultural norms and rules of transactions within intimate relationships. In turn, *tú* is perceived as the preferred form of address within intimate relationships and is thus perceived to possess high class qualities that promote cultural norms and rules of transaction in intimate relationships. Thus publicly addressing an intimate partner by *usted* is perceived as unconventional. Furthermore, the use of *usted* in this instance implicitly denounces the relationship as well as the other person. Consequently, the partner who is referred to by the *usted* form is perceived to possess low status because of his or her inability to reestablish the less formal *tú*. An example of such a situation occurs when intimate partners are engaged in conflict. In these situations, a public display of formality signals relational discord between the players. In this public display, intimate partners implicitly increase their interpersonal distance. To observers, this display signals a lack of *respeto* that indicates the inevitable end of the relationship.

For the receiver of the message, the formality of *usted* is a reflection on personal status and general class evaluation. In other words, being addressed in the *usted* form by an intimate partner is an implication of low class. In this case, the individual who is addressed by the *usted* form must portray a sense of high class (high status) in public. Not to do so would imply a weak sense of self. This notion is similar to Ting-Toomey's (1994) argument of "losing one's face." That is, to loose one's face indicates loosing one's dignity, honor, and strength. For the Mexican, this is not a desirable state. Thus the receiver may make several attempts to create an offensive strategy in order to combat the status of the initiator. For example, persons addressed by the *usted* form may attempt to impose a personal sense of *respeto* by reciprocating the formal *usted* form. In these cases, a competitive climate is fostered whereby *respeto* is at stake. Relational partners indirectly attack the other in order to gain *respeto*. Yet this act is futile because *respeto* cannot be reciprocated in this environment.

In sum, reverting back to the formal *usted* while involved in an intimate relationship where *tú* was readily used is undesirable. For Mexicans, status, intimacy, and distance are core factors in the formal and informal address. In these relationships, there is a mutual sense of *respeto* that is reciprocated between relational partners. When this sense of *respeto* is broken, relational partners attempt to reestablish former relational boundaries. The reciprocal relationship that occurs with immediacy (more formal : less intimate) indicates a struggle of status and power. Hence it becomes the responsibility of the receiver to create a strategy whereby status and power are matters of neither perception nor fact. When this shift is observed (from *tú* to *usted*), it further supports México's base of class hierarchy. In this case, the struggle to maintain status and power in a relationship requires the imposition of cultural norms and rules on fundamental human relationships.

Conclusion and Future Directions

In conclusion, historic and folkloric artifacts are symbiotic entities that perpetuate the life cycle of México's culture. The México-centric perspective is essential for the investigation and understanding of México's communication tradition.

It is clear that México's use of the Spanish language adheres to two main cultural elements: folklore and history. Yet to assume that these elements are mere artifacts is to deny México's manifestation through the speech of its people. First, the historical element perpetuates culturally specific nuances such as class distinction in speech. In this case, Mexicans use the Spanish language as a lever. Here, the use of the *tú* and *usted* (interpreted as the English *you*) forms indicates a status struggle, thereby perpetuating the overall cultural value of class distinctions. In the same vein, the folkloric aspect of the culture further combines religious beliefs and native tradition to convey cultural-specific messages to the natives. Here, narratives and rituals are used to perpetuate the life of the culture. In these cases, surrealism is used as a device to carry these norms and rules. Without this conceptual base, a study of México's communication culture is not fully understood.

It is imperative that communication research expand its cultural wings of inclusion. As mentioned above, the study of *Mexican* communication has been conducted in the United States. Although these studies provide rich information, they claim to investigate so-called cultural phenomena, but in the culture of the United States. In order to study the primordial aspects of México's communication culture, research must be conducted in México. To claim the opposite is to deny a culture the opportunity to manifest its uniqueness. Also, empirical data are needed to substantiate the hypotheses that appear in this work. Furthermore, the base of México's *respeto* must be recognized as a prominent element in the culture's tradition.

The Mexican communication system nurtures people who identify not only with the messages but also with their inherent values. For Mexicans, this includes an elaborate communication system that reflects the history and folklore to native Spanish-speakers. Such an elaborate system must be recognized as a main factor in México's cultural transactions. In essence, cultural behavior must be studied at its primordial level: a communication level.

References

Adler, D. A. (1979). *American ideals and institutions.* Belmont, CA: Wadsworth.

Anaya, R. A. (1994). *The legend of La Llorona.* Berkeley, CA: TQS Publications.

Atwood, R., & McAnany, E. G. (1986). *Communication and Latin American society.* Madison: University of Wisconsin Press.

Benítez, F. (1965). *A century after Cortés.* Chicago: University of Chicago Press.

Campos, M. O. (1969). *La oratoria en México.* Mexico City: Editorial F. Trillas, S.A.

Delgado, F. P. (1994). The complexity of Mexican American identity: A reply to Hecht, Sedano, and Ribeau and Mirandé and Tanno. *International Journal of Intercultural Relations, 18,* 77-84.

Dolson, D. P. (1985). The effects of Spanish home language use on the scholastic performance of Hispanic pupils. *Journal of Multicultural and Multilingual Development, 6,* 132-148.

Fairchild, H. H., & Cozens, J. A. (1981). Chicano, Hispanic, or Mexican American: What's in a name? *Hispanic Journal of Behavioral Sciences, 3,* 191-198.

García Márquez, G. (1968). *Cien años de soledad.* Argentina: Editorial Sudamericana.

Grant, M. (1987). *The rise of the Greeks.* New York: Scribner.

Gudykunst, W. B. (1988). Uncertainty and anxiety. In Y. Y. Kim & W. B. Gudykunst (Eds.), *Theories in intercultural communication* (pp. 123-156). Newbury Park, CA: Sage.

Hecht, M. L., Sedano, M. V., & Ribeau, S. R. (1993). Understanding culture, communication, and research: Applications to Chicanos and Mexican Americans. *International Journal of Intercultural Relations, 17,* 157-165.

Henry, S. (1990). English only: The language of discrimination. *Hispanic,* 20-31.

Jensen, R. J., & Hammerback, J. C. (1992). *Reies Lopez Tijeriena's "Letter from the Santa Fe jail."* Paper presented at the Speech Communication Association Convention.

Lewis, O. (1961). *The children of Sanchez.* New York: Vintage.

Lowenthal, A. F. (1987). *Partners in conflict: The United States and Latin America.* New York: Harper & Row.

Macías, R. F. (1993). Language and ethnic classification of language minorities: Chicano and Latino students in the 1990s. *Hispanic Journal of Behavioral Sciences, 15,* 230-257.

Mainous, A. G., III. (1989). Self-concept as an indicator of acculturation in Mexican Americans. *Hispanic Journal of Behavioral Sciences, 11,* 178-189.

Paz, O. (1961). *The labyrinth of solitude.* New York: Grove.

Phillips-Lathrop, J. (1984). *Ancient Mexico: Cultural traditions in the land of the feathered serpent.* Dubuque, IA: Kendall/Hunt.

Ross, S. (1988). *Is the Mexican revolution dead?* Albuquerque: University of New Mexico Press.

Sayer, C. (1990). *The Mexican day of the dead.* Boston: Shambhala.

Siméon, R. (1988). *Diccionario de la lengua Náhuatl o Méxicana.* Mexico City: Siglo Veinteuno Editores, S.A. de C.V.

Ting-Toomey, S., & Cocroft, B.-A. (1994). Face and facework: Theoretical and research issues. In S. Ting-Toomey (Ed.), *The challenge of facework: Cross-cultural and interpersonal issues* (pp. 307-340). Albany: State University of New York Press.

Whitaker, J. H., & Prieto, A. G. (1989). The effects of cultural and linguistic variables on the academic achievement of minority children. *Focus on Exceptional Children, 21,* 1-10.

8

Communication and Personal Relations in Brazil

Monica Rector
Eduardo Neiva

First Things First

The fact that South America belongs to the Hispanic world is relevant for the understanding of Brazilian culture and of communication studies dealing with interpersonal practices developed by our native scholars. Any approach to interpersonal relationships as a field of study must bear in mind the anthropological influence on its metatheoretical conceptions. The limits and obstacles faced by Brazilian scholars when building theoretical models for interpersonal relationships are difficult to understand unless one takes into account how the peculiarities of Brazilian culture came into being.

We realize that generalizing can be an attempt to create an abstract model for such a diversified conglomerate entity as South America. Nevertheless, it is undeniable that from the Hispanic *ethos,* Brazilians—and South Americans in general—in fact did acquire a supranational trace very active as a force in their everyday life. Technically as well as sociologically, this is referred to as Pan-Hispanism. History offers an explanation of how Pan-Hispanism works.

The Iberic Peninsula was divided into Spain and Portugal only for political reasons. The original elements of geographic unity, cultural blending, and a relational vocation were active parts of a heritage that was donated to Brazil. The framework of inherited rules encodes information for social actors; and interaction will be dependent upon the influence of macro organization principles on micro relations. In the course of history this can be seen in the way social time, as a support for personal relationships in Brazil, blends European notions and measuring tools with Amerindian values. Social time is not a direct and objective phenomenon that can be measured by simple, direct means. Brazilian society keeps a dual outlook. We glance at our wristwatches and settle an appointment that will not follow the rules of punctuality. This is no contradiction, but a blending of cultures that will not be understand without knowing the peculiar notions of time held by native Brazilians.

The Indians in the Northeast of Brazil measured time according to their cashew crop. The result was an experience of time directly linked to a cosmic dimension that would disregard human face-to-face interaction. Yet the succession of one crop after the other could not take care of rather small units such as days and hours. The cashew crop mattered drastically due to its vital function in the food cycle and as a diet staple. Apart from the crop, time was of little interest. Only rain and sun mattered for the production of food (Freyre, 1975, p. xxxiii). Time was lived as a ludic support in which obligations and social constraints could be transcended.

We can easily recognize the difference of this Hispanic heritage vis-à-vis Anglo-Saxon cultures where social time is not ruled by such large events but rather is seen as a continuous flow. Personal life in Hispanic countries can be lived at a slow pace, emphasizing today and leaving for tomorrow whatever is not particularly urgent.

If we compare this concept of time with the Anglo-Saxon experience, we will find sharp differences. A traditional business breakfast simply would not work in Brazil because, during the meal, the conversation would deal with everything but business. The meal is just an introduction for business to be done later. All of this expresses an important Brazilian cultural element, that is, the priority of socialization.

Westerners accustomed to punctuality respond negatively to the Latin American pattern of nonpunctuality. Time in the United States is a matter of punctual precision, whereas in Brazil as well as in most Latin American cultures it is an approximation, a displaced value. If they know and accept the cultural pattern, American businessmen will not be upset if a deadline is met a couple of days later. It is not lack of efficiency, but a different time value.[1] The reaction is not always negative. Americans may be pleased to go to a party where the invitation states the starting but not the ending time. In fact, the party will end when the last guest leaves. Different conceptions of time will entail different reactions. Life can be seen as an easy-going affair, whereas the rigidity of preciseness can be interpreted on the part of Brazilians as an undue pressure.

As a side effect of this prevailing conception of time in Hispanic cultures, we find the concept of *saudade*. This is a peculiar form of nostalgia that is combined with love and affection, and represents a larger-than-life longing arising from the present absence of pleasurable moments familiar from past experience, which we look forward to repeating in the future.

Studies on personal relationships in Brazil are bound up with the definition of the social background in which individual action does occur. Scholarship on Brazilian personal relationships needs to propose theories of collective representations as a necessary basis for understanding the conditions of face-to-face interaction. Anthropological and sociological frameworks, with their mandatory historical concern, have tried to deal with the rules for personal interaction in Brazil.

Brazil for Brazilians

Personal relationships cannot happen in a cultural void. Implicit rules guide interaction. In daily interaction, those rules are taken for granted (Gudykunst, 1983, p. 59) and we act as though an invisible hand pulled the strings for the scene. Yet culture should not be defined as rigid determination. Culture creates the possibilities of actions. Thanks to the projection of possibilities, we will meet the norm. In a general manner, cultures are ethic possibilities, and that is why we act as we do. Therefore, our acquired habits when approved culturally are considered proper and comfortable, and other habits are rejected. All cultures postulate themselves as ethical and moral possibilities. Personal relationships are impossible to understand outside their cultural framework.

Every culture presents itself as the unique and true system of representations. But if we compare cultures, we will see that there are no truths that could aspire to absolute universality, floating above the concrete expression of each particular culture. There are no generalizations about humankind that would not sound as clearly obvious. The only generalization is that there is no possible generalization.

As a result of collective instructions, cultural forms are laid upon human behavior. The idea of actions outside cultural frameworks is inconceivable. In that case, people would be less than empty baskets—not even instincts could exist, and no form of reasoning. Human nature is bound up with culture (Geertz, 1973, p. 73). Each human action is a shadow of the directions proposed by the specific culture in which it occurs.

Culture is total, but any action is partial. We are always moving in partial situations. Of itself, totality is inaccessible. Our behavior is an approximate process, ruled by possibility and as a result of the construction of hypothesis that can only point toward the whole. A set of rules, practices, and knowledge are in a state of dialogue with the actual contextual behavior. How do we know those norms? The interpretation of personal interaction has to provide an organizing answer for interaction. Personal interaction will make sense only if we have a rational motive for behavior. The first question then is: What is Brazil for Brazilians?

Our concern with communication in personal relations will lead to inquiring about how Brazilians define the social roles of Brazilians. Individuality is more than just the singular support in which a person, as a biological being, exists. First, we should understand that any social actor expresses the singularity of the individual, yet as a social being also exists as a *persona* that acts according to the social masks considered morally right and proper by society. How is individuality lived as a socialized *persona* in Brazil?

A distinctive trace of Brazilian life can be singled out in the tension between individuality and social hierarchy. As a country that aspires to be modern, Brazil cherishes liberty and individual freedom, but it is also true that archaic remnants of rural and patriarchal *ethos* still prevail. In an original manner, Brazil is a dual society where those apparently contradictory conceptions can easily coexist.

However egalitarian Brazilians would like to see themselves, it has been pointed out by Da Matta (1979) that rituals of distinction emphasizing social hierarchy are widely used in our daily life. The fact that an individual belongs to the higher strata of society will allow him to claim his privileged position saying: Do you know to whom you are speaking? If Brazil were not a dual society, with the emphasis laid upon individuality, the situation would be one of equality and it would take the form of this question: Who do you think you are?

We would like to take a more complex view of this problem. Social hierarchy is used as a means of empowering the individual. Such a particular blend of individuality does not rely exclusively upon the values of democratic ethos. Our special brand of individualism is a residue of Portuguese heritage.

The Portuguese arrival in Brazil by 1500 lead first to a dominion of Western Christian values. The Spaniards found well-developed cultures, such as the Aztec and Inca cultures that could resist Western invasion; the Portuguese, however, encountered Indian cultures that were less technically elaborate and could therefore be more easily overthrown. The way the Portuguese colonized Brazil was a result of arrogance based upon the ethnic origin of the rulers-to-be. Even the present system of property is derived from an act of appointment by the Imperial Crown of Portugal. Using the rationale that Brazil was too large to be colonized, the Portuguese distributed the *capitanias hereditárias,* splitting the country into areas that were donated by the Portugal Court, around 1532.

The *capitanias hereditárias* were administrative divisions created by D. João III, King of Portugal. Each *capitania* was handed over to an individual for colonization. The Brazilian territory was divided into 15 strips of land that varied from 180 km to 600 km. Twelve individuals, the *donatários,* received land, and some of them were granted more than one division. The donation was on a perpetual basis and the *donatários* had their rights as owners and governors of that land. A *donatário* did not have to respond legally to anyone. His obligations were only to the Portuguese Crown—for taxes and valuables such as gold and precious gems, for instance—and to the Church. The first move toward integration took the form of slavery. Forcing the natives to work on sugarcane plantations produced a cultural shock that deteriorated the relationships between natives and Portuguese. Therefore, the labor force had to be imported from Africa. The composition of Brazilian culture includes three major influences: the Western, through Portugal; the Native; and the African heritages. A rich and complex blend resulted. According to Manuel Diegues, Brazil is a culturally diversified and heterogeneous country. He identifies nine different cultural regions,[2] each of which has complex features due to the mixture of Portuguese, native, and African elements.

The kind of individualism that ruled Brazilian history takes a fierce form that does not respect the general principle of equality. As something inherited through Iberian and Portuguese values, the prevailing individualism can easily take the shape of an *anything goes* practice. In Brazil, due to the hardship of living, this became an instrument of defense and of upholding social hierarchy. Individualism took an authoritarian form, imposing discipline and respect. It was a weapon of defense and an efficient tool for law and authority. Justice was not a shared horizon. Privileges depended upon an individual's closeness to authority. There is a saying still current in Brazil: For our friends, everything;

for our enemies, the strictness of the law. Archaic forms can be present in contemporary personal relationships.

Individualism becomes the law and the individuals are not questioned or challenged, as long as they are bound through personal ties to authority or the top strata of social hierarchy. Individualism becomes an unchallenged rule. Azevedo (1950) says that "this individualism of Iberian origin is not, however, creative as in Anglo-Saxon individualism, nor does it possess the same significance or content. . . . [It] found in Brazil a new source of exaltation in the patriarchal and slaveholding regime of agriculture in the North or on the Plateau" (pp. 127-128). This tendency, with its strong streak of destructiveness and anarchy, can result in disrespect for the legal framework, and has been part of our history ever since the days of the *capitanias hereditárias.*

Individualism is at the root of traditional *personalism* and is now found in the public sphere, even in the life of political parties and their mechanisms of action. "In Brazil, the State appears as a providence which comes before individuals and to which they run for defense and protection" (Azevedo, 1950, p. 131). As a complement to this situation we can recognize the disguised predation in personal relationships among Brazilians from different social strata or in different positions in the social hierarchy.

Several social and economic models applied to Brazilian society simply do not work unless they take Brazil's cultural background into account. For instance, inflation remedies that follow the liberal and individualistic model fail, because they do not allow for inflationary prices being the result of extreme, predatory individualism. Fierce individualism results in a voluntary rat race of price hikes. This, combined with a paternalistic government that is in dire straits, simply does not fit into the classical and liberal theoretical model that comes from the Anglo-Saxon world. Whatever region of Brazil is studied, it requires a special quest for a theoretical paradigm that could account for the *málange* of this country. Studies on communication and personal relations are no exception to this rule.

In Search of a Paradigm

If a culture evokes a set of possible rules that are lived in daily interaction, the analysis of personal relationships should begin with the way the concrete group of social actors conceptualize their experience. Scholarly analysis should present an organized interpretation, which cannot be as clear to the social actor.

The theoretical grid furnished by common sense will be used to produce a higher level of interpretation. The data derived from common sense will be enhanced and enriched by the establishment of new relationships.

One could then review social practices in another light. Our interpretation of the historical residues that color Brazilian individualism allows us to recognize that family life, as the original *locus* of personal relations, is organized on a colonial hierarchical basis, in which the father plays a role akin to that of the *donatário,* as a lord who reigns over his subjects: wife and children. There is an apparent autonomy in the political-economical sphere counterbalanced by servitude in the domestic relations in the manner of a dual model that presents a necessary contradiction. The public sphere where individualism clashes is to be considered a threatening domain ruled by competition, whereas family life is viewed as a sanctuary, a shelter where authority is exercised with ease and by consent.

Modern life has changed this conception of personal relations. Postindustrialism drove women out of the family sanctuary to work outside of the house. Thus the hierarchical extended family was gradually reduced to the nuclear family of husband, wife, and children. The hierarchical pattern also suffered pressure from expanding individualism that granted similar roles to every member of the reduced family. As in so many industrialized cultures, family emerged as a collection of equals with equal rights, even though reduced to the role of consumers. Mass media addressed individuals living in the nonhierarchical core that became the nuclear family. Interpersonal relationships of family members were considered hierarchically equivalent. Migration toward big cities splintered the hierarchical foundations of traditional family life. There is no longer any guarantee of sanctuary inside family life. Spreading individualism was responsible for ever-growing intergenerational conflicts.

In industrial society, the mass media maintain permanent contact in order to offer guidance and alternatives to uprooted individuals. In a world where the threat of disintegration is constant, the offer of moral examples has to be constant as well. Cultural products shown in the media are a sociological means of giving to the members of society what industrialism and mercantilism suppressed. Narratives broadcast in prime-time soap operas (*telenovelas*) demonstrate examples that produce patterns of behavior.

Advertising has a different role to play. Advertising permeates social distinction. The possession of goods will differentiate social actors. Goods are then symbols, and vice versa. Media are powerful frames of reference in Brazil, occupying the place once reserved for parents—who now usually work outside of their homes. Parental figures are replaced by "nonparental" screen images that do not act according to traditional authoritarian roles.

Authoritarianism is depicted critically, and what prevails are screen images that are not repressive, obliging, or imposing. Traditional values are therefore in a process of change, the final social result of which is yet to be seen.

The framework of traditional values offered a public and transcendent solution for personal and even petty dilemmas. With this framework under stress, two consequences will follow: The preeminence of the public sphere will be constantly and gradually depreciated, and personal interaction will be ruled by immediacy, as a derivation of individualistic values. What now matters is the instant advantage or benefit. Due to a lack of permanent and timeless norms, interests that are short-run and selfish are becoming the collective norm. In Brazil, most problems that occur outside the home can be solved through the use of personal acquaintances. In order to do business and be successful one has to know people. Friendship is used as an exchange value, through giving and receiving. One easily admits that one needs a *pistolão,* a slang term that means, literally, a big pistol with considerable power, implying someone who would use his own personal acquaintances to introduce the claimer into a new ambience. Without such a personal touch, one gets nowhere.

Creativity and *improvisation* are considered key words and positive values for daily life. These forms of extreme individualism can also take a negative and perverted turn. As the public sphere is overtaken by private interests, corruption is a constant threat and has been noticeably tolerated; but this will certainly not last forever.

Antonio Bulhões (1990) has written a satirical essay, consisting of theatrical dialogues, called *Elogio da corrupção* ("In Praise of Corruption"), in which characters from Western culture, such as Plato, Leonardo da Vinci, George Berkeley, Ludwig van Beethoven, Immanuel Kant, and Bertolt Brecht, among others, have a discussion with Brazilian national characters and general types during a conference delivered by an imaginary professor. Bulhões's masterful text unveils corruption as a central issue for Brazilian life as well for as humankind as a whole.

As an expression of this sociological dilemma that runs through Brazilian life, the paradigms chosen to deal with personal relations gave major emphasis to efforts that attempted to establish structures underlying concrete and individual acts.

The Choice Between Paradigms

Communication, especially as presented by the mass media, was initially grasped through the extensive use of Marxist concepts. At first, Antonio Gramsci's theory of hegemony seemed adequate, but was replaced by derivations of the Frankfurt school. Gramsci's concept of hegemony provided a powerful tool for understanding relationships within a class system. In the course of time, Gramsci's ideas suffered a serious setback. They could provide an instrument for revealing class conflicts, ultimately related to economic struggles, but communication and personal relations were considered less relevant. The Frankfurt school's concepts helped to draw attention to the effects of media in society. During the 1970s, Michel Foucault (1972a, 1972b) had a powerful influence on Brazilian intellectuals. The macro-analysis springing from Marxism was no longer entirely satisfactory. It seemed necessary to treat power as both a class action and as a tool for seeing relations in "micro" everyday situations. This was the beginning of a structuralist wave that had great influence in the humanities and social sciences in Brazil. Nevertheless, Marxism retained some influence through the definition of the ideological role played by culture in forging daily life options. In the mid-1970s, Marxism and structuralism were competing paradigms. For the Marxists, the principles of Hegelian dialectics helped to explain the contradictions of the Brazilian social system, namely simultaneous neocolonialism and capitalism (Mota, 1977, p. x).

The importing of foreign behavior models was thought to be a result of cultural dependency, an ideological counterpart of the unfair Third World economic conditions. One should bear in mind that during the military dictatorship in Brazil, which lasted for 20 years after the coup d'etat in 1964, intellectual analysis became more than an act of interpretation. It was judged as a strict political choice on the part of scholars. Brazilian authors were prone to choose a class struggle perspective in a Marxist vein. It is therefore not surprising that North American theories, with their proverbial disregard of class struggle and their emphasis on race and gender, had little influence in Brazil. Race and gender were then thought to be minor issues, subsumed under the more general framework of class relationships.

Soon, political engagement on the part of scholars was no longer enough. The military dictatorship was not overthrown suddenly; it waned slowly. Taking sides over political issues did not guarantee a sound scientific analysis. For a growing number of scholars the old Marxist refrains, that everything is political, including science, no longer rang true. Structuralist methods qualified as an alternative path.

Nonverbal Communication

It is worth noting that distinguished research efforts of a structuralist orientation were carried out in nonverbal communication. As an object of study, the body became a basis for inquiring into personal relationships. Social aspects of bodily communication were highlighted. Rodrigues (1975) defined personal interaction as the result of an unconscious system of signification present in movements of the body. The starting point of Rodrigues's analysis depended on how Brazilians recognized the meaning of the word *nojo* (repulsion, nausea, and mourning). Using qualitative methodology, he asked in his interviews in what way an informant could tell a *nojento* (disgusting) circumstance. *Nojo* is more than mere psychological reaction. One could say that through this concept society and the body, as a support of individuality, express themselves. To think of the body means to think of it in terms of social structure, but in the socio-semiotic perspective of being a sender of messages that at the same time reinforces social order. Rodrigues concluded that hygiene could not be seen as a value in itself; it referred to socially accepted conventions. Repulsion toward something or somebody is codified. Code can be both a communicational concept and a key to personal interaction. In personal relations there is a transference of feelings coming from physical sensations, but not only that: There is also an intellectual order linked, through codes, to a physical order; for example, *to spit in the face* offends sacred principles of social structure, for a face is the principal sign of social identity. The limits of the self are extended beyond the singularity of the body. Through the codification of *nojo,* one separates Nature from Culture. Culture becomes aesthetic beauty and spiritual values. At the very moment that human bodies do not fulfill this demand, human beings are horrified with themselves. The awareness of culture, of belonging to a group, implies the rejection of nature as *otherness.* Personal relations should be understood as dependent upon codes that create a common horizon of interaction.

Other models have been used to handle nonverbal communication. The works of Johnson (1979) and of Harrison (1983) supplied useful information. For the study of gestures, the classifications by Ekman and Friesen (1969) were applied to Brazilian gestures (Rector & Trinta, 1986, 1990). Comparative studies profited from Morris's (1979) models and helped to confront European and Latin American reality. The European inheritance revealed similarities, whereas historical, ethnic, and social influences in Latin America established the differences. Against this background we recognize the effort of Brazilian indigenous research since the 1930s, involving folklorist studies and analysis from a definite psychological point of view (Rector & Trinta, 1986, pp. 64-75).

Proxemics

A major theory of Brazil was advanced by Roberto Da Matta (1979, 1985), who proposed an interpretation of personal interaction in Brazil based upon the way Brazilians conceived three spaces in mutual and dual opposition: the *house,* the *street,* and the *other world.* The complementary relationship among these spaces is a sign that Brazilian life requires constant compensation, which the social actor can obtain by moving from one space to another. According to Da Matta, Brazilian life shifts between the poles of a dilemma. Different rules are kept for each of these spaces. The *house* and the *street* are more than physical spaces, they are concepts that imply a certain morality and behavior. Sometimes one is so different from the other that they are mutually exclusive.

Da Matta states that this spatial division goes beyond strict proxemics. He is talking about provinces of action and social meaning, each harboring a whole conception of the social world, to the point of having a predominant time relation: At the house, time is cyclic; in the street, time is linear, rational, and progressive; in the other world, time is absolute and eternal. Home has a protective structure that shelters the members of the family from threats coming from the outside world. The rules of this world postulate an essentially male space (Da Matta, 1985, pp. 12-13). The duality of Brazilian society is shown in the dual structure that presumes different behavior. For Da Matta, the street world brings with it the impersonal face of society with its abstract and cold laws, whereas personal relations are an affair of the heart, ruled by affection and sentimentality (Da Matta, 1985, p. 15). A social actor will try to soften the hardness of the *street* through his private relations springing from the *home.* At this moment, the *home* and the *street* will interact, yet from the point of view of structural indications, the roles for social actors are clearly divided. Staying at home, the woman will reign as a sovereign queen, being called the *patroa* (the boss) by her husband, but on the other hand, this also means the acceptance of the male outside world, where relationships are to be established with women other than the wife. The expression *mulher da rua* (literally, woman from the street) is reserved for prostitutes. Da Matta's interpretation of Brazil captures with precision the way Brazilian tradition has organized personal relations.

Specific Themes

With the constant decline of Marxism as the predominant paradigm, themes that were considered minor came to the foreground. The result has been a tendency to split areas of investigation that are to be taken as separate worlds with their own rules. Whether or not this development will be fruitful or will lead to a sterile specialization, only time will tell. For the moment, we think that it is an analytical reaction to the complexity of Brazilian experience.

A Relational Experience

Relational end products are highly prized in Brazil and can therefore be taken as national symptoms. We might refer to some details of everyday life, like Brazilian cuisine whose main dish is *feijoada*. *Feijoada* is made of boiled black beans, spiced and cooked with different kinds of smoked and salted pork and sausages. All parts of the animal are put into the kettle; black slaves would cook with leftovers from the master's table.[3] The concoction is usually served with side dishes such as white rice, collard greens, oranges, fried flour (*farofa*) with bananas, sausages, or sometimes even with raw manioc flour. It is most assuredly a diverse mixture that has an evident symbolic and relational nature.

A comparable relational nature can be recognized in the *mulata,* a woman of mixed black and white descent. As a social category, the *mulata* is considered aesthetically beautiful, an object of desire, and an attractive sexual partner. Again, in symbolic terms, the relational constitution is predominant. The experience of pleasure has a distinct relational demand. The emphasis laid upon the enjoyment of life and the profusion of parties, holidays, and festivities is considered a paramount value. Collective joyfulness may even be mandatory in national events like Carnival.

Another major key trait of Brazilian life is the domination of that which is emotional, irrational, and mystical. Sensibility, imagination, and mystic religiosity permeate the thoughts and feelings of the people. Religious relations present two different aspects; they are either mystical and relate to superstition and even fanaticism; or they are formalistic, concentrating on practices, rites, and festivities (Azevedo, 1950, p. 120). Charity and kindness are unfoldings of this general outlook. Personal relations should be ruled by cordiality, politeness, and hospitality. One's sensitivity to the suffering of others, the ease with which offenses are forgotten or forgiven, a certain shamefacedness about one's own egotism, the rejection of racial prejudice, the absence of racial pride, the practice of tolerance, hospitality, liberality and generosity, and a distaste for radical solutions—these are emotional elements strongly marked in the national character (Azevedo, 1950, pp. 121-122).

There has a been a tendency to understand patterns of behavior in relation to geographic and regional belonging. One is tempted to establish the analogy between regional belonging and Da Matta's definition of *the house*. When the country is understood as an expression of the house, one would feel safe: The house is a shelter, where conflicts do not occur. The acknowledgment of regional differences has helped Brazilians build up a cultural identity. Specific behaviors are expected when meeting Brazilians from different areas.

Marked Personality Traits

Openness in character due to a reaction against Brazil's compulsory social force is counterbalanced by a tendency to discretion, introspection, and even secrecy in certain regions of Brazil, which are recognized all over the country. The so-called *mineirice* is an attribute that is part of the personal framework of the people from Minas Gerais. The people are simultaneously generous and shy and perceptive. The tendency is to be quiet and observe what is going on, expressing feelings through elusive metaphors. It is said that one never really gets to know what a *mineiro* (a local from Minas Gerais) is thinking.

The Paulista (from São Paulo) is discrete and reserved with a tendency toward action. The Carioca (from Rio de Janeiro) is good humored, irreverent, and has a taste for good living. The Gaúcho (from Rio Grande do Sul) is romantic, cavalier, and behaves with passionate enthusiasm, being sensitive and generous as well (Azevedo, 1950, p. 134). Whatever is said about regionalistic patterns of interaction, they are another way of defining differences in the all-encompassing national character.

Religiousness

The strong sense of religiousness emerges from a structural demand that comes from the opposition of spaces in Brazilian culture. The "other world" is a space complementary to the dichotomy of house/street that Da Matta (1985) defined as vital in providing guidance for personal relations in Brazil. Whereas the spaces of house and street bring about social distinction, the supernatural, the "other world" teaches resignation and renunciation and transcends the competition ruling the space of the street, as well as the structural opposition of we/them characteristic of the house.[4] Facing death, which will redeem and undo social injustice, all individuals are equals. The *terreiro* is the place of "other world" events, where people meet to perform rituals of reverence to the dead, our ancestors.

The social space of the *terreiro* is an Afro-Brazilian creation, but the *terreiro* does not serve the purpose of racial exclusion. Today, one finds devotees from all social strata and ethnic origins. In historical terms, the *terreiro* was the place where Afro religious rituals were celebrated. There, blacks could give continuity to their native African cultures, historically suppressed or despised by the *senhor* (master). The *terreiro* was the physical and psychological space in which African slaves and their descendants could be at home and could preserve an African heritage, free from outside pressures.

The *terreiro* started with black slaves from Nigeria (called *Nagô* in Brazil) at the beginning of the 19th century; it is a ritual model, an organized liturgic association (the *terreiro*) for preserving black *ethos*. The experience of the *terreiro* incorporates both urban culture and natural space. The *terreiro* has been further defined as a symbolic form in which lost territory is regained. *Reterritorialization* takes place (Sodré, 1988, p. 50). This is a major element in Brazilian personal relations: Identity is kept intact even within the confines of the oppressor.

It is impossible to disregard the relevance of black experience for all Brazilians, and not just because many Brazilians have African blood, but because African values were not restricted to a sealed ghetto. Black strategies have played more than a major role in Brazilian life; they expressed a tendency in this country that has been a bit hastily defined as syncretic, implying mixture and coexistence of influences. The African *orixás* (understood as gods and forces of nature) have their counterpart in Catholic saints. As Sodré (1988) states, however, Catholicism is now a religion committed to the industrialized world, whereas the *Nagô* cult emerges from a group inheritance based upon symbolic patrimonial values. So rather than intermingling, both religions live side by side. A popular proverb says: "The place of the priest is inside the church, the place of the *orixá* is in the *terreiro.*" The drama of integration happens without questioning the social structure that produced rejection and segregation. The common background remains intact. More than a physical territory, the *terreiro* is a center for liturgical activities and the irradiation of *axé,* a term that signifies strength. This force pervades and perpetuates the vital space and thus undergirds black identity that wants to rise above segregation and prejudice. Reinforced by rituals, *axé* also acquires a historical configuration, and becomes the physical place for transactions and small businesses.

From the *terreiros,* black experience reaches the rest of society, the oppressor. The *terreiros* are also the birthplace of such popular culture manifestations as *Samba-Schools, Blocos,* and *Ranchos.*[5] From the intimate space of the *terreiros,* poor and marginalized people from *favelas* (slums and shantytowns) move into the limelight of the Sambódromo, an avenue specially built by the political elite for the Samba-Schools' parades. Through a ritual of inversion the lower strata of society reach the upper echelon, briefly realizing all the hopes of justice kept in abeyance during the rest of the year. This moment of joy, music, dance, and colorful excess is more than lavish expenditure. Black identity has been recovered and maintained, but it is also a moment of magic communion with the rest of the country. Social distinctions seem abolished and, if only for a short time, everybody is united.

Conclusions

Most of the models proposed to interpret communication and personal relations in Brazil have a foreign origin, but they undertake the complex task of understanding this country admitting that national values find expression as psychosocial mechanisms. Sodré (1971, pp. 31-34) identifies five elements required to interpret Brazilian personal relations:

1. a spirit of compromise that accommodates dual and apparently mutually exclusive patterns of personal relations
2. a general optimism, such as boastful nationalism (*ufanismo*), and the belief that Brazilian natural resources and human potentialities are unmatched in the whole world
3. an extreme individualism, so that the individual with talent, culture—and therefore intellectual and social prestige—is considered worthy of a distinguished position in society
4. a taste for verbosity as a consequence of an elitist education and sterile erudition
5. a willingness to compromise on racial relations in a conciliatory way

Sodré's identification of five macro factors as necessary to understand micro relations in Brazil is bound up with the insight that foreign models of behavior transposed from mass media go hand-in-hand with the surviving residues of old Brazilian culture. The blend could be difficult, but in the end it produces a unique pattern for personal interaction. Underlying these five macro principles, one recognizes an appeal to common sense as one of the means to overcome conflict. Conflicts are undesired: They should be subsumed under the Brazilian traditions of optimism, tolerance, and good nature.

The tendency to reject contradictions and conflicts is also spread throughout society. Conciliation brings with it the idea that the isolated individual is a threat to the system. The five macro factors are complementary in such a way that one experiences them as a homogeneous totality. As a counterpart of this cultural tendency in Brazilian society, one can single out miscegenation. Miscegenation affirms that the whole is larger than the parts, whose relations point to the totality. Nevertheless, ambiguity can be a borderline rule.

In reference to Edward Hall's conception of low- and high-context frameworks, where high-context cultures provide a tight and homogeneous structure, with constraint demands (Gudykunst, Stewart, Lea, & Ting-Toomey, 1985, p. 76), one could say that Brazilian culture can be defined as essentially ambiguous. High or low context can prevail, depending upon the concrete situation. Brazilian society is a dual society, where such contradictory experiences can live with each other. Authoritarian rites are despised. But at the same time, in Brazil, where personal relations tend to be established under the sign of cordiality, interpersonal authoritarian acts are also inclined to happen.

Anyone interested in studying personal relations in Brazil from the point of view of communication should look for the as yet unpublished dissertations being produced in Brazilian universities. These dissertations are available in a yearly publication from the Ministry of Education through CAPES (Coordenação de Aperfeiçoamento de Pessoal de Nível Superior), and in various journals such as *Intercom, Revista Brasileira de Comunicação.* Under the topic *Documentação,* this journal offers a current bibliography in the field of communication. Several of the items dealing with personal relations are scattered throughout the field of communication under headings such as mass communication, communication and politics, organizational communications, rural communication, verbal communication, culture, law in communication, communication media, research in communication, radio, public relations, and television. The researcher will see that Brazilian scholarship has up to now chosen to treat personal relations as an index of the framework of rules that define the country.

Notes

1. In fact, the cultural interaction can produce change. In previous decades, Brazilians have increased their business relations with Americans. As a result, Brazilian businesspeople have adapted to the American conception of time and business appointments have been kept on time.

2. The nine regions are: Agrarian Northeast from the Coast, Rural Mediterranean, Amazonian, the Mining Zones of the Highlands, Center-West, Rural Extreme-South, the Foreign Zone of Colonization, the Coffee Plantation Area, and Urban-Industrial Brazil.

3. One must remember that this is not an eating preference restricted to a single ethnic group. In fact, *feijoada* is a truly national dish, eaten with relish and delight by all Brazilians from North to South, regardless of their ethnic or social extraction. However similar it may seem to some of the American soul foods, *feijoada* is not strictly identified with Brazilian blacks. Also, *feijoada* is a dish in which diverse ingredients are mingled, rather than a general style of preparing food. It would be interesting to see a comparative study of the way American and Brazilian cultures interpret these similar dishes. We presume that this is an expression of how the racial question has been treated in each country.

4. The relationship between *house, street,* and the *other world* are complementary codifications that do something besides demarcate separate regions. Brazilians will shift from one region to another without much trouble or discussion. Then one can know what to expect in their personal relations. We will point out once more that personal relations are therefore seen as a code, a central communicational concept.

5. *Blocos* and *Ranchos* are minor groups in relation to the *Samba-Schools*. All of them parade during Carnival, but the *Samba-Schools* are organized groups of about 3,000 people each.

References

Azevedo, F. de. (1950). *Brazilian culture: An introduction to the study of culture in Brazil.* New York: Macmillan.

Bulhões, A. (1990). *Elogio da corrupção.* Rio de Janeiro: Siciliano.

Da Matta, R. (1979). *Carnavais, malandros e heróis; para uma sociologia do dilema brasileiro.* Rio de Janeiro: Zahar.

Da Matta, R. (1985). *A casa & a rua; espaço, cidadania, mulher e morte no Brasil.* São Paulo: Brasiliense.

Ekman, P., & Friesen, W. V. (1969). The repertoire of non-verbal behaviour categories: Origins, usage, and coding. *Semiotica, 1*(1), 9-98.

Foucault, M. (1972a). *The archeology of knowledge.* New York: Harper & Row.

Foucault, M. (1972b). *Power and knowledge.* New York: Pantheon.

Geertz, C. (1973). *The interpretation of cultures.* New York: Basic Books.

Freyre, G. (1975). *O brasileiro entre os outros hispanos: Afinidades, contrastes e possíveis futuros nas suas inter-relações.* Brasília: Ministério da Educação e Cultura, Instituto Nacional do Livro.

Gudykunst, W. B. (Ed.). (1983). *Intercultural communication theory: Current perspectives.* Beverly Hills, CA: Sage.

Gudykunst, W. B., Stewart, Lea P., & Ting-Toomey, Stella. (Eds.). (1985). *Communication, culture, and organizational processes.* Beverly Hills, CA: Sage.

Harrison, P. A. (1983). *Behaving Brazilian: A comparison of Brazilian and North American social behavior.* Rowley, MA: Newbury House.

Johnson, S. (1979). *Nonverbal communication in the teaching of foreign languages.* Unpublished doctoral dissertation, Indiana University, Bloomington.

Morris, D. (1979). *Gestures, their origin and distribution.* New York: Stein & Day.

Mota, C. G. (1977). *Ideologia da cultura brasileira.* São Paulo: Ática.

Rector, M. (1989). Semiotic of mass communication in spatial reality. In Walter A. Koch (Ed.), *Evolution of culture* (pp. 143-156). Bochum: Universitatsverlag Dr. Norbert Brocjmeyer.

Rector, M., & Trinta, A. R. (1986). *Comunicação não-verbal: A gestualidade brasileira.* Petrópolis: Vozes.

Rector, M., & Trinta, A. R. (1990). *Comunicação do corpo.* São Paulo: Ática.

Rodrigues, J. C. (1975). *O tabu do corpo.* Rio de Janeiro: Achiamé.

Sodré, M. (1971). *A comunicação do grotesco; introdução à cultura de massa brasileira.* Petrópolis: Vozes.

Sodré, M. (1988). *O terreiro e a cidade, a forma social negro-brasileira.* Petrópolis: Vozes.

CHAPTER

9

Communication in
Personal Relationships in Iran:
A Comparative Analysis

Fred Zandpour
Golnaz Sadri

The purpose of this chapter is to provide a theoretical framework through which communication patterns in Iran can be predicted and explained. We have drawn upon the literature from intercultural communication, as well as interpersonal and traditional mass communication, in order to develop a model of national communication patterns. The proposed model utilizes a set of contextual, structural, stylistic, and interactive variables that could be used for testing and enhancing communication among people from different cultures. In addition to focusing on personal relations, the model can be utilized to collect data on mediated communication, including news, information, literature, art, entertainment, selling, and promotion.

It must be noted that the people of Iran come from a wide of variety of ethnic, religious, linguistic, and geographic backgrounds with unique histories and cultures. Although there are considerable local differences among different groups of Iranians, in this chapter we have focused on only those common characteristics that tend to distinguish Iranians from people of other nations. The communication implications of these cultural characteristics are examined and, when possible, compared to those of other countries. The underlying assumption in this chapter is that Iranian behavior emanates from a national culture, affecting all aspects of their communications. The following section will provide a brief overview of culture with some examples from Iran. The next section deals with communication implications of these cultural traits and how they manifest themselves in Iran, followed by a set of communication characteristics as they apply to Iran and other countries.

Ways of Viewing Culture

Past research has demonstrated the significant role that national culture plays in shaping the nature of personal communications (Bond, Leung, & Wan, 1982; Forgas & Bond, 1985; Gudykunst & Nishida, 1986; Gudykunst & Ting-Toomey, 1988b) as well as commercial communications (Zandpour et al., 1994; Zandpour, Chang, & Catalano, 1992). The term *culture* has been defined as how the world is perceived and organized by a group of people and how this perception is passed on interpersonally and intergenerationally (Condon & Yousef, 1983; Hall, 1983; Prosser, 1978; Singer, 1987).

Culture originates in a person's social environment and is learned (Hofstede, 1991). It includes a common code or language, heritage, history, social organization, norms, knowledge, attitudes, values, beliefs, objects, and patterns of perception that are accepted and expected by an identity group and it is expressed in verbal and nonverbal cues (Hall, 1969; Hecht, Andersen, & Ribeau, 1989). In addition, it is suggested that culture guides the actions and responses of individuals in every walk of life including survival, advancement in the world, and satisfaction in life.

People from different cultures have different orientations toward individualism, authority, uncertainty, and femininity (Hofstede, 1980, 1983, 1991), as well as space and time (Hall, 1983). We begin with individualism.

Individualism Versus Collectivism

The first dimension of culture that we consider is labeled individualism versus collectivism and has been shown by theorists across disciplines to be of practical significance (Bellah, Madsen, Sullivan, Swidler, & Tipton, 1985; Hui & Triandis, 1986; Marsella, DeVos, & Hsu, 1985; Parsons & Shils, 1951; Tonnies, 1963; Triandis, 1988; Westen, 1985). Individualism refers to a loose social framework in which people are primarily concerned with themselves and their immediate families. Collectivistic cultures are more concerned with the group as a whole, and the group might be defined as the extended family or the organization. In such cultures, the group takes care of its members in exchange for loyalty (Hofstede & Bond, 1984; Gudykunst & Ting-Toomey, 1988b).

Whereas individualistic cultures draw upon the "I" identity as a primary focus, the collectivistic cultures draw upon the "we." Individualistic cultures emphasize individual goals, whereas collective cultures stress that group goals have precedence (Gudykunst, 1991). The emphasis in individualistic societies is focused on a person's unique qualities, initiative, and achievement, whereas emphasis is placed on group identity and consensus in collective societies. People in individualistic cultures tend to apply the same value standards to all, whereas people in collectivistic cultures apply different value standards for members of their ingroups (groups to which one belongs) and outgroups (Gudykunst, 1991; Gudykunst & Ting-Toomey, 1988b).

Members of individualistic cultures form specific short-term friendships, while members of collectivistic cultures form friendships that are predetermined by stable relationships developed early in life (Hofstede, 1980). Because individualistic cultures have many specific ingroups including family, religion, and social clubs, groups exert less influence on their members than those of collectivistic cultures (Triandis, 1988).

In summary, collectivistic cultures place emphasis on group identity and goals; value group consensus and long-term relationships; and tend to apply different value standards to members of groups to which they belong.

On Hofstede's (1980) dimensions, Iran has a low average score of 41 on individualism, thus falling toward the collectivistic end of this continuum. This is in sharp contrast to the United States and most North European cultures, which rank high on individualism. There are a number of manifestations of collectivism in Iranian culture. In a typical conversation, it is more common for Iranians to talk in terms of "we" rather than "I." To illustrate, Iranians might say, "We usually do it this way" or "We like things that way" instead of saying "I like it this way" or "I do things that way." In fact, an individual who continually adopts the individualistic term "I" is likely to be viewed as egocentric or conceited in typical Iranian social circles.

Another indication of the collectivistic ideology in Iranian culture is the importance of the extended family. Iranians assume great responsibility for their children, their parents, and, to a lesser extent, other members of their family such as their aunts, uncles, and cousins. It is common for children to live with their parents until they marry and form families of their own, regardless of the age at which this occurs, even when they are 30 or even 40 years old. Parents also often live with their offspring during their more mature years. Thus three generations residing under the same roof is viewed as the norm. As part of this emphasis on the importance of the extended family and the value of familial relationships, Iranians like to engage in collective activities such as travel. Holidays to the seaside, perhaps to visit the Caspian Sea to the north of the country, are likely to be organized around larger groups; again, three generations vacationing together would be a very typical picture.

Members of one's ingroup other than one's family, such as friends, distant relatives, and acquaintances, are also a very important part of the typical Iranian's life. Entertaining all members of one's ingroup is a predominant focal point in social exchanges. Consequently, the area in an Iranian person's home that is devoted to entertaining guests is one of the most important areas of the house. This area is typically separated from the family room and is given a separate name, which means "guest room" when translated into English. The guest room is one of the best decorated rooms in the house and is always kept clean and tidy.

Much of the social life revolves around food and eating together. The Iranian new year, weddings, birthdays, and other celebrations almost always involve the preparation of very elaborate foods, which are shared and enjoyed collectively. Even during occasions of sadness, such as death or religious mourning, sharing food plays an important part. In fact, to refuse food when offered in an Iranian person's house would be viewed as rude. Similarly, to visit an Iranian person's house and not be offered some form of food or refreshment would also be viewed as rude.

The ingroup and extensive network of family and friends is not viewed exclusively as an important resource in terms of social exchange, but is also relied upon very heavily in the context of business and professional transactions. For example, Iranians usually prefer to conduct business with individuals with whom they are familiar or with individuals to whom they have been introduced by other members of their ingroup. Doctors, dentists, and lawyers, as well as gardeners and mechanics, are often referred on this basis.

Another feature of the Iranian culture that distinguishes it somewhat from the American culture is that what others in the group say is very important. Individuals listen to the advice they are given by members of their ingroup. Elders and those in positions of authority or respect are expected to give advice and take on this role without being explicitly asked to do so.

Uncertainty Avoidance

A second dimension of national culture identified by Hofstede (1980) is labeled uncertainty avoidance. Uncertainty avoidance refers to the extent to which people feel threatened by ambiguous situations and have created beliefs and institutions in an attempt to avoid such uncertainty and ambiguity. Individuals attempt to cope with uncertainty through a number of different means, such as technology, legislation, and religion. The tolerance for uncertainty varies considerably among people in different countries. Extreme uncertainty has the potential to create an intolerable level of anxiety (Gudykunst, 1988).

As a result, societies develop different ways of coping with uncertainty. Methods of coping with anxiety partially emanate from the cultural heritage of societies. Uncertainty avoidance can, to some extent, be linked to the political system that societies adopt. The underlying assumption that arises from the acceptance of freedom is the acceptance of uncertainty in the behavior of oneself and others that can lead to stress and anxiety (Hecht et al., 1989). Totalitarian ideologies try to avoid uncertainty by increasing the formal rules for behavior (Hofstede, 1980) and exhibit a low tolerance for deviant groups.

On uncertainty avoidance, Iran and the United States both ranked as below average, obtaining scores of 59 and 43, respectively, in comparison to a mean score of 64 for all of the countries included in the study. Clearly, Iran obtained a higher score on uncertainty avoidance than did the United States. There are a number of indications of a tendency to avoid uncertainty in Iranian ideals and behaviors. One such indication is the importance that the majority of Iranian parents place on the future of their children. This investment in the future or desire for a secure and prosperous life is expressed in different ways. For many Iranians, education is a highly valued commodity, and parents encourage their children to pursue a good education. Other Iranian parents may encourage their children to adopt a trade or to pursue a business and, where possible, they will even provide the financial support to enable their children to do so.

A second indication of uncertainty avoidance is the reliance on advice offered by certain authority figures in society. One important source of advice and guidance is religion in Iran, and individuals such as clergy who have access to such information are sought after, particularly in times of personal crisis.

There is also a tendency with Iranians to seek closure on issues and topics of importance. Hypothetical conversations and debates that leave issues unanswered are less typical in Iran than in the United States. Thus Iranians are likely to avoid "what if" questions and to pursue a route that leads more directly to concrete answers. There is also a desire for unanimity on issues; individuals with very divergent views and behaviors are observed as unusual or strange, rather than interesting.

The avoidance of uncertainty in the behavior of others is accomplished by the setting up of a pattern of ritual behaviors and conversational patterns, referred to as *taarof,* that offers prescribed behaviors and comments in response to various social exchanges. For example, Iranian etiquette requires that where an age differential exists in social exchanges, the younger party should take the initiative in greeting the older person. The older person would be expected to pursue an appropriate topic of conversation, which might include the offer of some form of advice.

Power Distance

The third dimension identified by Hofstede (1980) is power distance. Power distance may be defined as the degree of comfort with the unequal distribution of power in institutions (Hofstede & Bond, 1984). This dimension relates to the level of tolerance of social inequality and the amount of authority one person has over another. Individuals from high power distance cultures accept authority and inequality, which can also arise from differences in prestige and wealth as well as power, as an inherent part of society. In such societies, superiors and subordinates consider one another to be different in some significant way. On the other hand, low power distance cultures like to minimize status differences whenever possible (Gudykunst & Ting-Toomey, 1988b).

Power distance affects nonverbal behavior, because high power distance may severely limit interaction. High power distance cultures often prohibit free interclass dating, marriage, and contact, which are taken for granted in low power distance cultures. In high power distance cultures, subordinates tend to show more bodily tension and smile more in an effort to appease superiors and to appear polite (Andersen & Bowman, 1985; Hecht et al., 1989).

Like most Asian countries, Iran ranks as above average on power distance, obtaining a mean score of 58 in comparison to an overall mean score of 51 for the 39 countries surveyed, whereas the United States ranks as below average (40). Manifestations of high power distance in Iran can be observed in the importance of the roles played by various authority figures in Iranian culture. For instance, parents, elders, teachers, and the clergy play a very important part in the formulation of decisions such as marriage, buying a house, and choosing a profession or a field of education. Similarly, arranged marriages were the norm until fairly recently. Perhaps the fact that parents do not always choose a spouse for their children is a symbol of cultural change; nevertheless, what one's parents think about a potential spouse is a very important factor in the decision-making process for the majority of young Iranians. Choosing a house is usually considered to be a very personal decision in Western cultures, yet for some Iranians a seemingly ideal house may be rendered inappropriate for purchase if it is not sanctioned by a respected member of the family.

Attaining a position of authority or superiority in society is highly prized by the typical Iranian. Hence this is at times conferred upon people without necessarily being earned and is considered a symbol of respect. For instance, individuals who are highly respected members of a certain ingroup may, over time, have a certain title—such as doctor or general—conferred upon them without having, in fact, earned the degree or position. This is generally a sign of great respect, occurs under exceptional circumstances, and in no way implies that the respective individual assumes the professional role attached to the title.

Masculinity Versus Femininity

The fourth and final dimension identified in Hofstede's (1980) study is that of masculinity versus femininity, also referred to as quantity versus quality of life. Masculine cultures tend to be more concerned with assertiveness, success, and acquisition of material things, whereas feminine cultures emphasize the importance of relationships and show sensitivity to and an overall concern for the welfare of others in society. Evidence of a masculine orientation in society as a whole might be reflected in a higher tolerance of assertive behaviors. Masculine cultures are also likely to exhibit a greater concern for money and material things in comparison to feminine cultures.

On the dimension of masculinity versus femininity, Iran ranks as a relatively feminine culture, with a score of 43, while the United States ranks as above average on masculinity (62); the mean across all the countries surveyed was 51 (Hofstede, 1980). Indications of femininity may be observed in the fact that Iranians value friendship and dignity over material things. Like most Asian cultures, the notion of face-saving and respect from others in society is heavily relied upon in defining one's social identity. Because the opinions of other people in society, particularly members of one's ingroup, are important, many personal decisions are affected by the views of others. For example, when choosing a profession, for many Iranians the level of monetary and other extrinsic rewards plays a secondary role to various intrinsic rewards such as having a profession that is considered respectable and honorable by the relevant members of society.

Femininity as a cultural value can also be observed in the importance attached to giving and charity in Iranian culture. When a person wants some event to take place in his or her life and feels that its attainment is beyond his or her individual power, a traditional Iranian ritual is to make a certain charitable donation in exchange for its occurrence. This is referred to as a *nazre.*

Another sign of femininity is the degree of hospitality of the typical Iranian household. Iranians go to great lengths to welcome family and friends to their homes. As noted earlier, it would be considered terribly impolite to go to an Iranian person's home and to leave without the offer of some form of refreshment.

High Context Versus Low Context

Hall's (1976) notion of high context and low context has been used extensively in cross-cultural research on interpersonal communication (Gudykunst & Ting-Toomey, 1988b). This theory refers to the extent to which explicit verbal information is relied upon in communication. High-context cultures rely heavily on contextual cues like age, status, ceremonies, and the like. By contrast, low-context cultures strongly utilize detailed factual information that is explicitly conveyed through either a verbal or a written medium (Gudykunst, 1991; Gudykunst & Ting-Toomey, 1988b; Hall, 1976). Although verbal individuals are perceived as attractive in low-context societies, less verbal people are perceived as more attractive in high-context societies.

High-context cultures are more sensitive to nonverbal communication, including inarticulate moods and subtle gestures (Gudykunst, 1988, 1991; Hall, 1983). When people communicate, they make assumptions about how much the listener knows about the subject under discussion. In low-context communication, the listener is assumed to know little and must be told almost everything, whereas in high-context communication it is assumed that the listener is already familiar with the subject and does not need to be given much background information (Hall, 1983).

High-context cultures provide a context and a setting and let the point evolve (Hall, 1983). High-context cultures value spiral and correlational logic, indirect verbal interaction, group value orientation, and contextual nonverbal styles of communicating (Gudykunst, 1988).

Individuals from high-context cultures tend to have extensive information networks among family, friends, colleagues, and clients, whereas individuals in low-context cultures tend to compartmentalize their personal relationships, their work, and many aspects of their day-to-day lives (Hall, 1983; Gudykunst, 1988; Ting-Toomey, 1985).

There is evidence that the low-context and high-context cultural framework can explain differences in preferred conflict handling styles (Chua & Gudykunst, 1987; Ting-Toomey, 1985). In general, members of low-context cultures tend to prefer a direct mode of dealing with conflict, such as the use of confrontational strategies or solution-oriented strategies, whereas high-context members tend to prefer an indirect mode of resolving conflict, such as the use of smoothing strategies or avoidance strategies (Gudykunst, 1988).

In a low-context culture, individuals are better able to separate the conflict issue from the person involved in the conflict. Members of low-context cultures can disagree with one another over an issue and yet be able to remain friends afterwards (Gudykunst, 1991). On the other hand, in a high-context culture the instrumental issue is closely tied to the person who originated the issue. To disagree openly with or to confront someone in public is a severe blow and an extreme insult, causing both sides to lose their respect or face. This has been found to be especially true in an organizational context, with superior-subordinate communication (Ting-Toomey, 1985).

Face-negotiation is an overt communication process in the low-context system like that of the United States. The arguments and persuasions in a conflict situation would typically follow a linear logic pattern. Face-negotiation in the low-context system is based on an immediate reward, whereas in the high-context culture, face-negotiation follows a cumulative, long-term process. Because members are interlocked in a group-value perspective, every face-support or face-violation act on another person will have larger social and group implications. The arguments and disagreements in a conflict situation are likely to be ambiguously expressed and the face-giving and face-saving appeals typically follow a spiral logic pattern. Eventual face-honoring and face-compensating is important for the maintenance of both social and personal relationship develop-ments (Ting-Toomey, 1988).

Members of low-context cultures are more likely to separate issues from persons and to adopt an instrumental orientation toward conflict resolution. Conversely, members of high-context cultures, who mainly perceive the world in synthetic, spiral logic terms, would be more likely to punctuate the same conflict event as expressive-oriented in focus. For these individuals, the conflict issue and the conflict person are the same (Ting-Toomey, 1985).

In summary, high-context cultures tend to rely more on nonverbal cues as opposed to detailed factual information. In addition, members of high-context cultures tend to be collectivistic and, where possible, they avoid direct confron-tation, preferring instead to save face. They typically do not separate the issue from the person; consequently, to attack a particular notion implies an attack on the person offering it.

The Iranian culture, like that of most Asian cultures such as Japanese, Chinese, and Korean (Gudykunst, 1988, 1991; Gudykunst & Ting-Toomey, 1988b; Hall, 1983) falls toward the high-context end of the continuum. There are a number of contextual parameters that are relied upon in Iranian social transactions that we would like to discuss here. First, the way one looks is an important nonverbal cue to most Iranians, implying social class, good taste, and a certain level of superiority in society. Consequently, Iranians spend quite a lot of time on personal presentation. Typically, they like to dress appropriately for each situ-ation and almost always like to appear clean and tidy. As an extension of one's personal appearance, there is the appearance of one's home. It is important to an Iranian that his or her house looks clean, tidy, and inviting. Iranians will generally go to quite a degree of trouble when they are expecting guests to visit their house, making sure that the physical surroundings are clean and also making sure that the food that is to be served to their guests is well prepared and looks appetizing.

Other contextual information that is relied upon in defining one's social identity includes the car that one drives. As in many other cultures, an Iranian person's car qualifies as a status symbol, communicating style, wealth, and good taste.

Titles and labels that define one's place in society are viewed as important pieces of contextual information. It was noted previously that to have a title is valued to such a degree that to bestow this on a person who may not have earned the title is viewed as a sign of great respect (e.g., referring to someone as an engineer, boss, or chief).

As with other high-context cultures such as the Asian cultures, in Iran it is also important to avoid confrontations with members of one's ingroup. Typically, Iranians tend to be very polite, humble, and gracious with such members. The same standards are not always used in transacting with members of one's outgroup. For example, in driving or dealing with strangers, Iranians may not always act as politely and graciously.

Monochronic or Polychronic Perception of Time

Another way of distinguishing among cultures is through the way members of each culture perceive and organize time. Cultures may be labeled as either monochronic or polychronic. Individuals from monochronic cultures adopt a linear, schedule-driven view of time and focus on doing only one thing at a time. On the other hand, individuals from polychronic cultures adopt a more circular view of time and are comfortable with being involved in many things at once (Hall, 1969).

Individuals in monochronic cultures tend to need a great deal of information when communicating with one another. They show commitment to the job at hand and adhere closely to plans. They respect privacy, emphasize promptness, and are accustomed to short-term relationships (Hall, 1983). Polychronic cultures are usually high-context. They typically exhibit a greater commitment to family, friends, and close business associates than to privacy. Individuals from such cultures tend to build lifetime relationships. They prefer personal relations to promptness and change plans often and easily (Hall, 1983).

The majority of Iranians operate on a polychronic time scale. Typically, Iranians do not have long-term plans and tend to operate effectively in the moment. On a social level, it is fairly common to visit friends and family on a surprise basis. Both socially and professionally, it is considered acceptable to have a last-minute cancellation of plans, far more so than in monochronic cultures.

During a conversation with an Iranian, one might expect one or more interruptions, either by phone or by another person. An Iranian person may be comfortable with talking to several people at the same time whereas his or her American counterpart is unlikely to experience comfort with such a situation. As with members of other polychronic cultures, Iranians may experience

difficulties in meeting deadlines, thus seeming to be disorganized to members
of monochronic cultures.

Interpersonal Space:
High Contact or Low Contact

Hall (1969) suggests that spatial organization represents one of the key
elements of a culture. He suggests that each person has an invisible bubble of
personal space that expands and contracts depending on his or her relationship
to the people nearby, and his or her emotional state and cultural background.
Spatial changes give a tone to communication, accenting it and at times overriding the spoken word. If a person gets too close, an individual from a
low-contact culture has the tendency to back up. In high-contact countries, the
interaction distance is much less; people stand closer to one another to talk and
transact business (Hall, 1973).

The immediacy dimension on one side shows actions that simultaneously
communicate closeness, approach, and accessibility. At the other extreme is
behavior expressing avoidance and distance (Andersen, 1985). Highly immediate behaviors in the U.S. culture include smiling, touching, eye contact, open
body positions, closer distances, and more vocal animation. Some scholars call
this nonverbal involvement, intimacy, or expressiveness (Patterson, 1983).

Cultures that display considerable interpersonal closeness are high-contact
cultures. Examples are South America and South and Eastern European. These
create immediacy by increasing sensory input (Hecht et al., 1989). In addition,
differences are reported regarding touching behavior between Latin America
and the United States (Shuter, 1976). On the other hand, low-contact cultures
prefer less sensory involvement (Sussman & Rosenfeld, 1982). Examples
include Asia, North America, and Northern Europe. Like the Arab, Mediterranean, and Latin cultures, Iran is predominantly a high-contact culture as opposed
to Asian and Western cultures, which are generally low-contact (Hall, 1969).

Implications for Communication:
The Case of Iran

The present section aims to outline how the aspects of culture discussed above
may affect communicative patterns in Iran. Communication may be defined as

the process by which we understand others and, in turn, try to be understood by them. Accordingly, it is a dynamic process, constantly changing and shifting in response to the total situation. In addition, communication involves sharing and interchange; transmission of information, ideas, emotions, skills; and so on, through the use of verbal and visual symbols. It also serves to reduce uncertainty (see Littlejohn, 1983, p. 7) and to satisfy needs (Katz, 1974). Based upon the discussion of differences across cultures, it is possible to provide a number of theoretical generalizations about patterns of communication in Iran.

Iranians do not stress self-assertion and individual expressiveness

Gudykunst, Yoon, and Nishida (1987) point out that in collectivistic cultures communication with outgroup members is more synchronized, and behavior is governed by situational norms, not individual needs. In individualistic cultures, the level of intimacy and self-disclosure is a result of a person's desire to form a relationship with others. One would therefore expect lower levels of affection and inclusion motives (Rubin, 1992) for Iranian people than for individualistic people.

Iranians emphasize adherence to culturally defined social expectations and rules rather than encouraging the expression of individuality through the articulation of words. Much emphasis is placed on conformity to the already established social relationships defined by the position in society of the individual speaker. For example, Iranian women can freely talk as sisters, mothers, wives, or neighbors, but they are seldom expected to discuss their feelings as an individual.

In addition, Iranians place less emphasis on the use of the name of a person with whom they are communicating. They are also less likely to use first-person or second-person pronouns during a typical conversation (see "Human Interest," Carbone, 1975) as compared with most Western cultures.

Humility is very characteristic of the communication patterns of most Iranians. They seldom feel comfortable in taking credit for their achievements, good taste, or choice and tend to become embarrassed as a result of excessive praise. If you compliment Iranians on a gift they have given you, they will tend to downplay the gesture by remarking that the gift is unworthy of the recipient. There are a number of other expressions of humility that Iranians typically adopt to express their affection for another person; for example, "I would die for you."

Iranians rely more on nonverbal communication
than on the articulation of words

The people of Iran, like those of Asia (Hecht et al., 1989), expect communicators to understand inarticulate moods, subtle gestures, and environmental cues
that people from low-context cultures simply do not process. In this respect,
Iranian communication is receiver-centered (Yum, 1991). That is to say, the task
of understanding is placed on the listener and his or her interpretation, in contrast
to the Western cultures that place emphasis on the message sender's delivery
skills and so forth.

Iranians' attitude toward speech and rhetoric, like that of Asians (Gudykunst
& Kim, 1984; Oliver, 1971), is characteristically a holistic one—words are
perceived as part of and inseparable from the total communication context.
Consequently, even periods of silence embedded between words carry meaning.
Verbal individuals are perceived as attractive in Western cultures, but in Iran,
less verbal people are perceived as more attractive. In fact, Iranians border on
having a mistrust of words, like Asian cultures (Oliver, 1971); they prefer silence
to improper words that might offend the other party (Hall, 1983). As an
illustration of the differences attached to the importance of speech across
cultures, research conducted in the United States has shown that speaking fast
enhances the speaker's credibility (MacLachlan, 1982; Miller, Maruyama,
Beaber, & Valone, 1976; Petrie, 1963). By contrast, in Iran, slow speakers are
likely to be perceived as more competent than fast speakers because the
deliberate nature of their speech suggests they are taking more care in the
preparation and production of their message. This preference for slower rates of
communication is similar to that of Asian cultures (Lee & Boster, 1992). This
may explain why Iranians are more likely to use complex and longer sentences
than Americans (see "Listenability," Carbone, 1975).

Because words are not relied upon heavily, we would also expect Iranian
people to use more nonverbal communications such as head nodding, bowing,
hugging, and kissing (see "Alertness" and "Haptics" in Sillars, Pike, Jones, &
Murphy, 1984). As an example, in Iran it is customary to greet friends and family
with a kiss on each cheek.

Showing affection may also be expressed through symbolic means. If an
Iranian person invites you to his or her home and wishes to show how important
you are, this will be expressed through the means of hospitality. There will, as
mentioned previously, be a great deal of attention paid to elaborately prepared

foods and lavish service. Gifts also play an important nonverbal role in Iranian society, in the expression of warmth, affection, and even respect. Gifts are exchanged on birthdays, and the first visit to someone's home is usually accompanied by the giving of a very elaborate gift. At the new year, *Nowruz,* which is the first day of spring, it is customary for the older members of a family to give gifts in the form of cash to younger members.

Expressions of anger and discontent are also expressed nonverbally through the process of ignoring the object of the hostility. Silence becomes an important tool for younger and less respected members of society who, by society's standards, are not in the position of talking to their seniors as equals. Such behavior would be considered a transgression against the expected normative standards.

Iranians are not direct and assertive

An important communication goal in Iran, as in most collectivistic societies, is to avoid being embarrassed or embarrassing members of your ingroup in the course of symbolic exchanges. Eventual face-honoring and face-compensating is important for the maintenance of both social and personal relationship developments (Gudykunst, 1988). This is attained by being indirect and ambiguous in communications (Lee & Boster, 1992). Like the French and Asians (Hall, 1983), Iranians often do not spell out the details. They will often talk around the point they wish to make and expect the listener to be intuitive enough to discover the hidden message being communicated. For example, the use of metaphor and satire (*Tanz*) is very prevalent in Iranian arts and literature. Furthermore, by being deliberate in one's speech, additional time is available to qualify potentially face-threatening messages nonverbally (Lee & Boster, 1992).

Iranians are more likely to use abstract (Carbone, 1975) ideas as opposed to concrete facts in their communication as compared with Americans and Northern Europeans. Iranians often tend to speak in general terms and to make statements with implicit meanings as opposed to being explicit, which is a common practice among Americans and Northern Europeans. As a result, in a typical Iranian conversation a great deal of background information will be provided about the topic, which may appear to be more than that needed by Western standards.

Considering the structure of messages (McGuire, 1957), Iranians invariably present the more pleasant aspects prior to the less pleasant parts of an issue. There is also a tendency to avoid the presentation of bad news where possible.

Doctors may attempt to avoid giving very negative pieces of information to their patients. In some instances in which a close family member dies, the communication of this information may be postponed for months and even years.

The Iranian use of subdued and ambiguous verbal expressions is not limited to situations in which one might express negative emotions such as disagreement, embarrassment, doubt, or anger. Even when expressing strong personal affection, a style of hesitancy and indirectness (Sillars et al., 1984) is commonly preferred. As mentioned previously, like Asians (Gudykunst & Kim, 1984), Iranians communicate excessive verbal praise or compliments with feelings of embarrassment.

Iranians demonstrate anxiety when confronted with uncertainty

In order to remove the uncertainty in a given communication episode, Iranians often resort to intuitive explanations of events and speculations, sometimes on the basis of little factual information. Like most Asian cultures (Gudykunst, 1988), they have a need for formal rules and a low tolerance for deviant groups or inconsistent beliefs. Iranians are less likely to present all sides of an issue and often use one-sided arguments (Zandpour, 1990).

Observance of typical communication patterns among Iranians might reveal this greater desire to reduce uncertainty by the manner in which communication tends to be very ritualistic. Iranians have a pattern of communication referred to as *taarof*, which essentially prescribes certain responses to various comments. For example, in many instances if Iranian individuals receive a compliment on some aspect of their appearance, they will respond by suggesting that beauty is in the eyes of the beholder. Such prescribed patterns of communication are observed much less frequently in U.S. communications.

Iranians respect authority

In Iranian institutions there is a highly centralized authority structure. In Iran, it is considered inappropriate to downplay status differences in ways that are considered highly appropriate in the United States. For example, Iranians do not generally call their instructors, supervisors, or elders by their first names. Moreover, in the official Iranian language (Farsi), the second person has two forms, similar to the *you* and *thou* as previously used in the English language. Persons in positions of higher status and authority should be referred to using only the *thou* form. Further, older people are referred to by younger members of society in terms of *thou;* they are relied upon to give advice and implicitly take on this role. It would be considered rude for a younger person to challenge directly the view of an older Iranian person.

As in other Asian countries, in Iran the individual in a public forum is somewhat cold, formal, ritualistic, and preoccupied with status. An Iranian person will generally pay a great deal of attention to who you are and not necessarily to what you are saying. As an illustration, a person with a title such as doctor or general will probably be listened to more carefully than a person without such a qualification or status. However, there is also a private self, that is observed in an informal world that is warm, close, friendly, and egalitarian. Iranians seem to have no trouble shifting from one world to the other, which is similar to individuals from Asian cultures (Hall, 1983).

In power-discrepant circumstances, Iranians show more bodily tension and smile in an effort to appease superiors and to appear polite. Again, this pattern is replicated in most of the Asian cultures (Andersen & Bowman, 1985; Hecht et al., 1989). In such situations, individuals remain alert and polite by being quiet and supporting the speaker with frequent nodding and other affirmative gestures.

As a result of this respect for authority, we would expect powerful and credible sources of information to be more effective in Iran than in Western cultures. The Iranians' love for authority and social approval may also be observed by a slight and indirect exaggeration of their credentials in some instances, by the person him- or herself or by another person. Iranians also like to be told in public that they are right about a particular issue. To improve the chances of this occurring, the dominant or most accepted position on a particular issue is usually adopted.

In social interaction, we expect to observe more frequent use of asymmetrical or superior-subordinate relationships (Watzlawick, Beavin, & Jackson, 1967) among Iranians than among Westerners. Asymmetric interaction serves the dual purpose of maintaining one's status and conferring status and respect on another person.

Iranians tend to avoid dealing directly with conflict

Iranians value harmony: A fundamental communication goal in Iran, as in other collectivistic societies, is to avoid being embarrassed and embarrassing others in the course of symbolic exchanges. A premium is placed on the maintenance of personal relationships (Triandis, Bontempo, Villareal, Asai, & Lucca, 1988; Wheeler, Reis, & Bond, 1989). In individualistic societies, face-threatening remarks are not considered as detrimental as they are in collectivistic societies, because the maintenance of ingroup relations is less important (Triandis, 1988). Iranians, like other collectivistic (Lee & Boster, 1992) cultures, sometimes avoid making face-threatening comments by being indirect and ambiguous in their communications. In general, Iranians greatly enjoy being approved and praised by others.

When dealing with members of their ingroups, Iranians prefer indirect styles of dealing with conflict, like the Asian cultures (Gudykunst, 1991). This allows all those involved in the communication to save face. Iranians tend to perceive conflict as expressive-oriented in focus. As for Asians (Ting-Toomey, 1985), for Iranians the conflict issue and the conflict person tend to be the same. In Iran, one tool that is sometimes adopted in avoiding a conflict episode is to pay attention to only certain pieces of information, which appear favorable, and to ignore all other pieces of data. The listener may thus remain comfortable and avoid direct conflict.

This is in sharp contrast to the Western cultures, which are more likely to view the world in analytic, linear, logical terms. Because issues and persons are commonly perceived as dichotomous concepts in the West, individuals from such cultures are more likely to perceive a conflict event as primarily instrumental-oriented. Hence Americans and Europeans prefer a direct mode of resolving conflict, such as the use of confrontational strategies or solution-oriented strategies (Gudykunst, 1988). In a low-context culture, such as the United States, individuals are better able to separate the conflict issue from the person involved in the conflict. In these cultures individuals can fight over an issue and yet be able to remain friends afterwards (Gudykunst, 1991), something that is very unlikely in Iran.

Iranians are oriented to the past

In terms of time orientation or *chronemics* (Williams, 1989), Iranians tend to focus on the past. They give more attention to causes, and, like Asians (Jung-Sun, 1962), they perceive events or objects that have similar signs or symbols as sharing a common relationship. Similarly, their causal pattern of thought does not build on linear time, but instead uses visual space and relies on analogies and associations (Ting-Toomey, 1985) with the past, which is used to speculate about the future. Unlike Americans, Iranians are very interested in general background information and historical antecedents regarding the issue they are dealing with. The Western cultures (such as the United States, Great Britain, and

Germany), by contrast, have present-orientations that pay relatively little attention to either traditions or speculation (Gudykunst & Ting-Toomey, 1988b).

The Western communication style is typically short and concise. Americans, for example, have a narrow focus when eliciting information and show little interest in general background information but prefer to obtain the information that they need to know promptly (Hall, 1983). Again, stylistically, we expect Iranians to be more abstract and general (Carbone, 1975) in their communications than people from the United States and Northern Europe.

There are a number of manifestations in Iranian culture of this attention to the past. Iranians value and respect their traditions and cultural heritage. Like people of many other cultures, Iranians who emigrate to other countries like to maintain their traditions and pass these on to their children. As part of their respect for tradition, Iranians also respect and pay attention to history and historic events. Whereas in the West old ideas are sometimes viewed negatively because of their lack of perceived currency, in Iran old fables and stories are abundant and relied upon in the explanation of current issues and events.

Iranians demonstrate their emotions

Iranians may be seen to be highly demonstrative of their emotions. They tend to create a sense of immediacy by increasing the level of sensory input in a communication situation, as opposed to communicators from North America, Northern Europe, and Asia (Sussman & Rosenfeld, 1982), who tend to prefer less sensory involvement. Iranians use all of their senses and talk and communicate with their whole bodies. Their faces and gestures are expressive and reflect the intensity of their involvement with each other. When observing a typical Iranian conversation, it would be normal to observe elevated volume or even shouting when important or interesting points are being conveyed.

In emotional situations Iranians are more likely to use vocal language to substitute for words, such as crying in the course of a conversation; it is considered acceptable for Iranian men to cry. Iranians communicate their emotions nonverbally through the use of their hands and animated facial expressions. We expect to see higher frequencies of movement of hands and arms, nodding or shaking of the head, leaning toward the communication source, and occasional interruptions of the speaker among Iranians. In addition, Iranians may express their emotions through repetition (Carbone, 1975) of words or sentences.

Unlike the Asian and Western cultures (Patterson, 1983), when friends meet or part in Iran, they shake hands, embrace, and sometimes kiss each other. Similarly, we expect to see more frequent use of emotional appeals attempting to entice the receiver's values and feelings, as opposed to rational appeals with empirical and logical evidence (McGuire, 1969) in communications by Iranians. In addition, like the traditional Japanese culture (Chu, 1991), we expect the Iranian communication themes to center on sadness and sometime fear.

Iranians communicate from a close distance

Iranians tend to stand and sit closer to each other than do most Americans. In their interactions, they are totally engrossed in their discussions. Typically, Iranians have a smaller zone of interpersonal space than Americans do and are not highly territorial; instead, they thrive on constant interaction and high information flow. In addition, Iranians rely more heavily on personal communication whenever possible, as opposed to more formal methods of communication such as letters or telephone calls. Examples of high-contact interactions and communications in Iran include holding hands, whispering, and sitting close to one another.

Conclusion

In summary, we can classify Iranian communication patterns into six groups: style, interaction, message structure, context, type of appeal, and nonverbal. In terms of style, Iranians are more likely to provide abstract and general information as opposed to detailed facts. They are less likely to provide or be interested in expressions of individuality. We expect them to use less vocabulary diversity and more repetition of words and sentences. In addition, Iranians prefer to communicate from a close distance.

In terms of interactive variables, Iranians are expected to place emphasis on the credibility of the communication source, as opposed to the message content and the evidence that is presented. They tend to utilize asymmetrical communication, taking a superior-subordinate position such as in parent-child or teacher-student relationships. Further, communication in Iran tends to be receiver centered, placing emphasis on the receiver's interpretation and understanding, as opposed to emphasizing delivery skills.

Considering message structures, Iranians are less likely to be explicit, letting the receiver draw his or her own conclusions. They are more likely to present pleasant and agreeable information first and even to withhold threatening and negative information. Iranians tend to focus on the side of an issue that is more consistent with their group's thinking and are less likely to deal with the opposing sides of the issue.

As far as context is concerned, Iranians are past oriented; they tend to provide extensive background information. They are receiver centered in the sense that the receiver must use contextual cues in order to interpret the information, because he or she tends to be provided with very little detailed and concrete information.

Iranians often resort to emotional and fear appeals to change the attitudes and behavior of others. It is common to focus on sadness and tragedy. They tend to display their emotions through their body movements, facial expressions, and the tone and volume of their voice. Iranians rely heavily on nonverbal communication, use vocal variety, touch, and communicate from a close distance.

References

Andersen, P. A. (1985). Nonverbal immediacy in interpersonal communication. In A. W. Siegman & S. Feldstein (Eds.), *Multichannel integrations of nonverbal behavior.* Hillsdale, NJ: Lawrence Erlbaum.

Andersen, P. A., & Bowman, L. (1985). *Positions of power: Nonverbal cues of status and dominance in organizational communication.* Paper presented at the International Communication Association, Honolulu, HI.

Bellah, R. N., Madsen, R., Sullivan, W., Swidler, A., & Tipton, S. (1985). *Habits of the heart: Individualism and commitment in American life.* Berkeley: University of California Press.

Bond, M., Leung, K., & Wan, K. (1982). How does culture collectivism operate?: The impact of task and maintenance contributions on reward allocation. *Journal of Cross-Cultural Psychology, 13,* 186-200.

Carbone, T. (1975). Stylistic variables as related to source credibility: A content analysis approach. *Speech Monographs, 42,* 99-106.

Chu, C.-N. (1991). *The Asian mind game.* New York: Maxwell Macmillan International.

Chua, E., & Gudykunst, W. (1987). Conflict resolution style in low- and high-context cultures. *Communication Research Reports, 4,* 32-37.

Condon, J. C., & Yousef, F. (1983). *An introduction to intercultural communication.* Indianapolis, IN: Bobbs-Merrill.

Forgas, J., & Bond, M. (1985). Cultural influence on the perception of interaction episodes. *Personality and Social Psychology Bulletin, 11,* 75-88.

Gudykunst, W. B. (1988). Uncertainty and anxiety. In Y. Y. Kim & W. B. Gudykunst (Eds.), *Theories in intercultural communication* (pp. 123-156). Newbury Park, CA: Sage.

Gudykunst, W. B. (1991). *Bridging differences.* Newbury Park, CA: Sage.

Gudykunst, W. B., & Kim, Y. Y. (1984). *Communicating with strangers: An approach to intercultural communication.* Reading, MA: Addison-Wesley.

Gudykunst, W. B., & Nishida, T. (1986). Attributional confidence in low- and high-context culture. *Human Communication Research, 12,* 525-549.

Gudykunst, W. B., & Ting-Toomey, S. (1988a). Culture and affective communication. *American Behavioral Scientist, 31,* 384-400.

Gudykunst, W. B., Ting-Toomey, S., with Chua, E. (1988b). *Culture and interpersonal communication.* Newbury Park, CA: Sage.

Gudykunst, W. B., Yoon, Y., & Nishida, T. (1987). The influence of individualism-collectivism on perceptions of communication ingroup and outgroup relationships. *Communication Monographs, 54,* 295-306.

Hall, E. T. (1969). *The hidden dimension.* Garden City, NY: Anchor/Doubleday.

Hall, E. T. (1973). *The silent language.* Garden City, NY: Anchor/Doubleday.

Hall, E. T. (1976) *Beyond culture.* Garden City, NY: Anchor/Doubleday.

Hall, E. T. (1983). *The dance of life: The other dimension of time.* Garden City, NY: Anchor/ Doubleday.

Hecht, M., Andersen, P., & Ribeau, S. (1989). Cultural dimensions of nonverbal communication. In M. Asante & W. B. Gudykunst (Eds.), *Handbook of international and intercultural communication.* Newbury Park, CA: Sage.

Hofstede, G. (1980). *Culture's consequences.* Beverly Hills, CA: Sage.

Hofstede, G. (1983). Dimensions of national cultures in fifty countries and three regions. In J. Deregowski, S. Dziurawiec, & R. Annis (Eds.), *Explications in cross-cultural psychology.* Lisse, The Netherlands: Swets & Zeitlinger.

Hofstede, G. (1991). *Cultures and organizations.* London: McGraw-Hill.

Hofstede, G., & Bond, M. (1984). Hofstede's culture dimensions: An independent validation using Rokeach's value survey. *Journal of Cross-Cultural Psychology, 15,* 417-433.

Hui, C. H., & Triandis, H. C. (1986). Individualism-collectivism: A study of cross-cultural researchers. *Journal of Cross-Cultural Psychology, 17,* 225-248.

Jung-Sun, C. (1962). A Chinese philosopher's theory of knowledge. *A Review of General Semantics, 9,* 215-232.

Katz, P. (1974). *Acculturation and social networks of American immigrants in Israel.* Unpublished doctoral dissertation, State University of New York at Buffalo.

Lee, H. O., & Boster, F. (1992). Collectivism-individualism in perceptions of speech rate. *Journal of Cross-Cultural Psychology, 23,* 377-388.

Littlejohn, S. W. (1983). *Theories of human communication.* Belmont, CA: Wadsworth.

MacLachlan, J. (1982). Listener perception of time compressed spokespersons. *Journal of Advertising Research, 22,* 47-51.

Marsella, A. J., DeVos, G., & Hsu, F. (Eds.). (1985). *Culture and self: Asian and Western perspectives.* New York: Tavistock.

McGuire, J. W. (1969). The nature of attitude and attitude change. in G. Lindzey & E. Aronson (Eds.), *Handbook of social psychology* (2nd ed.) (Vol. 3). New York: Random House.

McGuire, W. (1957). Order of presentation as a factor in conditioning persuasiveness. In C. I. Hovland (Ed.), *Order of presentation in persuasion.* New Haven, CT: Yale University Press.

Miller, N., Maruyama, G., Beaber, R., & Valone, K. (1976). Speed of speech and persuasion. *Journal of Personality and Social Psychology, 34,* 615-624.

Oliver, R. (1971). *Communication and culture in ancient India and China.* Syracuse, NY: Syracuse University Press.

Parsons, T., & Shils, E. A. (1951). *Towards a general theory of action.* Cambridge, MA: Harvard University Press.

Patterson, M. L. (1983). *Nonverbal behavior: A functional perspective.* New York: Springer.

Petrie, C. R. (1963). Informative speaking. *Speech Monographs, 30,* 79-91.

Prosser, M. H. (1978). *The cultural dialogue: An introduction to intercultural communication.* Boston: Houghton Mifflin.

Rubin, R. B. (1992). A cross-cultural examination of interpersonal communication motives in Mexico and the United States. *International Journal of Intercultural Relations, 16,* 145-157.

Shuter, P. (1976). Proxemics and tactility in Latin America. *Journal of Communications, 26,* 45-52.

Sillars, A. L., Pike, G., Jones, T., & Murphy, M. (1984). Communication and understanding in marriage. *Human Communication Research, 10,* 317-350.

Singer, M. K. (1987). *Intercultural communication: A perceptual approach.* Englewood Cliffs, NJ: Prentice Hall.

Sussman, N. M., & Rosenfeld, H., (1982). Influence of culture, language, and sex on conversational distance. *Journal of Personality and Social Psychology, 42,* 66-74.

Ting-Toomey, S. (1985). Toward a theory of conflict and culture. In W. B. Gudykunst, L. P. Stewart, & S. Ting Toomey (Eds.), *Communication, culture, and organizational processes.* Beverly Hills, CA: Sage.

Ting-Toomey, S. (1988). Intercultural conflict styles: A face-negotiation theory. In Y. Y. Kim & W. B. Gudykunst (Eds.), *Theories in intercultural communication.* Newbury Park, CA: Sage.

Tonnies, F. (1963). *Community and society.* New York: Harper & Row.

Triandis, H. C. (1988). Collectivism vs. individualism. In C. Bagley & G. Verma (Eds.), *Personality, cognition, and values: Cross-cultural perspectives of childhood and adolescence.* London: Macmillan.

Triandis, H. C., Bontempo, R., Villareal, M., Asai, M., & Lucca, N. (1988). Individualism and collectivism. *Journal of Personality and Social Psychology, 54,* 323-338.

Watzlawick, P., Beavin, J. H., & Jackson, D. (1967). *Pragmatics of human communication.* New York: Norton.

Westen, D. (1985). *Self & society: Narcissism, collectivism, & the development of morals.* Cambridge, MA: Harvard University Press.

Wheeler, L., Reis, H., & Bond, M. (1989). Collectivism-individualism in everyday social life. *Journal of Personality and Social Psychology, 57,* 79-86.

Williams, F. (1989). *The new communications.* Belmont, CA: Wadsworth.

Yum, J. O. (1991). The impact of Confucianism on interpersonal relationships and communication patterns in East Asia. In L. Samovar & R. Porter (Eds.), *Intercultural communication.* Belmont, CA: Wadsworth.

Zandpour, F. (1990). Candidate evaluation: Selectives versus comparatives. *Mass Communication Review, 17,* 34-46

Zandpour, F., Chang, C., & Catalano, J. (1992). Stories, symbols, and straight talk: A comparative analysis of French, Taiwanese, and US TV commercials. *Journal of Advertising Research, 32,* 25-38.

Zandpour, F., Campos, V., Catalano, J., Chang, C., Cho, Y. D., Hoobyar, R., Jiang, S., Lin, M., Madrid, S., Scheideler, H., & Osborn, S. T. (1994). *TV commercials and culture.* Paper presented at the International Communication Association Annual Conference, Sydney, Australia.

CHAPTER

10

Interpersonal Communication
in Communalistic Societies in Africa

Andrew Moemeka

> Both in its outward forms and in substance communication . . . lies
> at the heart of the cultural identity of a people since it is cultural
> values which create the symbolic bonds and ensure and preserve the
> cohesion of a society.
>
> *Jean-Louis Reiffers et al., 1982*

"Humanity," points out Geertz (1965) "is as various in its essence as it is in
its expression" (p. 36). Simply stated, cultures differ as much as the process
by which cultures are expressed and given substance. In order to set an
appropriately relevant scene for our discussion on interpersonal communication in communalistic societies (communities) in Africa, it is necessary to
define *communalism, community,* and *African culture.* This will provide clear
referents necessary to understanding the sociocultural environment in which
communication functions under communalism.

Communalism is the principle or system of social order in which the supremacy of the community is culturally and socially entrenched. The individual is
not important in his or her own right. Individuals are an integral part of the
whole—the community—and derive their place in the context of the community.
Community welfare undergirds actions, and affectiveness (in addition to effect-

edness and effectiveness) underscores communication intentions. Therefore standardized coordination behavior (Cushman, 1989) prevails; and adherence to communication rules (tacit but socially sanctioned understandings about appropriate ways to interact in given situations) is a strict requirement; noncompliance provokes strict social punishment. Unlike in collectivism where the concern of the individual is with the adaptability of self-presentation image (Gudykunst & Ting-Toomey, 1988), in communalism the concern is with the authenticity of community-presentation image. Hence the guiding dictum is, "I am because we are." Meanings and understandings are mostly projected through specific nonverbal codes (e.g., eye behavior, body movements, signs, and silence), as well as through the use of idioms, proverbs, and wise-sayings. This high-context communication (Hall, 1976) environment produces situations in which very little is said to imply much; co-orientation is achieved through mental application of codes and contexts sometimes "external" to ongoing communication; and appropriate feedback is expected as a matter of course.

The community in Africa is usually like a small town where the relationships among the people are characterized as *Gemeinschaft,* that is, intimate, familiar, sympathetic, mutually interdependent, and conspicuously manifested in a shared social consciousness. Inhabitants are usually descendants of one major common ancestor—a super-grandparent—and therefore regard themselves as close relatives, sharing their joys and sorrows. Administrative arrangements within the town are based on distinct and more closely related affinities that derive from offspring ancestors. Such finite internal groups may see themselves as communities, but because they do not have an existence independent of the town, they do not present themselves to the outside world as communities, but as units within the Community (see Appendix for more details).

African Culture refers to the fundamental characteristics of social order that are common to all Africa, even in the face of unique differences. For example, marriage in Africa is not contracted between a young man and a young woman; it is contracted between the families of the two young people. But while some ethnic groups believe in paying dowry, others believe in paying bride-price. The social drama of how marriage is contracted is an example of African Culture; the ritual of who pays for what is an example of African cultures. It is the existence of unique ethnic differences in the face of universally accepted African traits that has led to the idea of cultural dualism in Africa (see Appendix for more details). But this existence does not invalidate the fact that there are irrefutable fundamental factors of social order that are uniquely African, that obtain everywhere on the continent, and that have an overwhelming impact on the communicative behavior of Africans anywhere. The most basic of such funda-mental factors have a major bearing on the discussion that follows.

Communalism and Communication

In communalistic cultures, communicative acts are engaged in fundamentally to confirm, solidify, and promote communal social order. In such cultures, communication is always a question of attitude toward one's neighbor. There-fore, who says what to whom, when, under what conditions, and for what purpose is determined largely by the community's interaction rules. The accep-tance or rejection of information; the flow, content, and context of communica-tion; as well as the appropriate level at which exchange of ideas should occur and the appropriate atmosphere for specific types of communication, are nor-matively determined based on how they will affect established relationships. This is not to say that interpersonal communication and relationship in all communalistic societies are the same in format, content, context, and structure. There are distinct differences in the application of basic cultural demands.

All communities in Nigeria require children to respect and obey their parents. But elements of the expected respect and how they are manifested differ from community to community. Here are some examples of different formats for greeting parents as a mark of respect: Among the Ishan of the Midwest, while sons say, "I bow to receive your blessing," they bend down as if wanting to touch their toes, making it easy for their parents to lay their right palm on their back and bless them—daughters say the same thing but kneel down and bow; the Yoruba of the West prostrate themselves fully in total submission, while saying so in words, and then stand up quickly to receive their parents' acknowledgment and blessings; the Hausa of the North stoop down, half raising their right hands with clenched fist, acknowledging their parents' authority and superiority, and say so in numerous praise-words; the Itsekiri of the South-West go down on one knee and say, "I adore you"; and the Efik of the South-East genuflect and say something that has no direct English translation but has been taken to mean "Are you up?" or "Did you sleep well?"

These rituals, which reflect differences in degree rather than in substance, must be performed every day, preferably early in the morning; otherwise, at any other time during the day that the child first comes in contact with its parents. These are traditional communication rules (not choices) that must be obeyed. Compliance with these rules is required by tradition because it indicates the expected normal relationship between parents and children in which children acknowledge and accept the authority of their parents, and parents accept the responsibility for the welfare of their children. Acting out these rules usually sets a happy tone for the day's interactions. Noncompliance, which most times reflects serious strains in a parent/child relationship, provokes social sanction. In other words, the child would be socially castigated and sometimes physically punished or sentenced to a fine for noncompliance, irrespective of the faults of the parents. Therefore the requirement that children must "respectfully" greet their parents and in culturally sanctioned form, also serves as a cultural detector of possible relationship problems. But the child has no excuse whatsoever for default; the child must follow the cultural norms and state his or her case afterward.

The above example reflects one aspect of what has been called cultural dualism in Africa, that is, the coexistence of fundamental and universally accepted cultural factors or traits in Africa alongside ethnic differences in application that can be seen from community to community. What follows is a discussion of the impact of such fundamental cultural factors or traits on communication patterns and behavior in communalistic Africa, where individual community differences that gave rise to the concept of African cultures do not invalidate the authenticity of basic cultural communicative behaviors that are distinctly African (African Culture) and are discernible everywhere on the continent. Readers will most certainly notice some significant similarities (and differences in details) between the African communication environment and those of other communalistic societies in Asia, Latin America, and the Caribbean.

Cultural values and attitudes are informed by the philosophical foundations of African Culture, which are basic to the understanding of all aspects of the culture. In Africa, vertical communication follows the hierarchical sociopolitical ranks within the community. What a person says is as important as who he or she is. In other words, social statuses within the community carry with them certain cultural limitations as to what to say, to whom to say it, how to say it, and when to say it. On the other hand, horizontal communication is relatively open and usually occurs among people of the same age (sometimes, only of the same sex), those who work together, live in proximity, or belong to the same ethnic group. In this system of communication, the strength of existing relationships affects what a person says as much as what is said determines the type of relationship that would exist between and among individuals.

The two major systems of communication—verbal and nonverbal—that obtain everywhere in the world, also obtain in communalistic Africa, but they are utilized in a unique way. Although elders in Africa have the right to communicate mostly verbally, young children and youths in general are, by tradition, expected to communicate mostly nonverbally. Because younger generations are presumed to have limited experience in life, they are expected to watch and listen, and to act according to what is judged to be best for them in the context of the overall welfare of the community as indicated by the elders. This norm is buttressed by many cultural adages. For example, the Wolof of Senegal affirm that, "The child looks everywhere and very often sees nothing, but the elderly person while sitting down sees everything." The Aniocha of Nigeria, though conceding that some children may see something, hold the view that such children have no cultural right to announce personally or say publicly what they have seen. They must "tell it" through the elders. Hence the saying that, "The child may own a cock, but it must crow in the compound of the elder."

Communication in authentic communalistic Africa, that is, in rural Africa, is almost entirely through the interpersonal mode carried out in dyads, small groups (e.g., family meetings), and large groups (e.g., village meetings). The marketplace, the village school, and social forums, as well as funeral occasions, also serve as very important channels for messages and exchange of information (Moemeka, 1981, p. 46). In addition, ballads, stories, and praise-songs are used to relive the exploits and experiences of past and present generations and thus help to educate and guide the younger generation culturally.

It is not only word-of-mouth and nonverbal acts that are extremely important in communication in traditional settings; also important are some instruments of nonverbal communication that are of very significant cultural value. Three such instruments that are regarded as the sine qua non in the process of using information and communication to induce effective communal participation in the government of the community and in the preservation of the people's shared identity are the Gong, the Flute, and the Drum. Though utilized differently in different communities, the widespread use of these instruments attests to their cultural significance. In spite of some ethnic differences in utilization, they all play three universal roles—informing the community, mediating interpersonal and group communication, and serving as part of the paraphernalia of cultural instruments for entertainment. The gong in particular is most often seen as an indispensable instrument in the process of disseminating civil- and social-order messages. Using the gong to gain attention, the gongman then delivers important messages—which usually include explicitly stated punishment for noncompliance—from the leader and/or community council. When the flute and the drum are used for purposes other than entertainment, they are acknowledged as "emergency" communication channels. In this capacity, they usually play the role of serving as channels for informing the community of serious impending dangers, death of the leader, catastrophes, flagrant violations of taboos, visits of important dignitaries, declarations of war, and for summoning the community to emergency meetings.

In truly authentic communalistic African communities (the encroachment of Western values has diluted the African tradition in urban settings and cities), communication, whether horizontal or vertical, verbal or nonverbal, or for social, religious, or political matters, is carried on strictly according to the established norms (communication rules) of the community. These norms are, on the whole, based on a number of fundamental principles (to be discussed below) that have been shown to have strong philosophical implications that underscore the rationale for the unique communication pattern in communalistic cultures (Moemeka, 1984).

The Supremacy of the Community

The most important characteristic (fundamental principle) of a communalistic society is the pride of place given to the Community as a supreme power over its individual members. The community as a unit takes precedence over its members. Individual needs and aspirations are viewed as extensions of community needs and aspirations and are examined in the light of the welfare of the community. This holistic perspective holds true whether the need is for saving an individual from deprivation or for rejoicing with him or her for unique success, for carrying out a community service or for taking part in social events. Yet the desires, wants, and needs of the individual members of the community are not, as it might seem, subjugated to those of the community; rather they are merged with community needs in a holistic attempt aimed at ensuring effective prioritization. Not only is this true of physical or material needs; it is also true of emotional and communication needs. For example, personal matters, no matter how urgent and important, are required to be postponed, if they conflict with community needs. Some individual grievances are played down and others ignored, if they are at variance with the interest of the community. If what a person has to say is not in the best interest of the community, the person would be bound by custom to "swallow his (or her) words." Of course, the affected individual may whisper complaints into the ears of those who may be able to help in such other ways that would not conflict with community interest.

The welfare of the community of which the individual is an integral part takes precedence over that of individuals. The understanding, of course, is that such communal welfare will eventually be of direct benefit to all the individuals who make up the community and upon whom the community depends for its existence. In some communalistic communities, especially in Africa, the high pedestal on which the community is placed imposes limitations and demands on what the individual can say about the community, to whom, when, and how. In general, all community members are expected to present the community in a good light in all places, at all times. One may criticize individual members of the community; but the community itself should remain sacrosanct. Individuals live, and individuals die; but the Community endures.

This unquestioning loyalty and regard for the community that individuals respect as the raison d'être for their own existence creates a patriotic desire to work hard and be useful to the community, and to try to outdo others in the service of the community. Communication between and among members of the community always revolves around (in the words of the late President Kennedy) what the individual can do for the community, and not what the community can do for the individual. Discussions, conversations, and jokes that surround the unique position of the community as a supreme authority are generally about the frequency, quality, and value of each one's contribution and how such contributions have impacted on the community. Individuals are always urging one another not to be left out. If they cannot contribute directly (e.g., paying a ransom in the name of the community), they should at least do so indirectly (e.g., being such a good farmer or good wrestler that their names are heard in other communities around). Such indirect contributions boost the image and prestige of the community.

Those who can and do make positive contributions to the community are hailed as "good" sons and daughters and respected in the community. Those who can, but fail to make positive contributions are usually "lashed with the tongue" at gatherings and meetings; able-bodied members who are not able to make any positive contributions, because they cannot, are made fun of and classified as lazy and ne'er-do-wells. The tacit implication here is that no one, except invalids, is excused. As long as "they also serve, who only stand and wait," no service to the community, no matter how small, is unappreciated. Both the harsh and the "soft" criticism above are aimed at pressuring both the "recalcitrants" and the "indolents" into paying their traditional dues—services—to the Supreme Authority, even at the risk of their own comfort and happiness. Parents are castigated if their children consistently fail to meet this demand; sarcastic remarks are made before friends and relatives about their loved ones who fail to meet this demand; and wives are jeered or sneered at if their husbands default. All this is directed at making these close relatives put pressure on loved ones who "owe the community." The principle of the supremacy of the community demands selfless service to, and/or productive and self-enhancing activities on behalf of, the community. It deplores being *in the community* without being *with the Community.*

For some ethnic groups, especially the Igbo of Nigeria, not physically living in the community does not absolve one from the responsibility of treating community affairs as top priority issues, and with full dedication and commitment. Sons and daughters who live in cities and urban centers far away from their traditional communities meet on a regular basis to discuss the problems and progress of their ethnic communities back home, and of their own pseudo-communities where they live. Not only do they, as much as possible, interact in their city and urban environments as they would back home (see The Utility of the Individual, below), but more important, they make direct financial and moral contributions—helping in settling disputes, constructing roads and town halls, renovating and/or building schools—to the development of their traditional communities. Full participation in the activities of these pseudo-communities is mandatory; delinquencies and/or irregular defaults incur financial penalties, and total self-exclusion from participation and/or consistent defaults lead to ostracism, both in the city and in the community back home.

The Utility of the Individual

Communalistic societies strongly believe that people are not only mirrors for one another—that is, instruments that help individuals to see how others see them—but are, in fact, providential guides for one another; that is, useful companions who help individuals through various ways and means to live as Providence would have them live. As the Igbo of Nigeria put it, "Humans are God to one another." These are two of the underlying cultural reasons for the importance of the individual under communalism. The third is service to the community as an entity.

If the community depends on the individual for its existence, it goes without saying that the individual is acknowledged as very important. But individual importance is only in the context of the welfare of the community. This may sound ambiguous, but it is simple to explain. Although the community takes precedence over the individual, it also has the responsibility to protect the individual. Because the individual is a product of his or her community and has been brought up within the norms and mores of that community, the individual's interests and those of the community are, generally speaking, almost never in conflict. The members of the community therefore see themselves not as slaves of the community, but as part and parcel of the community that they serve and whose unity, peace, good government, and progress will eventually be of direct benefit to each of them.

Tradition confers on every adult male member (among the Aniocha of Midwestern Nigeria, this right applies to *all adult members*) of the community the right to say how he thinks the community should be governed. When public issues are opened for discussion, the individual is given a hearing if he wants to contribute. In fact, tradition demands that he should "say his mind" in order to be seen as contributing to the government and welfare of his community. It is only after a decision has been taken and given a ritual binder that further opinions and views from the individual become irrelevant. Before then such views and opinions are regarded as very important, because it is the synthesis of such individual views and opinions that form the basis of community decisions.

The utility of the individual is the principle that, through the exercise of communal responsibility, most reinforces the inherent social unity nature of communalistic societies everywhere, especially in Africa. The community enjoins each of its members to be their neighbor's keeper. In this way, it discharges its responsibility for guiding and guarding the welfare of individuals. The man without food is fed by his neighbor; the widow has a right to expect to live on the generosity of the community; the farmer who suddenly falls sick midway through the farming season has his farmwork completed for him by the community; the child who misbehaves is conscious that it would be punished, not just at home by its parents, but on the spot, by the first adult to find out what it has done. This cultural trait, which transcends ethnic and linguistic groups in Africa, finds explicit philosophical justification and expression in some aspects of African oral literature and proverbs. The Fante of Ghana transmit this value with the proverb, "The poor kinsman does not lack a resting place"; the Igbo of Nigeria with, "Two children of the same mother do not need a lamp to eat together even in the darkest corner"; and the Zulu with, "Hands wash each other to keep the fingers clean" (Moemeka, 1989, p. 6). These adages, which are sociocultural in nature but have very strong religious undertones, call for (a) honesty and trust in interpersonal and group relationships and (b) willing acceptance of the cultural demands for service to the community and help to one's neighbor.

Living a "clean" life is of utmost importance. Antisocial acts like dishonesty, adultery, cheating, and stealing are seen as serious crimes in authentic communalistic communities. And those caught committing any of these "crimes" are punished, not only physically but also emotionally. Even after they have been officially punished, they are continually harassed with name-calling, sarcastic remarks, and repulsive treatment, and are generally seen as unworthy members of the community. False accusations and lying are also abhorred and incur both physical and emotional punishments. For example, those found to have falsely accused others or to have told lies are made to walk the streets of the community publicly recanting their statements and apologizing both to the community and to those falsely accused. Such "criminal" acts not only affect the standing of the perpetrators but also damage the image and reputation of their immediate families. Hence parents spare no effort in teaching and exhorting their children to abide by the norms of the community; and friends caution one another against overstepping the bounds of liberty and doing anything that would taint their relationship.

Individuals may sometimes question but rarely refuse a request for help, even from indolent members of the community. If and when such requests are questioned and refused (this hardly ever happens on a community level), it is usually to teach a positive lesson. Tradition demands that those who are in need should be helped by those who can do so. Those who "have" are required to help those who do not. This requirement is not meant only for those who are very well-off. It states that if an individual has "more" than the one who needs help, then the individual is expected to lend a helping hand according to his or her "strength." It is not how much help is given, but rather whether the help given is commensurate with what the helping individual is capable of giving. On the other hand, the needy are not expected to take undue advantage of the benevolence of individuals or of the community. They must be seen to be doing *all they can* to help themselves before they can culturally justify asking for help.

The individual is also expected to express his or her utility to the community in a practical way, through service. Such services might be manual, moral, financial, and/or intellectual. Communalistic communities have been known to build schools, construct roads, and offer scholarships to deserving children with money contributed by members of the community both at home and in places away from home. Such contributions, usually known as "development dues," are mandatory but are levied in proportion to financial standing. Most community members take pride in paying such development dues because doing so is reflective of their usefulness to the community. Even the few who may not feel particularly happy about paying have reported experiencing a unique sense of self-satisfaction and belonging after they have paid.

Because payment of such dues constitutes the major element in the development of most communalistic communities, individuals prevail on one another to meet the financial obligation. The total burden of such development activities is not put wholly on the rich; neither are the poor unduly overburdened. Following the adage that "the head of the elephant is as heavy on the elephant as the head of the ant is on the ant," contributions are demanded from all, each according to financial strength. This way no one is left out or overstressed, and each is seen as expressing his or her utility to the community.

The Sanctity of Authority

Every communalistic society, big or small, monolithic or multiethnic, has a leader. The title of such a leader differs from community to community; so also does the amount of power bestowed on the office. Whatever the circumstance, however, the leader is the first citizen of the community and is always given the honor and prestige befitting that position. In many communities, the leader is both the temporal and the spiritual head, and is therefore seen as representing divine providence. Among the Yoruba of Nigeria, for example, a popular maxim regarding the leader calls him "the King, the Commander and the Wielder of Authority, next to the Almighty" (Okediji, 1970, p. 205). This eulogizing maxim agrees with the proverb among the Ashanti of Ghana, who say of the leader that "after the elephant there is no other animal." Yet this high honor reserved for leaders in communalistic societies must be deserved. As long as the leader lives an exemplary life, the honor and prestige of the office is accorded him; otherwise he would not only lose the leadership but also fall into disrepute. The leader is expected to be above reproach. The community expects of him no less than what the status and honor bestowed on him demand. Therefore, even for the leader, the demands of the supremacy of the community are in force. He leads, but he is not above, the community.

Community leadership is of two main types—hereditary and rotational. Hereditary leadership is that which passes from father to eldest surviving son. Such leaders are therefore born, and their positions ascribed. Rotational leadership is that which is earned or achieved, based on certain qualifying criteria. When the incumbent passes away, the position is taken up by the most qualified member of the community. Sometimes, rotational leadership is assigned in turn to different sections of the community, each of which then decides, when it comes to its turn, who, according to specified criteria, should be the overall community leader. In truly authentic communalistic communities, leaders do not rule; they merely reign. The act of governing is carried on through a cabinet of elders who, in fact, make the decisions (after discussing with the leader) that the leader announces. The existence of a cabinet of elders is particularly important for hereditary leadership that, as has happened many a time, might be thrust upon an infant son or a teenaged daughter of a deceased leader. When this happens the cabinet becomes the de facto leader, and the infant child or teenaged daughter is recognized as the de jure leader.

One aspect of leadership structure that obtains only in very few communalistic societies (or in any other society for that matter) is the special place given to women among the Aniocha communities of Midwestern Nigeria. Here, the community ascribes leadership of the womenfolk on any woman, usually above middle age, identified by women elders as the most trusted, honest, and caring, and with enough charismatic qualities. She leads the womenfolk, on the advice of women elders, in matters relating to women's affairs, their expectations and aspirations, and their contribution to the welfare of the community. She is an adviser to the overall leader of the community. She is revered as the Mother of the Community, and, like the overall leader, she is given special respect and honor as long as she lives an exemplary life and meets the demands of the community. This unique arrangement ensures that women are brought fully into the government of the community, thus giving effect to the very essence of communalism.

Apart from the above formal forms of leadership (authority), all communalistic societies believe in the fluid type of leadership structure that derives from the philosophy of gerontocracy, that is, government (or leadership) by elders. In the sociocultural arena, leadership is the responsibility of everyone—from the very oldest in the community to the very young who are old enough to know the difference between "good and bad." Anyone who finds him- or herself in a situation in which he or she is the oldest person around, is expected to assume the leadership position and to protect the group and/or lead it to the successful completion of ongoing activity. And all those over whom the individual exercises this normative "on-the-spot" leadership are expected to recognize and respect the leader's authority. Gerontocracy thus requires that each individual should act as leader to those who are younger (whether or not they are relatives) in all aspects of the community's life. This finds expression in a number of communicative behaviors. The leader has the duty of correcting, advising, admonishing, and helping those under his or her care; the leader also is culturally empowered to mete out, on the spot, appropriate punishment for antisocial behavior. Those being led are required not only not to talk back to the leader, but also to respect and listen to him or her. They may criticize the leader, but privately; they may report the leader to an older person, but not engage in a direct confrontation. The leader is held fully responsible for the actions of those under him or her, and answers to the community for whatever is and/or is not done. So the leader deserves the respect of the group.

The primary authority in anyone's life is one's parents because they occupy the first leadership position in the life of the individual. And in communalistic communities, parents rank second only to the overall leader of the community. Even though "it takes a village to raise a child" under communalism, parents bear the primary responsibility for the upbringing and behavior of their children. As a result, the culture gives parents an almost unlimited right of supervision and control over their children. Children are required to serve their parents until they themselves get married; to respect and obey them in all things including when to marry, whom to marry, and how to treat their spouses; and to take full and personal care of their parents in old age. Children who quarrel with or disregard their parents are looked upon with disdain by members of the community; those who verbally abuse or hit their parents are charged with parental assault by the community and severely punished. Any neglect of aged parents is socially and culturally despicable and is regarded as a violation of the sanctity of parenthood—a violation that is culturally repugnant and punished with both verbal and nonverbal condemnation.

Religion as a Way of Life

Religion is an all-important part of the social order of communalistic societies. By *religion* is meant not only Christianity, but also Islam, Buddhism, Judaism, Sikhism, and the numerous other traditional ways by which people of different societies express and manifest their relationship to God. Religion pervades life in traditional Africa and is used as a tool for safeguarding social order and for protecting social norms and communication rules (Moemeka, 1994). "Wherever the African is, there is his religion; he carries it to the fields where he is sowing seeds or harvesting a new crop; he takes it with him to the beer party or to attend a funeral ceremony" (Mbiti, 1969, p. 2). What is true of Africa, is true of virtually all communalistic societies.

Because religion pervades community life in such societies, there is no formal distinction between the sacred and the secular; between the religious and the nonreligious; or between the spiritual and the material areas of life. The "explicit" dichotomy one finds in collectivistic and individualistic societies between the secular and the religious does not exist in communalistic societies. Communalism demands that people's lives reflect a solid blend of the secular and the religious. Hence what is a crime in law is a moral vice and a religious sin; what is a duty is a moral obligation and a religious imperative (Moemeka, 1984, p. 45).

The role that religion plays as a tool for the maintenance of social order is manifest in the hold that it has on the people, especially on the young. In Africa, for example, the symbols representing the gods through which the people seek the favors of Almighty God are physically near, and their presence is felt everywhere—in the village square, in the marketplace, along the footpaths, in the streets, and in the home. This symbolic proximity, which strongly implies the actual presence of the gods and their watchful eyes over individual and communal behavior, helps to ensure that rules and regulations are obeyed and that norms and mores are observed, making the task of maintaining social order easier than it would have been without the impact of religion. This is why, even though both the secular and the religious are not only seen as important but are expected to merge in people's behavior, the religious would appear to have a slight edge. This is so, because the "best" way of behavior at any one point in time is dictated by the accepted norms of the community, which, in turn, are based on the religious beliefs of the people.

As already pointed out, religion pervades life in communalistic communities. It therefore does not seem a useful exercise to detail specific communication implications of the religious principle. Every norm, every mos, and every principle or act is predicated on a religious base. People's behaviors are thus guided not only by social and/or cultural rules and regulations but, more important, by religious expectations. What individuals say and how they say it is heavily influenced by religious imperatives and moral obligations. It is, in fact, religion that helps give very positive effect to the other fundamental principles of communalistic social order.

Respect for Old Age

All authentic communalistic societies (those that have not yet reached the point of no return in their enforced march toward collectivism and/or individualism) believe in gerontocracy—government or leadership based almost solely on the number of years one has spent on this earth. The longer one lives, the wider one's traditional as well as social span of authority within the community, and, of course, the more the community expects of one. In traditional Africa, old age is honorable and old men and women are treated with dignity and respect. The elderly are seen as the true repositories of wisdom and knowledge and, therefore, as assets of great value to the community. As a result, their cultural right to lead is seen as providential. The future of the community, though not placed in their hands, is intricately linked with the type and quality of advice they give; and they are ultimately held almost solely responsible for whatever is done or not done in the community. It must be remembered, though, that there is also the fluid structure of authority or leadership that gerontocracy demands. But in general the overall leader and the elders take all the blame and all the praise for the fortunes of the community.

Even in modern Africa (torn between collectivism and communalism), old age still has its aura of authority and dignity. Even though political power rather than age determines who should have authority under modern representative forms of government, the place of the aged is still regarded as culturally sacrosanct. So strong is this belief that the Fante of Ghana transmit it from generation to generation with the adage, "The word of the elder is more powerful than thunder." In order to assure a constant flow of the words of wisdom from them, the elderly are given a place of honor in the government of the community, and their advice, in general, is not easily set aside or ignored. They are expected to guide the community, leading it to actions that will fall in line with the cherished traditions of the people.

The second reason why the elderly are given a special place of honor is that African tradition holds strongly to the belief that living to a "ripe" age is providential reward for a life of justice, fair play, high levels of integrity, honesty, and chastity—a life well spent observing and respecting the norms and mores of society. As a result, the elderly are seen as examples for the youth to emulate. And to drive home this expected elder-youth sociocultural relationship, different ethnic groups have admonition adages and proverbs warning against insouciance toward the value of the elderly. For example, the Ashanti of Ghana warn that "when a child does not listen to the words of his father (elders), he eats food that has no salt"—meaning that going against the advice of elders would lead the young to outcomes that are, at best, superficial. The Igbo of Nigeria have an even stronger warning. They hold that "a child who demands to be his own master (to be left alone to do what he or she feels is good) sleeps in the cold"—meaning that self-gratification on the part of the young irrespective of repercussions on others and on society, leads to dire consequences later in life. And they reinforce this adage with another that points out that "what the young cannot see even if they climbed the tallest of palm trees, the elderly can see clearly without even standing up."

The exalted position that the culture has bestowed on old age gives communalistic communities a learning environment in which the experienced and knowledgeable are culturally encouraged not only to guide the community, but also to educate and guide the inexperienced and the young. This learning environment finds expression in meetings (community and family), moonlight storytelling, impromptu village square discussions, street and footpath one-to-one conversations, and settlement of disputes (community and family), to mention but a few. Because of their usual success in guiding the community as a whole, and the younger generation in particular, the aged are seen to have carved out a niche for themselves as a reference point for judging and guiding behavior, both communal and individual.

Conclusion

The five basic principles discussed above underlie traditional African culture, and reflect, in general, the type of social order that obtains in strictly communalistic societies. Once assimilated by the individual, each of these principles communicates its own values and thus helps to guide individual and societal behavior according to the culture of the community. For example, the principle of the Utility of the Individual demands reward for considerate behavior, concern for the underprivileged, abhorrence of selfishness, love of one's kinsmen, respect for life, and the right to participate in community affairs. All these reflect the wise-saying that, "It is people who make people become people"; or, as the Japanese strongly believe, "One becomes a human being only in relation to another person." The implication here is that only in helping others and treating them as an important part of the society can one really and truly acknowledge one's own utility. The basic injunction of the Utility of the Individual is that the community should recognize every member as useful and that every member should be concerned about the welfare of every other member and of the community. It implicitly demands life-enhancing communal leadership of the community.

Some of the values of Respect for Old Age have already been mentioned. Other values, most of which are also related to the values of the Sanctity of Authority, also reflect the uniqueness of the communication patterns and expression in communalistic societies. For example, the two principles would seem to create what Western communication observers have called the dominance-submission communication environment, but what communalists see as an environment in which "water finds its own level." This not only reduces conflict situations, but also brings into focus the normative injunction for reciprocal sensitivity toward one another. Of course, the demands of these fundamental principles are not one sided. Just as the culture gives those in authority the right to demand the respect and obedience of those over whom they exercise authority, so does the culture give the subordinates the right to be treated with dignity and respect. For the sake of social order, to each is given the appropriate cultural due. Just as the culture requires the younger generation to listen to and learn from the elders, so does it demand from the elders appropriate actions to provide conducive learning experiences for the younger generation. And to guard against any dereliction of duty with regard to this cultural expectation, the Igbo of Nigeria constantly remind themselves that

> To foresee danger and not to forewarn
> Is the bane of Elders
> To be forewarned and not to listen
> Is the bane of Youths.

The collective impact of the fundamental principles gives positive effect to the bonds that sustain communalistic societies. These bonds, which find expression in unique ways of establishing friend and mate relationships (Moemeka & Nicotera, 1993, pp. 107-124, 169-186), in conflict management (Olsen, 1978, p. 308), uncertainty avoidance (Gudykunst & Ting-Toomey, 1988, p. 192), social penetration (Gudykunst & Nishida, 1983), and power distance (Hofstede,

1980), to mention only a few, are the shared symbols, rituals, values, and beliefs of the members of such societies, and it is in these that the meaning of communality is contained. These bonds are strengthened and revitalized when those to whom the people look for guidance and leadership live what the community considers exemplary lives.

References

Cushman, D. (1989). Interpersonal communication within a rules theoretic position. In S. King (Ed.), *Human communication as a field of study: Selected contemporary views.* Albany: State University of New York Press.

Geertz, C. (1965). *The interpretation of cultures.* New York: Basic Books.

Gudykunst, W. B., & Nishida, T. (1983). Social penetration in Japanese and North American friendships. In R. Bostrom (Ed.), *Communication yearbook 7.* Beverly Hills, CA: Sage.

Gudykunst, W. B., & Ting-Toomey, S. (1988). *Culture and interpersonal communication.* Newbury Park, CA: Sage.

Hall, E. T. (1976). *Beyond culture.* Garden City, NY: Doubleday.

Hofstede, G. (1980). *Culture's consequences: International differences in work-related values.* Beverly Hills, CA: Sage.

Mbiti, J. S. (1969). *African religions and philosophy.* London: Heineman.

Moemeka, A. A. (1981). *Local radio: Community education for development.* Zaria, Nigeria: Ahmadu Bello University Press.

Moemeka, A. A. (1984). Socio-cultural environment of communication in traditional/rural Nigeria: An ethnographic exploration. *Communicatio Socialis Yearbook III,* 41-56.

Moemeka, A. A. (1989). Communication and African culture: A sociological analysis. In S. Boafo (Ed.), *Communication and culture: African perspectives.* Nairobi, Kenya: WACC/ACCE.

Moemeka, A. A. (1994). *Socio-cultural dimensions of leadership in Africa.* Paper presented at the Global Majority Retreat at Rocky Hills, CT.

Moemeka, A. A., & Nicotera, A. M. (1993). The friendship formation process in Nigeria: A preliminary study of cultural impact, communication pattern, and relationship variables. In A. M. Nicotera & Associates, *Interpersonal communication in friend and mate relationships.* Albany: State University of New York Press.

Okediji, O. (1970). *Sociology of the Yoruba.* Ibadan, Nigeria: Ibadan University Press.

Olsen, M. (1978). *The process of social organization* (2nd ed.). New York: Holt, Rinehart & Winston.

Reiffers, J.-L., et al. (1982). *Transnational corporations and endogenous development.* Paris: UNESCO.

Appendix

African Culture: There are three views on the concept of culture in Africa—ethnocultural pluralism, cultural dualism, and Africanity. Ethnocultural pluralism denies the existence of purely authentic African Culture, arguing for the concept of African cultures. Cultural dualism stresses the impact of Western culture in Africa, and argues that contemporary Africa stands between African tradition and Western tradition. In other words, not only is the concept of African cultures no longer completely sustainable, but more important, the concept of an African Culture is no longer tenable. The existence of universal African cultural traits along side numerous unique ethnic traits is also referred to as cultural dualism (Moemeka, 1989). Africanity argues in favor of the existence of authentic African Culture that is easily identifiable and has a powerful impact on the behavior and worldview of the African. It does not deny the existence of ethnocultural pluralism or of cultural dualism, but gives prominence to the reality of African Culture, present all over Africa and functional over and above the unique cultures of different ethnic groups in the continent. This chapter takes a stand in favor of, and provides concrete examples in support of, Africanity or authentic African Culture.

Community can be characterized in different ways but all such characterizations emphasize one or the other of the following: defined boundary, common ancestry, and common interest. Hence there are communities of interest (sociocultural, socioeconomic, sociopolitical); communities of ideas (paradigmatic groupings in the intellectual world); and communities of common heritage (ethnic communes, villages, small towns). These categories are, of course, not mutually exclusive. For example, those who live in a village occupy a defined area with limited boundary, usually have a common ancestor, and have an overriding common purpose. In this chapter, *community* is operationalized as a cultural group of people who have a common ancestor, and the majority of whose members live close together in an identifiable location. The community as used here is synonymous with the Town and is under the supervision of a Leader or a King and his chiefs. The town is made up of Villages under the supervision of Village Heads who are accountable to the king. The villages are made up of Quarters under the supervision of Patriarchs, accountable to the village heads. The quarters are made up of Compounds of extended families under the supervision of Elders who are accountable to the patriarchs. See Moemeka (1984, p. 50) for a graphic expression of the political structure of a typical African community.

CHAPTER 11

Interpersonal Communication in Totalitarian Societies

Catalin Mamali

Interpersonal relationships and communication are always developed in a specific cultural context that has its own values, norms, and even institutions to cope with different types and levels of interpersonal relationships. Several studies have proved that personal space, interpersonal relationships, and communication display a cultural variability. Interpersonal relationships themselves have different functions in relation to the wider society. These functions might be described as a continuum running from the function of providing a certain degree of social autonomy within a social system for those involved in personal relationships, to the function of facilitating social contacts with the wider society. Briefly, they may function either as a social

AUTHOR'S NOTE: I would like to express my appreciation to Kate Neckerman, the Executive Director of POROI where I had the opportunity to work on this chapter as an independent scholar, and to Kathy Fait and John Fuller for the hospitality of their residence in West Branch, IA.

shield against undesired social relationships, or as a social facilitator for wider social interactions, as means for integration within the macro-social structures. Metaphorically, it is possible to say that interpersonal relationships might function as synapses between individuals and the wider society.

Interpersonal relationships and their scientific study might imply a certain ideology, as Sennett (1977) and Parks (1982) argue from different perspectives. Sennett, who introduced the term *ideology of intimacy,* argues,

> The reigning belief today is that closeness between persons is a moral good. The reigning aspiration today is to develop individual personality through experiences of closeness and warmth in relationships with others. The reigning myth today is that the evils of society can all be understood as evils of impersonality, alienation and coldness. To sum up these: there is an ideology of intimacy: social relationships of all kind[s] are real, believable, and authentic the closer they approach the inner psychological concern of each person. (p. 259)

Parks (1982) reviews many studies on interpersonal communication and considers that even if "the ideology of intimacy" has directed attention to many important areas, it has ignored "two phenomena of fundamental importance: (1) information control—the use of privacy, secrecy, and deception by individuals and groups; and (2) the individual and social functions of 'weak' or non-intimate relationships" (p. 89).

The main argument of these authors is based on the perspective of "weak social ties" (Blau, 1974; Granovetter, 1973). From a sociological perspective, the "weak ties" are considered to be necessary for social integration:

> Since intimate relations tend to be confined to small and closed circles, . . . they fragment society into small groups. The integration of these groups in the society depends on people's weak ties, not on their strong ones, because weak social ties extend beyond intimate circles and establish the intergroup connections on which macrosocial integration rests. (Blau, 1974, p. 623)

Developing Sennett's argument regarding the practical consequences of the ideology of intimacy and Granovetter's idea on the functions of "weak ties," Parks (1982) argues that,

> The closed and limited communication networks engendered by the ideology of intimacy inhibit large scale social action. They deprive individuals of information about the actions of those outside their own circle. They make it more difficult to recruit members in social action movements. . . . Finally, the ideology of intimacy

discourages social action by implying that it can accomplish nothing of real significance. (p. 98)

I think that the ideas concerning the "strength of weak ties" and of the "ideology of intimacy" point out real and important issues regarding some implicit assumptions about the value of personal relationships held by some theoretical models, and the research pitfalls that might be generated by these assumptions if they are not transformed into explicit hypotheses that can be tested. On the other hand, it seems that the critique of the ideology of intimacy, itself, overlooks some important issues. First, it does not distinguish between the ideology of intimacy implied by different theoretical models of interpersonal relationships and communication worked out by different researchers in their studies on self-disclosure, close relationships, loneliness, accuracy of communication, and the existence or nonexistence of such an ideology at the level of everyday knowledge of the individuals who develop personal relationships in different sociocultural contexts. If such an ideology of intimacy exists at the level of commonsense mentality in different cultures, and very probably it does exist in many cultures, it is necessary to study it and to determine what its influences are on macro-social participation and mobilization. Second, if the ideology of intimacy implied in different scientific models on interpersonal relationships has its own pitfalls, which already have been described (Blau, 1974; Blum, 1964; Grama, 1973; Mihu, 1967, 1970; Parks, 1982; Sennett, 1977), it is necessary to point out that the opposite ideology, which I will call *the ideology of collectivistic and depersonalized relationships,* also has its own pitfalls both theoretically and pragmatically, even though these have not yet been submitted to a systematic empirical inquiry. The ideology of collectivistic and impersonal relationships basically maintains that personal development is not only a consequence but also that it must be subordinated to collective goals, unity, and strength. Third, it is important to ask about all these micro ideologies, which could exist both at the level of the implicit assumptions of research models as to the level of common sense: Are these ideologies reinforced or even systematically promoted by the political power? Is the political power programmatically oriented toward a specific ideology of social relations? And if it is so, is it using repressive force in order to impose a certain type of social relationships considered to be a basic criterion for the evaluation of all other social relationships?

The specific case of communist totalitarian societies is characterized by a state ideology that is officially represented as the only legitimate ideology. The political power, and mainly the party elite, claims that it has to be internalized or at least respected by all members of the society. This state ideology has among its core elements the idea that class relationships are the most important social relationships and that they consequently guide all other social relationships.

The implications of these ideological and political representations for research and the practice of interpersonal relationships deserves a systematic analysis. I will discuss the main theoretical and practical implications of this ideology.

The Supremacy of Class Relationships

Within totalitarian societies of the communistic type, *class relationships are politically and ideologically represented as the most important social relationships.* These representations and their practical consequences are justified theoretically by the Marxist theory of social classes and of class struggle. The basic statement of Marx and Engels on this issue is expressed in the *Manifesto of the Communist Party:* "The history of all hitherto existing society is the history of class struggle" (Marx & Engels, 1971a, p. 81).

According to *the theory of class struggle,* the ruling class also provides the most influential intellectual framework for the whole society: "The ideas of the ruling class are in every epoch the ruling ideas, that is: the class which is the ruling material force in society, is at the same time the ruling intellectual force" (Marx & Engels, 1963/1927-1932, vol. 5, p. 35). At both theoretical and practical levels this argument is completed by the idea of the organization of the proletariat, which "*alone* is a really revolutionary class" (Marx & Engels, 1971a, p. 89; italics added) *into one political party,* consequently the only truly revolutionary political party.

Within totalitarian societies the Communist Party, which has a *Central Authority* (*Statuses of the Communist League,* draft written under the direction of Marx & Engels: Marx & Engels, 1971b, p. 120), became the single political party and tried to control all of social life. The Communist Party tried to function not just as a political party but as the entire, total political organization. Thus it became in all totalitarian countries a *political oxymoron:* a part that claimed to be the total power and the single legitimate political power. Schapiro (1960, pp. 231-285) maintains that the design for the details of the Communist Party and its dictatorship was carried out by Lenin, and it was Stalin who transformed this political elite into a self-reproducing bureaucratic machine. Marxist ideas about the class struggle and the political algorithm to take and maintain the power (as it is explicitly described in the *Manifesto* and as its details have been worked out by Lenin and Stalin) have many implications for the dynamic of social relationships, including the area of interpersonal relationships. Most of these implications have become manifest characteristics in all the countries in which the Communist Parties came into power.

The political style of every Communist Party and the specific norms and patterns of interpersonal relationships that were widely spread into a given society before the coming of communist rule are among the main factors that have determined a certain variability of the restrictions imposed on the dynamics of interpersonal relationships by the political and ideological representations of class struggle.

Class relationships, including the class struggle and interests, are the ultimate and the most important criteria for judging the value of all other social relationships, including interpersonal relationships. According to this political and ideological representation, all social relationships, including family and personal relationships, are subordinated to class relationships. In other words, interpersonal relationships and communication were socially judged by their rapport with class interests. In the most extreme cases, interpersonal relationships and communication had the ontological status of means of class relationships or by-products of class relationships. Even the motivation for personal relationships was ideologically conceived as deriving from class interests. In case of conflict between the motives for interpersonal relationships on one hand and class interests on the other, both individuals and social groups were supposed to promote the class interests.

The Ideological Legitimacy of the Ruling Class

The ideological and political representations assert that the revolutionary class and its political party have a legitimate right to control the degree to which all social relations—including interpersonal relationships—support party policy in order to enhance class relationships and interests. Among the first and general "measures" associated with the "political supremacy" of the proletariat and "its most advanced and resolute section"—the Communist Party—is the *"centralization of the means of communication"* (Marx & Engels, 1971a, pp. 91, 97; italics added). The centralization of the means of communication has the latent possibility of being developed into a strong control over the content, channel, and partners of communication. This possibility became a terrible reality in all communist countries. Chirot (1986, p. 268) considers that the "Leninist socie- ties," and mainly those with Stalinist regimes, are characterized by the following five dimensions: low commitment to equality, high commitment to heavy industrialization, high centralization, high repression, and low openness to the outside world. Chirot argues that "societies living under Leninist regimes have far more aspects of their daily lives regulated by the state than in the typical capitalist-democratic regimes" (p. 263).

The centralization of the means of communication has evolved in communist societies from party control of public communication to party control of inter- personal, private, and even intimate communication. It is necessary to distin- guish this type of control and centralization, which has explicit political and ideological goals, from the moral problems generated by the development of "techniques of direct observation of living persons" (Shils, 1959, p. 114) and what Miller (1970) called "the assault on privacy" in the case of "the information based society." Miller distinguishes two major consequences: "the individual's loss of control over personal information" (p. 25) and "the individual's loss of control over the accuracy of his informational profile" (p. 32). Miller considers that the growing centralization of individualized information is related to the increasing number of people who "by having access to it are capable of inflicting damage through negligence, sheer stupidity, or lack of sensitivity to the personal privacy of others" (p. 32). All these consequences and motives and many others are possible within a totalitarian society. But there are some qualitative differ- ences between open societies and relatively closed and overcentralized societies regarding the use and abuse of all these techniques. I will mention just a few of them. First, control is produced in a systematic way at the request of the political power that has the monopoly over the institutional informational system of the society. This system is intentionally used to extend the control of political power over personal information regarding as many members of the entire society as possible. Second, the individual usually has *no control* over his "informational profile," which is preserved in his file, and he has *no access* to it. Third, the higher the political status and repressive power of a social actor, the greater are the possibilities for obtaining, producing, and/or asking for information about others and even for intentionally modifying the informational profiles con- tained in others' files. These social actors may decide about the nature of the information that can be publicly circulated (as informal rumors that are formally planned, or just as formal information) about others. Fourth, in closed and overcentralized societies a strong sociocognitive segregation is produced between the statuses of observer and observed: The higher the position in the structure of political power, the greater are the social and technical resources of the observer status. In a way, the dual nature of the cognitive status of every person, which is defined by the interplay between the statuses of natural observer and observed played by the person in his or her social space, is strongly altered and in many cases split (Mamali, 1982).

These characteristics are supposed to influence basic processes of interpersonal relationships and communication. For example, it seems that what Berger (1979) and Berger and Bradac (1982) called "uncertainty reduction strategies" might be strongly influenced at micro and macro social levels. In order to use the categories worked out by Berger it is necessary to distinguish between those actors who have similar statuses in the power hierarchy, and those who do not hold similar statuses. In the first case a formal structure, organization, or actor could either act directly or manipulate an interpersonal relationship or situation to obtain indirect informational control over a person. The active strategies (no direct interaction between the observer and the target; however, the observer takes measures to acquire information indirectly) might be used by officials to get information on the personal relationships, beliefs, and attitudes of target persons. The "interactive strategies" that involve direct interaction could be used by "uncovered," transparent officials who may provoke direct interactions with the target. Such interactions might imply different degrees of violence, promise, and/or threat. In totalitarian societies, these strategies used by the political system conform to the well-known Orwellian statement: "BIG BROTHER IS WATCHING YOU." At the other extreme are the interpersonal relationships and communication among individuals who try to protect their interaction from the observing strategies of the political power and its technical and social instruments. From this perspective it is possible to assume that in such societies most individuals will try to adjust their strategies to reduce uncertainty regarding not only the characteristics of their partners (targets) but also regarding the possibility of being observed by the instruments of political power. Most individuals try to protect their personal relationships from the watching instruments of BIG BROTHER.

As Duck (1982) and Duck and Miell (1986) argued, a major concern of persons in dissolving relationships is a focus on the possibility that the secrets revealed to their partner during the relationship will be used to harm them. This concern is very probably increased in closed and centralized societies where interpersonal conflicts could be intentionally used to obtain greater control over the individuals.

The state police control over interpersonal relationships and communication was achieved not only in public spaces but also within private spaces (houses). Most of the new dwellings were typically built and administered in such a way that their inhabitants could be under permanent control.

Individuals Are Interchangeable Units

Class interests and class behavior are the basic criteria of social differentiation. Within the same social class, individuals are interchangeable.

The problem of depersonalization is approached from many perspectives, ranging from micro to macro, and even to the global level. The theory of self-categorization (Turner, 1985), which focuses on the process of social self-categorization, argues that

> group behavior is assumed to express a change in the level of abstraction of self-categorization in the direction which represents a depersonalization of self-perception, a shift towards the perception of the self as an interchangeable exemplar of some social category and away from the perception of self as a uniquely differentiated person. (p. 100)

Depersonalization could be produced in many social situations that imply social categorization, but in totalitarian societies of the communist type, class membership, together with its political and ideological representations, is associated with a high degree of depersonalization of a great number of individuals. This depersonalization marks not only the social presentation and self-perception of individuals, but also the social perception of interpersonal behavior. Due to the political and ideological representations, interpersonal relationships among individuals are socially reconstructed as relationships among members of the same or of different social classes.

A common slogan in totalitarian societies of the communistic type regarding this issue is: "Nobody is irreplaceable." In Galtung's (1980) terms this represents a basic limitation to "personal growth": "The more replaceable a human being is, the less he is a *person* in the social context, and the more similar he is to a spare part, a machine tool, or any other thing or commodity" (p. 47).

It is very probable that under such conditions, individuals will try to find a way to avoid depersonalization and to keep their identity. How is it possible to maintain a personal identity in such conditions? It seems that the identity validation model worked out by Ting-Toomey (1986) could also be applied to this question. Its three basic elements—identity salience, perceived identity support, and communication—conceived of as the identity negotiation process between the self and relevant others (pp. 122-123), could be used to understand the function of interpersonal networks in repressive systems. In such conditions the "perceived identity support" is rarely based on explicit expressions of support, and it is frequently limited by the strong boundaries between formal and informal, and public and private relationships.

Formal Reinforcement of Collectivistic Orientations

The formal reinforcement of collectivistic orientations refers mainly to the ideological and political representations of the relations between collective and individual. Within totalitarian societies of the communist type the goals, interests, personal relationships, and development of the individual were systematically and unconditionally subordinated to the goals, interests, social relationships, and unity of the collective. The collectivistic ideology was not only very explicit, but it was also reinforced by formal and even repressive means.

In different areas of social psychology, the theoretical construct *individualism-collectivism* is considered by many researchers as a very important one, and its study has produced meaningful results in both intra-cultural and cross-cultural studies (Hinkle & Brown, 1990; Hofstede, 1980, 1983; Hsu, 1981: Triandis, 1988; Triandis et al., 1986; Triandis et al., 1988; Wheeler, Reis, & Bond, 1989; Yang, 1981). Triandis (1988), in contrasting collectivism to individualism, points out the following traits, among others: in collectivism personal goals are subordinate to ingroup goals, stronger stress is put on formal norms and duties, beliefs are consensual with the ingroup, and the collectivists are more socioemotional. In the case of collectivistic groups, the individuals (and especially those with collectivistic attitudes) "feel concerned about their communities and ingroups [and] feel proud of their group achievements," whereas individualists "find it completely rational to 'do their own thing' and to disregard the needs of their communities, family, or work group [and] feel proud of their achievements and success in competition" (Triandis et al., 1988, pp. 325, 335). Most of studies indicate that some cultures are more collectivistically oriented (Chinese, Costa Rican, Indonesian) and others are characterized as highly individualistically oriented (the United States and The Netherlands) (e.g., Hofstede, 1983; Hsu, 1981, Triandis et al., 1986; Wheeler et al., 1989).

Cultural values are not the only source of collectivistic orientations. Another major source is the ideological and political representations about social relationships, with an extreme case being that of state and party ideologies as was and still is the case with totalitarian societies of the communist type. This is why it is necessary to study the ideology of collectivism and depersonalization within such societies. This study is facilitated by the coherent *pedagogical theory and practice of collectivism* worked out by Makarenko between 1920 and 1938. He started his type of action-research in 1920 at a school for juvenile delinquents near Poltava, where he created a colony called Maxim Gorki. Later, he became deputy director for the "working colonies" (working camps) from Kiev. Makarenko was not a social psychologist (his formal training was in pedagogy), but he worked out a theory of collectivistic education and he implemented it. In his conception, the main goal of education is not the individual but the collective:

> The Soviet education has to be based on a completely new logic: *from the collective to the individual.* The object of the soviet education could be only the collective as a whole. Only by educating the collective we might hope to find an organizational form for the collective within which the (isolated) personality will be the most disciplined and the freest possible one. (Makarenko, 1963, Vol. 2, p. 330)

For Makarenko the collective is a group of persons united by a common goal, activity, and organization, all of which are subordinated to the needs of the communist society. The main—even the only—desirable structure of the collective is formal. He also distinguishes between a primary collective (a small group) and the general collective. In his case, the general collective was the working camp (the colony). The primary group has always to be subordinated to the general collective and the general collective to the demands of the wider society. By that time, the wider society was ruled by a unique political party with a supremist ideology and a dictatorial leader (Stalin). Makarenko insisted on the relationship of dependence and obedience (submissiveness to the higher level). He was much more interested in creating relationships of submissiveness than egalitarian relationships:

> I paid a special attention to this aspect (the creation of submissive relationships rather than equalitarian relationships) and this is why I tried to apply a complicated system of dependence and submissiveness relationships within a collective. (Makarenko, 1963, Vol. 1, p. 156)

In an educational game called "Thief and Informer," conceived by Makarenko, the players were dealt cards inscribed "thief," "informer," "investigator," "judge," or "executioner." The informer had to guess who the thief was. If his guess was wrong he was severely punished; if his guess was right "his sufferings were at an end, and those of the thief began." What was the new logic of this game? Makarenko argued that

> the main charm of the game consisted in *the alternation of suffering and revenge.* A harsh judge or ruthless executioner, on becoming informer or thief, got his own back from the reigning judge or executioner, who now remembered against him his former sentences and inflictions. (Makarenko, 1973, p. 129; italics added)

Makarenko played the game, too, and enjoyed it. The roles rotated, and the alternation of suffering and revenge was produced within an unchanged authoritative structure in order to increase the strength of intra-collective ties and the collective's instrumental value for achieving the goals of the larger society.

This explicit collectivistic ideology, including its educational program, was identical with the official ideology. It had been produced as a pedagogy of the relationships between individuals and the collective during Stalin's dictatorship and it was used in different forms and degrees in all totalitarian societies of the communist type. Because of these characteristics, the alternation of leading and subordinated roles achieved in such groups is very different from that produced in encounter groups (Rogers, 1970) or in those groups that apply the principle of synectics (Gordon, 1961). It seems that through their internal rules and their explicit subordination to external authorities, including the "general collective," Makarenko's collectives and their ideology were prototypes of much more brutal procedures, such as those used in many political prisons, including those in the Soviet Union (Solzhenitsyn, 1968a, 1968b, 1985), Romania (Goma, 1990; Ierunca, 1990), and other countries. On a larger scale, individual behavior and interpersonal relationships are strongly and intentionally dominated by what Orwell called *oligarchic collectivism.*

The Politization of Social Relationships

George Orwell's psychosocial imagination introduced the term *Newspeak* to describe the transformation of language in totalitarian societies. In Newspeak, war is peace, freedom is slavery, ignorance is truth, love is hate.

Orwell's idea is that "the political chaos is connected with the decay of language" (Orwell, 1946/1987, p. 367). In the case of totalitarian societies, Newspeak becomes an instrument of political control. In totalitarian societies of the communist type, the political and ideological representations of the ruling class and its elite generate a radical change in the language of social relations. I am not referring only to the problem of the wooden language apparent mainly in political speeches, but to the transformation of the daily language of social relationships. This phenomenon is not a new one. Rorty (1989), approaching the problem of the "contingency of language," argues, "The French Revolution had shown that the whole vocabulary of social relations, and the whole spectrum of social institutions, could be replaced almost overnight" (p. 3).

This kind of replacement systematically applied to the language of social relations involves many layers. I will mention only those that seem to be very important to the dynamic of interpersonal relationships and communication.

First, names for the leading party positions were generated: "first secretary," "general secretary," "party secretary." Every time an individual moved into an important party position, all friends and former colleagues were supposed to mention this political function when addressing him or her. The name of the political function often even replaced a person's last and first names during interpersonal communication in public or in private spaces. At the level of language, the personal identity was dissolved into the political status.

Second, the older appelatives—for example, Mr. or Mrs.—were replaced in a compulsory way in all public institutions by *Tovaras* or *Tovarasa*, from the Russian *Tovarish* (Comrade). Even though there was a Romanian word for Comrade (*Camarad*), it was replaced by the Russian *Tovarish*. If a person were to use "Mister" instead of "Comrade" in an institution (e.g., school, factory), the person would be asked to renounce the older appelative, and threatened and even punished. Step by step this official and imposed vocabulary of social relationships was challenged by a kind of linguistic resistance. For example, in this specific case the individuals tried to discriminate during their interpersonal communication, mainly in public and institutional settings, between those who were visibly on the side of power and those who were not, by using different forms of address: *Tovaras* and *Tovarasa* (comrade) for those in the first category, and "Mrs." and "Mr." (Lady and Gentleman) for the second. In this way, social space and social relationships were once again differentiated by the use of these appelatives. These appelatives were also used as social signals. If the question, "How is he (she)?" was followed by the answer, "He (she) is a Comrade," it became a warning, a different way of saying "Be careful!" If the answer was,

"She is a Lady," it meant "It is OK." The expression, "He is *Un Tovaras Just*" (a Just Comrade) was used—at least in many social situations in Romania—as a strong warning signal indicating a clear political commitment to the party line by the person called "a Just Comrade." Because these linguistic strategies became increasingly frequent and were used to guide and to protect personal relationships against the instruments of BIG BROTHER, and because they were considered to be a form of disobedience during the eighties in Romania, a formal norm proposed by Ceausescu was published that replaced the nonparty forms of address ("Lady," "Gentleman") with a *Cetateanca* and *Cetatean* ("Citizen," from *Citoyen*, used during the French Revolution). This new compulsory form of address did not work and soon became a target of political jokes. Such means of address have similar functions in relationships between political categories as the *shibboleth schema* (Hopper, 1986) has for dialect differences. It is possible to label these types of address *political shibboleths:* linguistics tests and boundaries used by individuals in order to communicate their political identity and to differentiate among those who belong to the governing power and those who do not. Political shibboleths could be used by individuals to orient themselves within a repressive system.

Third, *a grammar of social relations* was developed in the totalitarian societies; it was characterized by a strongly asymmetrical use of pronouns. More specifically, the grammar of social relations refers first of all to the way in which the pronouns (singular and plural) are used to point out close or distant relations, symmetrical or asymmetrical relations, and formal or informal relations. This part of the grammar of social relations is very visible, particularly in those languages that differentiate between the *singular* and *plural* forms of the second person pronoun, *you* (which is not differentiated in modern English). The second person plural pronoun is used even when addressing just one person. This is the case with many languages, among them Bulgarian, French, Italian, German, Romanian, and Russian. H. L. Mencken (1980) wrote about this problem in *The American Language:*

> In "Twelfth Night" Sir Toby Belch urges Sir Andrew Aguecheek to provoke the disguised Viola to combat by *thouing* her. In our own time, with thou passed out entirely, the confusion between you in the plural and you in the singular presents plain difficulties. (p. 546)

In other modern languages the difference between "you in the plural" and "you in the singular" still plays an important role in the grammar of social relationships. Traditionally, the "you in the plural" is used to express respect related to age, professional status, social power, or the fact that those who are interacting are not personally close. This was the case for Romania, too, before 1945. But the "you in the plural" has become—especially within institutions—a verbal means of reinforcing the status of formal authorities at each level of power. Thus, as a general rule, whenever a person who had a higher status within the power structure addressed a person with a lower status, the person with the higher position used the singular form of you (*tu*), whereas the person in the lower status was supposed to use the polite (plural) form of you (*Dumneavoastra*). The singular form was almost always used from the top down to the bottom of the political and bureaucratic hierarchy, while from the bottom up to the higher levels the polite form was used regardless of the work experience, age, sex, or educational level of the actors. The main criterion was political and administrative power. The use of the singular form by the person in the lower status, when the person in the higher status also used the singular form, was not perceived as a claim for symmetrical verbal relationships but as a sign of disobedience, which was punished. It is interesting to note that sometimes the plural and singular forms were used in a strategic way to deceive a third party about the true personal relationship between the speakers. The pronoun seems to be an important means to "converge" or "diverge linguistically" (Gudykunst, 1986, p. 157) during intra- and intergroup communication. One of the axioms of the theory of intergroup communication focuses on this problem:

> People will attempt to maintain their speech patterns or even diverge linguistically away from those believed characteristics of their recipients when they (a) define the encounter in intergroup terms and desire a positive group identity, or (b) wish to dissociate personally from another in an interindividual encounter, or (c) wish to bring another's speech behaviours to a personally acceptable level. (Gudykunst, 1986, p. 157)

Individuals' attempts to converge or diverge linguistically within an environment dominated by overcentralized political representations could be considered as ways to express inter-categorical attitudes from political alignment to political dissent.

These political and ideological representations were reinforced not only by norms and by the formal structures, but also by a police system. Havel has described this system in his letter addressed in 1975 to Husak (General Secretary of the Czechoslovak Communist Party):

The system of existential pressure, embracing totally the whole society and every individual, either as a specific everyday threat or as a general contingency, could not, of course, work effectively if it were not backed up—exactly like the former, more brutal forms of pressure—by its natural hinterland in the power structure, namely by that force that renders it comprehensive, complex and robust: *the ubiquitous, omnipotent state police.*

For this is the hideous spider whose invisible web runs right through the whole of society; this is the point at infinity were all the lines of fear ultimately intersect; this is the final and irrefutable proof that no citizen can hope to challenge the power of the state. And even if most of the people, most of the time, cannot see this web with their own eyes, not touch its fibres, even *the simplest citizen is well aware of its existence, assumes its silent presence at every moment in every place, and behaves accordingly, that is, so as to ensure the approval of those hidden eyes and ears.* (Havel, 1987, p. 7; italics added)

This system was used in all communist countries in Eastern and Central Europe. In some cases it was stronger (the Soviet Union, Romania, East Germany, Bulgaria), in others not so strong. But its basic traits were similar. This ideological and existential framework of personal relationships has its own evolution. For the problem of interpersonal relationships and communication *two stages* seem to be very important: (a) *the stage of direct control* over interpersonal relationships achieved in the first years of the communist dictatorship; (b) *the stage of an indirect, hidden, even refined control* over interpersonal relationships and communication when the communist regimes had established their strong watching system. The historic order of these two stages does not exclude the use of direct means to control personal relationships in the second stage or the use of more indirect and manipulative means in the first stage.

Conclusion

Interpersonal relationships and communication within totalitarian societies still represents a field that has not been studied in a systematic way. One of the main reasons is the repressive nature of such social systems. At the same time, the dynamics of interpersonal relationships and communication have been preserved by many meaningful traces, such as memoirs, diaries, and especially letters. These traces, together with the literature produced by dissident writers, could be extremely useful for the theoretical reconstruction of the characteristics of interpersonal relationships and communication within such societies.

This chapter tries to make explicit the main assumptions of the "ideology of collectivism" and of the political and ideological representations that influenced the nature and dynamics of interpersonal relationships and communication within communist societies. The ideological and political framework of interpersonal relationships and communication is defined by the following traits:

- class relationships are formally considered as the most important social relationships in such societies
- the ruling class and its political elite are supposed to have an ideological legitimacy to control all the social relationships among the members of the society and between them and the outside world
- individuals and the relationships among them are considered to be interchangeable social units
- the political power has the right to reinforce formally and even brutally the collectivistic orientation of individuals and social groups
- the language of social relationships is politicized

References

Berger, C. (1979). Beyond initial interaction: Uncertainty, understanding, and the development of interpersonal relationships. In H. Giles & R. St. Clair (Eds.), *Language and social psychology.* Oxford, UK: Basil Blackwell.

Berger, C., & Bradac, J. J. (1982). *Language and social knowledge.* London: Edward Arnold.

Blau, P. (1974). Parameters of social structure. *American Sociological Review, 39,* 615-635.

Blum, A. F. (1964). Social structure, social class, and participation in primary relationships. In A. B. Shostak & W. Comberg (Eds.), *Blue collar world.* Englewood Cliffs, NJ: Prentice Hall.

Chirot, D. (1986). *Social change in the modern era.* New York: Harcourt Brace Jovanovich.

Duck, S. W. (1982). *Relationships 4: Dissolving personal relationships.* London: Academic Press.

Duck, S. W., & Miell, D. (1986) Charting the development of personal relationships. In R. Gilmour & S. W. Duck (Eds.), *Emerging field of personal relationships.* Hillsdale, NJ: Lawrence Erlbaum.

Galtung, J. (1980). *The true worlds. A transnational perspective.* New York: Free Press.

Goma, P. (1990). *Gherla.* Bucuresti: Editura Humanitas.

Gordon, W. (1961). *Synectics, the development of creative capacity.* New York: Harper.

Grama, D. (1973). *Preferinta interpersonala.* Bucuresti: Editura Stiintifica.

Granovetter, M. S. (1973). The strength of weak ties. *American Journal of Sociology, 78,* 1360-1380.

Gudykunst, W. B. (1986). Toward a theory of intergroup communication. In W. B. Gudykunst (Ed.), *Intergroup communication.* London: Edward Arnold.

Havel, V. (1987). Letter to Dr. Gustav Husak, Secretary of the Communist Party. (1975). In J. Vladislav (Ed.), *Vaclav Havel or living in truth. Twenty two essays published on the occasion of the award of the Erasmus Prize to Vaclav Havel.* Amsterdam: Meulenhoff.

Hinkle, S., & Brown, J. R. (1990). Intergroup comparisons and social identity: Some links and lacunae. In D. Abrams & M. A. Hogg (Eds.), *Social identity theory: Constructive and critical advances.* New York: Springer.

Hofstede, G. (1980). National culture revisited. *Behavior Science Research, 18,* 285-305.

Hofstede, G. (1983). Dimensions of national cultures in fifty countries and three regions. In J. Deregowski, S. Dziurawiec, & R. Annis (Eds.), *Explications in cross-cultural psychology.* Lisse, The Netherlands: Swets & Zeitlinger.

Hopper, R. (1986). Speech evaluation of intergroup dialect differences: The shibboleth schema. In W. B. Gudykunst (Ed.), *Intergroup communication.* London: Edward Arnold.

Hsu, F. L. K. (1981). *American and Chinese: Passage to differences* (3 ed.). Honolulu: Hawaii University Press.

Ierunca, V. (1990). *Fenomenul Pitesti.* Bucuresti: Humanitas.

Makarenko, A. S. (1963). *Opere pedagogice alese* (Vols. 1 & 2). Bucuresti: Editura Didactica si Pedagogica.

Makarenko, A. S. (1973). *The road to life. An epic in education* (Trans. and Introduction by P. Licthenberg). New York: Oriole Editions.

Mamali, C. (1982). Democratization of the social research process. In P. Stringer (Ed.), *Confronting social issues: Application of social psychology.* London: Academic Press.

Marx, K., & Engels, F. (1963). Marx-Engels *Gesamtausgabe, Erste Abteilung.* In H. Selsman & H. Martel (Eds.), *Reader in Marxist philosophy.* New York: International Publishers. (Original work published 1927-1932)

Marks, K., & Engels, F. (1971a). *Manifesto of the Communist Party.* In K. Marx, *On revolution* (Ed. & Trans., S. K. Padover). New York: McGraw-Hill.

Marx, K., & Engels, F. (1971b). *Statutes of the Communist League.* In K. Marx, *On revolution* (Ed. & Trans., S. K. Padover). New York: McGraw-Hill.

Mencken, H. L. (1980). *The American language.* New York: Knopf.

Mihu, A. (1967). *Sociometria, eseu critic.* Bucuresti: Editura Politica.

Mihu, A. (1970). *Sociologia Americana a grupurilor mici.* Bucuresti: Editura Politica.

Miller, A. R. (1970). *The assault on privacy: Computers, data banks, and dossiers.* Ann Arbor: University of Michigan Press.

Orwell, G. (1987). *Nineteen eighty-four.* London: Secker & Warburg. (Original work published 1946)

Parks, M. R. (1982). Ideology in interpersonal communication: Off the couch and into the world. In M. Burgoon (Ed.), *Communication yearbook 5.* New Brunswick, NJ: Transaction Press.

Rogers, C. (1970). *Carl Rogers on encounter groups.* New York: Harper & Row.

Rorty, R. (1989). *Contingency, irony, and solidarity.* New York: Cambridge University Press.

Schapiro, L. (1960). *The Communist Party of the Soviet Union.* New York: Random House.

Sennett, R. (1977). *The fall of public man.* New York: Vintage.

Solzhenitsyn, A. (1968a). *Cancer ward.* New York: Farrar, Straus & Giroux.

Solzhenitsyn, A. (1968b). *The first circle.* New York: Harper & Row.

Solzhenitsyn, A. (1985). *The Gulag archipelago, 1918-1956: An experiment in literary investigation.* New York: Harper & Row.

Ting-Toomey, S. (1986). Interpersonal ties in intergroup communication. In W. B. Gudykunst (Ed.), *Intergroup communication.* London: Edward Arnold.

Triandis, H. C. (1988). Collectivism vs. individualism: A reconceptualization of a basic concept in cross-cultural psychology. In G. Verma & C. Bagley (Eds.), *Cross-cultural studies of personality, attitudes and cognition.* London: MacMillan.

Triandis, H. C., Bontempo, R., Betancourt, H., Bond, M., Leung, K., Brenes, A., Georgas, J., Hui, H. C., Narin, G., Setiadi, B., Sinha, J. B. P., Verma, J., Spangenburg, J., Tonzard, H., &

Montmollin, G. (1986). The measurement of etic aspects of individualism and collectivism across cultures. *Australian Journal of Psychology, 38,* 257-267.

Triandis, H. C., Bontempo, R., Villareal, M. J., Asai, M., & Lucca, N. (1988). Individualism and collectivism: Cross-cultural perspectives on self-ingroup relationships. *Journal of Personality and Social Psychology, 54,* 323-338.

Turner, J. C. (1985). Social categorization and the self-concept: A social cognitive theory of group behavior. In E. G. Lawler (Ed.), *Advances in group processes: Theory and research* (Vol. 2). Greenwich, CT: JAI.

Wheeler, L., Reis, H. T., & Bond, M. H. (1989). Collectivism-individualism in everyday social life: The middle kingdom and the melting pot. *Journal of Personality and Social Psychology, 57,* 79-86.

Yang, K. S. (1981). Social orientation and individual modernity among Chinese students in Taiwan. *Journal of Social Psychology, 113,* 159-170.

PART
IV

CONCLUSION

CHAPTER

12

Cross-Cultural
Interpersonal Communication:
Theoretical Trends and Research Directions

Stella Ting-Toomey
Leeva Chung

Individuals learn the norms and rules of appropriate or inappropriate interpersonal conduct, and effective or ineffective interpersonal behavior, within the webs of their culture. People learn the meaning of "friendship," "reciprocity," or "commitment" via the primary socialization process of their family system situated within a culture. Culture serves as the wider net in which salient interpersonal concepts are used and interpreted.

Culture, in essence, is a meaning system that is shared by a majority of individuals in a particular community. On a general level, it refers to a patterned way of living by a group of interacting individuals who share similar sets of

AUTHORS' NOTE: We want to thank Bill Gudykunst for his thoughtful comments on an earlier version of this chapter.

237

traditions, beliefs, values, norms, and behaviors. On a specific level, cultural values and norms influence the expectations that we hold in the development of our interpersonal relationship. They also affect the implicit stories and theories that we use to describe and explain our everyday relationships.

The purpose of this chapter is to address some of the theoretical trends and research issues in cross-cultural interpersonal communication. Although many chapters in this volume have addressed interpersonal concepts from a cultural indigenous perspective, no chapter has yet offered a synopsis of current theoretical trends and research issues in cross-cultural interpersonal communication. The objective of this chapter is to fill this gap. We hope our review of some of the current theories in cross-cultural interpersonal communication will offer beginning researchers a guide for further readings and reflections. We organize the chapter into three sections. First, we discuss the cultural variability perspective of individualism and collectivism and review some of the chapter ideas presented in Part III of this book. Second, we summarize some of the current theories that are related to cross-cultural or intergroup-interpersonal communication. Third, we conclude with suggestions for future theorizing and research in the area of cross-cultural interpersonal relationship development.

Cultural Variability Perspective

A cultural variability perspective refers to how cultures vary on a continuum in accordance with some basic dimensions or core value characteristics. Although there are many dimensions in which cultures differ (see Chapters 1, 2, & 3, this volume), one dimension that has received consistent attention from cross-cultural researchers around the world is individualism-collectivism. While the individualism-collectivism dimension has been used to explain *cultural-level* differences and similarities on interpersonal behavior, the dimension of construal of self has been used to explain *individual-level* differences and similarities on interpersonal conduct.

A Cultural-Level Approach

Countless cross-cultural studies (Hofstede, 1980, 1991; Schwartz & Bilsky, 1990) have provided theoretical and empirical evidence that the value orientations of individualism and collectivism are pervasive in a wide range of cultures. The value orientation approach has been researched for more than 40 years in multiple academic disciplines (e.g., Hall, 1976, 1983; Hofstede, 1980; Kluckhohn & Strodtbeck, 1961; Triandis, 1972).

Basically, *individualism* refers to the broad value tendencies of people in a culture to emphasize individual identity over group identity, individual rights over group obligations, and individual achievements over group concerns. In contrast, *collectivism* refers to the broad value tendencies of people in a culture to emphasize group identity over the individual identity, group obligations over individual rights, and ingroup-oriented concerns over individual wants and desires (Hofstede, 1980, 1991; Triandis, 1995).

Individualism is expressed in interpersonal interaction through the use of direct verbal assertions, up-front emotional expressions, and the emphasis of "control" and "openness" in interpersonal relating process. Collectivism, on the other hand, is displayed in interpersonal communication through the use of indirect verbal expressions, understated emotional disclosures, and the emphasis of "relational face" in interpersonal interaction process. "Relational face" refers to the proper considerations and respect accorded to the relational partner and her or his ingroups (see Ting-Toomey, 1994a, for a detailed discussion of cultural facework dimensions).

Ingroup (e.g., extended family, same caste, same work group), as a critical interpersonal factor, tends to influence a wide variety of interpersonal situations in collectivistic and individualistic cultures. The ingroup/outgroup boundary is conceptualized along lines such as perceived common fate, proximity, similarity (e.g., similar demographic factors, beliefs, attitudes), affinity, and perceived outside threats (Triandis, 1989). Overall, collectivists (more than individualists) tend to: (a) be concerned about the consequences of their behaviors on ingroup members, (b) be more willing to share resources with ingroup members, and (c) feel emotionally involved in the lives of ingroup members (Triandis, 1994, p. 165). Different norms (such as degrees of hospitality, formality, intimacy, and reciprocity) govern different ingroup/outgroup interpersonal behavior in different collectivistic cultures (e.g., Greece and Thailand).

In intercultural communication research, British, French, German, Scandinavian, Swiss, Australian, Canadian, and the U.S. cultures have been identified consistently as cultures high in individualistic value tendencies (Hofstede, 1980, 1991). Comparatively, strong empirical evidence has supported that many Asian (e.g., China, Japan, and Korea), Southeast Asian (e.g., Thailand and Vietnam), Mediterranean (e.g., Greece and Italy), Latino (e.g., Brazil and Mexico), Middle Eastern (e.g., Iran and Saudi Arabia), and African (e.g., Ghana and Nigeria) cultures can be identified clearly as group-based cultures (Gudykunst & Ting-

Toomey, 1988; Hofstede, 1980, 1991; U. Kim, Triandis, Kagitcibasi, Choi, & Yoon, 1994; Triandis, 1994, 1995). Different degrees and forms of individualism and collectivism exist in different cultures (Triandis, 1995).

For the past 10 years, researchers in anthropology, cross-cultural psychology, and intercultural communication areas (for reviews, see Fiske, 1991, 1992; Gudykunst & Ting-Toomey, 1988; Hofstede, 1991; U. Kim et al., 1994; Triandis, 1994, 1995) have used the individualism-collectivism dimension to explain a host of interpersonal-related concepts such as intimacy disclosure (Ting-Toomey, 1991b), romantic love (Dion & Dion, 1988; Gao, 1991, 1993), and conflict styles (Ting-Toomey et al., 1991). For example, Gao (1993) examines the meaning of romantic love in individualistic (i.e., U.S.) and collectivistic (i.e., Chinese) cultures. Based on triangulated interview and survey data analysis, she observes that for the U.S. romantic couples, shared interests and activities serve as important romantic intimacy indicators. For the Chinese couples, shared intellectual intimacy (i.e., partners helping each other to clarify ideas and provide guidance) acts as an important dimension in Chinese romantic relationship development. In addition, U.S. couples tend to value passionate love (see also Jankowiak, 1995, on cultural romantic passion) more so than the Chinese couples. Chinese couples, in comparison, tend to emphasize companionship love more so than U.S. couples. In another study, Ting-Toomey (1991b) examines "love commitment" and "intimacy disclosure" in large samples of students concerning opposite-sex friendship in France, Japan, and the United States. Through self-report survey data, she finds that U.S. citizens tend to report a higher degree of "love commitment" and "intimacy disclosure" than the other two samples. The same U.S. sample also reports more "relational ambivalence" (as expected of individualistic culture) about whether to continue the opposite-sex friendship than the other two groups. Though the cultural variability perspective has been used to explain cross-cultural differences on an aggregate group membership level, an emerging trend in cross-cultural interpersonal research focuses on individual-level differences of interpersonal relationship interaction.

An Individual-Level Approach

An alternative way to understand individualism and collectivism focuses on how individuals within (or across) cultures conceptualize the sense of "self." Markus and Kitayama (1991) argue that the placement of our sense of self-conception in our culture profoundly influences our interpersonal communication with others. Factors such as cultural ideologies and values, social change, media, generation, family socialization, ethnicity, gender, ingroup, and personality tendency shape an individual's construction-of-self process.

Individuals with a strong sense of *independent self* tend to see themselves as autonomous, self-reliant, unencumbered, change agents, and as rational choice-makers. Individuals with a strong sense of *interdependent self* tend to see themselves as ingroup-bound, role-based, interconnected, obligatory agents, and as harmony seekers. While independent-self individuals are more concerned with relational autonomy issues, interdependent-self individuals are more concerned with relational connection issues. While the former group is more concerned with personal commitment issues, the latter group is more concerned with social/network commitment issues. Furthermore, while independent-self persons tend to practice low-context interaction patterns and direct request messages, interdependent-self persons tend to practice high-context interaction patterns and indirect request messages (Gudykunst et al., 1996; M. Kim, Sharkey, & Singelis, 1994).

Both types of self-construal exist within a culture. Overall, however, independent (or "I identity") concepts of self are predominant in individualistic cultures, and interdependent (or "we identity") concepts of self are predominant in collectivistic cultures. The independent-/interdependent-self approach extends the line of research on cultural individualism-collectivism by accounting for *individual variations* within and between cultures. Most of the chapters in Part III of this book address issues of group orientation or collectivism from a cultural-level approach. However, we should also keep in mind the independent- and interdependent-self concepts when explaining people's behavior on an individual level.

Collectivistic-Related Themes

Although the individualism-collectivism dimension is a powerful dimension to explain differences and similarities in cross-cultural interpersonal behavior, the dimension also operates in a unique way within each culture. Almost all chapters in Part III of this book cover some cultural indigenous aspects of collectivism (see Chapters 4 through 11). This is not surprising given the fact that "about 70% of the population of the world lives in collectivistic cultures" (Triandis, 1990, p. 48). Ironically, however, almost all theories that have been developed in explaining interpersonal behavior are reflective of individualistic, Western ideologies (Ting-Toomey, 1991a). Thus one of the contributions of this book is in the generation of sensitizing concepts pertaining to collectivistic-oriented interpersonal communication. As Nishida (Chapter 5) crisply states: "In order to understand the communication behaviors of any culture, it is important to examine them in light of communication theories that have developed within the culture itself."

In reviewing the chapters in Part III, a major pattern emerges; that is, the importance of an emic (or cultural-specific) approach to collectivism. For example, concepts of "other orientation" (in Gao's Chapter 4), "corporativism" (in Nishida's Chapter 5), *"che-myon"* (face-related, in Lim & Choi's Chapter 6), *"respeto"* (in Garcia's Chapter 7), "the house," (in Rector & Neiva's Chapter 8), "collectivism" (in Zandpour & Sadri's Chapter 9), "communalism" (in Moemeka's Chapter 10), and "ideology of collectivism" (in Mamali's Chapter 11) are all reflective of the group orientation label of "collectivism."

Taken together, various authors in these chapters help to deepen our understanding of the concept of "collectivism" by providing rich insights and cultural-specific examples. Cultural emic taxonomies and interpretations are added to highlight the multidimensional facets of "collectivism." Interestingly, though some of the authors of this volume view the broad concept of collectivism as equivalent to their emic understanding of collectivism, other authors (see, e.g., Chapters 4, 6, 7) propose their own vocabularies in developing interpersonal communication theories anew.

On a more specific level, four collectivistic themes emerge in Part III. They are: the importance of *family, affect, facework,* and *social change* in conceptualizing cross-cultural interpersonal relationship development. For example, in examining Chinese personal relationships, Gao (Chapter 4) argues that "family is both a home and a community [to the Chinese]. Family [in the Chinese culture] serves as the primary and ongoing unit of socialization of each person . . . when friends become very close, Chinese say they're like members of the family." Thus the relational principle of Chinese friendship development is derived from that of the family. Similarly, in examining Mexican interpersonal relationship development, Garcia states that the family symbolizes a

> fundamental system of interaction. . . . For instance, the first words, *jefe* [father— "male chief"] and *jefa* [mother—"female chief"], imply the highest positions within a family system. Second, the words *viejo* [husband—"old man"] and *vieja* [wife— "old woman"] connote comfort or confidence and, therefore, are indicative of equal

positions of power. . . . Lastly, . . . the word *escuincles* [children—no direct English translation but roughly means "brat"] . . . connotes the lowest position in the system.

According to Garcia, the family "class" system permeates all other areas of social and personal relationship development in the Mexican culture.

The second theme, *affect,* also takes on specific cultural vocabularies, meanings, and nuances in these different group-oriented cultures. For example, Gao (Chapter 4) examines two fundamental interpersonal relationship constructs in the Chinese culture: *ren qing* and *bao. Ren qing* is translated as "human feeling" and can be defined in three different ways: feelings between individuals, an individual's natural inclinations, and interpersonal resources. Once *ren qing* is established, *bao* often follows. *Bao* as a verb also consists of multiple meanings such as "to repay," "to respond," and "to retaliate." *Bao* as a concept of "relational indebtedness" is based on the scope of *ren qing* (e.g., big or small) and the nature of a relationship (e.g., expressive or instrumental). In comparison, Lim and Choi (Chapter 6) examine the cultural conceptualizations of *jung* in Korean interpersonal relationship development. They use the word *jung* in contrast to the word "love." They clarify:

> The psychological basis of interpersonal relationships in Korea is twofold. One is love (or *sah-rang* in Korean), and the other is *jung.* Love, as in Western society . . . is purely affective. *Jung* is a much broader concept than love. In addition to the affective aspect of love, *jung* comprises the forces of inertia of a relationship. . . . *jung* is unconscious and voluntary. . . . [with] four properties: duration, togetherness, warmth, and solidarity.

In sum, *jung* is a "solid emotion" that exudes feelings of warmth and caring between persons in a relationship across time because of frequent contacts and perceived shared fates. While love is what makes a relationship intense and intimate, deep *jung* is what makes a Korean interpersonal relationship stable and mutually bonded.

In comparison, Rector and Neiva use the term *saudade* to describe relational affect in the Brazilian culture. *Saudade* refers to a "peculiar form of nostalgia that is combined with love and affection, and represents a larger-than-life longing." Brazilian relationship development emphasizes what is "emotional, irrational, and mystical. Sensibility, imagination, and mystic religiosity permeate the thoughts and feelings of the people." The religious orientation (see also Chapter 10 on religious influence on communalism) has two aspects: It is "mystical, and relates to superstition and even fanaticism; or . . . formalistic . . . [and relates to] cordiality, politeness, and hospitality." Thus the ideological and religious roots of a culture also profoundly influence how interpersonal affect, loyalty, or harmony are enacted and maintained in a collectivistic society.

The third theme, the conceptualization of *facework,* appears to be a critical construct in many of the chapters (see Chapters 4, 5, 6, 7, 8, 9, & 10) in Part III. For example, Gao (Chapter 4) comments on the concepts of *lian* ("face") and *mian zi* ("image"). Whereas *lian* refers to both social sanction and internalized sanction of one's interpersonal conduct, *mian zi* refers to one's claim for a positive social image. Both *lian* and *mian zi* serve to regulate proper and improper interpersonal behavior in the Chinese culture. Lim and Choi (Chapter 6) use the concept of *che-myon* or "face" to explain how *che-myon* is inevitable in every aspect of a Korean person's daily interaction. For the authors, *che-myon* is a double-face concept. It is the image of "personal self that is claimed and negotiated through social interactions. . . . It is [also] the image of sociological self that is defined by the society and must be protected by passing the normative standards of positiveness of relevant social values." Most Koreans value *che-myon* dearly. When they "hoist up" their *che-myon,* Koreans do not simply feel good. They feel actually more socially desirable. To maintain *che-myon,* Koreans need to be involved in the activities that are designed to fulfill their face-related social expectations. Such activities include visiting others and giving gifts, entertaining others, and helping others to pay for weddings and funerals, and more. Garcia (Chapter 7), in examining the concept of *respeto* as a conceptual base for Mexican interpersonal relationship, describes *respeto* (or "respect") as related to perceived relational status. It implies honor and dignity that one accords to another person in a higher position within the Mexican class system. By choosing the linguistic marker of *usted* (the formal form of address of *you*) or *tú* (the informal form of address of *you*), respect or face is given to one's interactional partner. Addressing someone by the improper form of *you* can pose serious face-threat problems in Mexican interpersonal interaction. Individuals can also use *usted* and *tú* strategically to change the structure of the relationship, thereby changing the *respeto* or intimacy level of the interpersonal relationship.

Finally, several chapters (see, e.g., Chapters 4, 5, 7, 8, 10, & 11) emphasize the importance of *social change* (especially from a traditional past to a modern future) on collectivism in China, Japan, Mexico, Brazil, an African "community," and in Romania. For example, Rector and Neiva (Chapter 8) examine the dualistic aspects of tradition and change in Brazilian personal relationship development. They observe that although the Brazilian people aspire to attain individual freedom, they are still bound by the hierarchical structure of a traditional, group-based culture to act in a certain manner. They summarize: "As a country that aspires to be modern, Brazil cherishes liberty and individual freedom. . . . In an original manner, Brazil is a dual society where those apparently contradictory conceptions can easily coexist." Thus, while collectivism continues to prevail in many of the group-oriented societies, it also transforms adaptively to meet the many challenges of the modern future.

We have reviewed the cultural variability perspective of individualism-collectivism in this section and identified some of the specific collectivistic themes that emerged in the chapters in Part III. We now turn to a discussion of some of the current theories that have been used in explaining cross-cultural interpersonal behavior.

Cross-Cultural Interpersonal Theories

The term *cross-cultural* is used in this section to refer to theoretical/research work that is comparative (e.g., comparing romantic love in China and the United States) in nature. The concept "interpersonal communication" is defined as interaction-related patterns that are linked to social and personal relationship development processes. We believe that the design of any good interpersonal research study starts with a meaningful research question. A meaningful research question is often generated with the guidance of a sound theory. We therefore believe that it is vital for novice researchers to be familiar with various existing interpersonal theories and to understand the various theoretical options that are available to them. The criteria for selecting a good theory to guide our cross-cultural interpersonal research effort include: logical consistency, explanatory power, parsimony (i.e., simplicity), inspiratory power, and cross-cultural validity. The propositions of a good theory should be logically consistent, explain a wide range of phenomena, be simple to grasp, be inspiring, and be applicable across cultures.

We discuss five cross-cultural interpersonal theories here: anxiety/uncertainty management theory, expectancy violations theory, face-negotiation theory, interpersonal facework theory, and communication accommodation theory. Each theory is identified based on the criteria of systematic theoretical development over the years and of a body of work revolving around *cross-cultural* and also intergroup-interpersonal relationship issues. We provide a synoptic discussion of each theory below.

Anxiety/Uncertainty Management (AUM) Theory

The anxiety/uncertainty management (AUM) theory (Gudykunst, 1988, 1993, 1995) suggests that effective intergroup/interpersonal communication is a function of the amount of anxiety and uncertainty individuals experience when communicating with others. *Anxiety* refers to the feelings of discomfort or awkwardness when two strangers (from different cultures or same culture) try to relate to each other. *Uncertainty* refers to the perceived unpredictability of the various intergroup/interpersonal situations. The concept of "management" refers to the importance of cultivating awareness or "mindfulness" (Langer, 1989) in dealing with unfamiliar values and interaction scripts.

Gudykunst and associates (for a detailed review, see Gudykunst, 1995) have been testing and refining AUM theory for the past 10 years. Altogether 47 axioms in the main theory and 47 axioms on cultural variability in AUM processes have been developed. Selected axioms have been tested in intergroup and interpersonal communication settings. For example, Gudykunst and Shapiro (1996) uncover that greater anxiety is experienced in intergroup (i.e., interethnic and intercultural) encounters than in intrapersonal encounters. Anxiety is associated positively with the degree to which social identities (i.e., group membership identities) are activated in the interaction, and the amount of uncertainty experienced. In addition, they also find that there is greater uncertainty in intergroup encounters than in intragroup encounters. Uncertainty is associated negatively with positive expectations, communication satisfaction, and quality of communication.

In another study, Hubbert, Guerrero, and Gudykunst (1995) observe that both anxiety and uncertainty decrease over time in intergroup encounters. However, the decrease does not fit a linear pattern (i.e., the pattern fluctuates across time). Finally, the ways that individuals gather information to reduce uncertainty differ in individualistic and collectivistic cultures. Members of individualistic cultures (e.g., the United States) seek out person-based information to reduce uncertainty about strangers, and members of collectivistic cultures (e..g, Japan) seek out group-based information to reduce uncertainty (Gudykunst & Nishida, 1986).

In sum, Gudykunst (1995) claims that anxiety and uncertainty exist in all cultures, but how people define these two terms varies across cultures. Cultural variability dimensions such as individualism-collectivism, power distance, uncertainty avoidance, and femininity-masculinity (Hofstede, 1991; see also Gudykunst & Matsumoto, Chapter 2, this volume) have been integrated into the AUM theory to explain social and personal encounters across cultures. In addition, AUM theory has been used to explain both cross-cultural (i.e., comparative analysis) *and* intergroup (i.e., intercultural analysis) interpersonal relationship situations.

Expectancy Violations (EV) Theory

An emerging cross-cultural interpersonal theory is Burgoon's (1992, 1995) expectancy violations (EV) theory. Although the theory has been around for more than 15 years (Burgoon, 1983), it is only in the past 5 years that the theory has been applied in the cross-cultural interpersonal settings.

According to Burgoon (1995), there are four focal constructs in the EV theory: expectancies, expectancy violations, communicator valence, and violation valence. "Expectancies" refers to our group-based and individual-based anticipatory patterns concerning individual members. "Expectancy violations" refers to the enacted actions that are sufficiently discrepant from initial anticipations and are therefore noticeable (e.g., personal space violations). "Communicator valence" refers to whether, on balance, the interaction with that particular communicator is viewed as rewarding (pleasurable) or costly (not pleasurable). Finally, "violation valence" refers to the positive or negative evaluations people assign to the violating action.

Burgoon (1992, 1995) suggests that though the concept of "communication expectancy" is a universal one, the meanings, the tolerable range, and the evaluations (positive-negative valence) of expectancy violations (e.g., the use of direct eye contact) vary from one culture to the next. Although many of the EV propositions have been tested within the "mainstream" U.S. culture, only a few studies have used this theory in cross-cultural and ethnic interpersonal settings. For example, Lobdell (1990) investigates friends' and family's reactions to sojourners who return from their travels with new values and mannerisms. She concludes that such expectancy violations serve to produce uncertainty and anxiety, which in turn produce negatively-valenced evaluations.

In another study, Chung and Ting-Toomey (1994) survey a large sample of Asian Americans concerning their ethnic identity and communication expectancy issues. They find that Asian Americans with strong ethnic identity tend to hold unfavorable attitudes toward outgroup dating. Conversely, Asian Americans with weak ethnic identity tend to hold favorable attitudes toward outgroup dating. While the strong ethnic exclusive group may tend to emphasize perceived differences between ingroup and outgroup (and, therefore, expect costly interaction), the weak ethnic exclusive group may tend to emphasize perceived similarities between the two groups (and, therefore, expect rewarding interaction).

Overall, it is interesting to note that the AUM and EV theories complement each other in their theoretical foci. For example, both AUM and EV theories emphasize internal cognition and affect in approaching interpersonal encounters. When communicators' expectations are violated in intercultural settings, anxiety and uncertainty are experienced. Yet though AUM theory emphasizes the importance of the management of anxiety/uncertainty, EV theory emphasizes the interpretations of such violation as possibly rewarding or costly.

Face Negotiation (FN) and Interpersonal Facework (IF) Theories

As social beings, most of us have the experiences of blushing, feeling embarrassed, feeling awkward, feeling shame, or feeling pride. Many of these feelings are face-related issues. When our social poise is attacked or teased, we feel the need to restore or save face. When we are being complimented or given credit in front of others for a job well done (i.e., in an individualistic culture), we feel that our self-respect is enhanced and stroked. Losing face and saving face are some of the key concepts under this "face negotiation" umbrella.

Several approaches have been developed over the years concerning the study of face and facework (e.g., Brown & Levinson, 1987; Cupach & Metts, 1994). We focus our discussion on two approaches here: the face negotiation (FN) theory (Ting-Toomey, 1985, 1988, 1994a) and the interpersonal facework (IF) theory (Lim, 1994; Lim & Bowers, 1991). The first approach emphasizes the influence of culture on facework, the second approach focuses on the influence of the interpersonal relationship on facework.

Using a cultural variability approach to the study of face and facework, Ting-Toomey (1988) proposes a theoretical model, the face negotiation (FN) theory (with 7 assumptions and 10 propositions), of face and facework. According to Ting-Toomey (1985, 1988), face is conceptualized as an individual's claimed sense of positive image in a relational and network context. Facework is defined as the communicative strategies that are used to enact self-face and to uphold, support, or challenge the other person's face. Face and facework are basically about projected self-respect issues and other-consideration issues.

In a nutshell, Ting-Toomey's (1988) face negotiation (FN) theory assumes that (a) people in all cultures try to maintain and negotiate face in all communication situations; (b) the concept of "face" is especially problematic in uncertainty situations (such as request, embarrassment, or conflict situations) when the situated identities of the communicators are called into question; (c) the cultural variability dimension of individualism-collectivism influences members' selection of one set of facework strategies over others (such as autonomy face vs. approval face, and self-oriented face saving vs. other-oriented face saving); and (d) individualism-collectivism in conjunction with other individual, relational, and situational variables influence the use of various facework strategies in intergroup and interpersonal encounters.

Overall, research by Ting-Toomey and associates (Cocroft & Ting-Toomey, 1994; Ting-Toomey, 1994c; Ting-Toomey et al., 1991; Trubisky, Ting-Toomey, & Lin, 1991) indicates that though individualists tend to use more self-oriented face-saving strategies, collectivists tend to use more other-oriented face-saving strategies. In addition, individualists (e.g., U.S. respondents) tend to use more direct, face-threatening conflict styles, and collectivists (i.e., Taiwan and China respondents) tend to use more indirect, mutual face-saving conflict styles. The concepts of "social face" (i.e., concern for approval from others) and "perceived self-pride/status" (i.e., concern for self-oriented pride) have been found to influence facework strategy selection in Japan and the United States (Cocroft & Ting-Toomey, 1994). Social face is negatively associated with antisocial facework strategies, and perceived self-pride is positively associated with antisocial strategies (i.e., the use of defensive/confrontative acts). Males (from both Japan and the United States) also report the use of more antisocial and controlling facework strategies than females. It is important to note that all these studies have been conducted in acquaintance relationships (e.g., classmate relationships) and that they assessed perceived responses to different facework or conflict situations.

From a conversational constraints perspective, the line of research by M. S. Kim et al. (1994) on construal of self and of conversational constraints also provides additional evidence for face negotiation theory. For example, M. S. Kim et al. (1994) uncover that individuals with independent self have higher perceived importance for conversational clarity than individuals with interdependent self. In addition, interdependent self persons have higher perceived importance of not hurting the hearer's feelings and avoiding devaluation by the hearer in conversation than independent self persons. While the concepts of independent self reflect individualistic value tendencies, the concepts of interdependent self reflect group-oriented value tendencies.

Imahori and Cupach (1994) investigated embarrassing situations in Japan (a collectivistic culture) and the United States (an individualistic culture) via the open-ended written response method. They discovered that U.S. college students tend to mention accident-prone (e.g., tripping, falling) embarrassing predicaments, Japanese college students tend to mention social-based embarrassing mistakes (e.g., such as walking into the wrong bathroom and getting caught). U.S. students are also more concerned with outgroup (such as passing acquaintance) embarrassing situations, and Japanese students are more concerned with ingroup (such as family and close friends) than outgroup reactions. In addition, the U.S. sample tends to use self-face diffusing strategies (such as humor) as coping responses, whereas the Japanese sample tends to rely on either remediation (such as verbal regrets) or avoidance to cope with embarrassing, face-threatening situations. Lastly, the U.S. group focuses on the experience of personal stupidity in predicaments, while the Japanese group emphasizes the experience of social shame. The line of research on cross-cultural embarrassing predicaments provides further support concerning FN propositions on self-face and other-face concerns in individualistic and collectivistic cultures.

In extending Brown and Levinson's (1987) model of discourse politeness, Lim and Bowers (1991) propose that all human beings have three distinct face wants: autonomy face (the want not to be imposed upon), fellowship face (the want to be included), and competence face (the want that their abilities be respected). According to Lim's (1994) *interpersonal facework (IF) theory,* different types of face want promote the different uses of facework strategies. Based on three interpersonal relationship parameters (i.e., status difference, relational intimacy, and role right to perform face-threatening acts), 10 propositions have been formulated in the IF theory. In particular, the role of interactional intention is incorporated as an important mediating variable between the three relational parameters and the use of different facework strategies. Past research (Lim & Bowers, 1991) indicates that of all the three relational parameters, relational intimacy acts as a strong predictor to the selection of specific facework strategy types.

Although Ting-Toomey's (1988) FN theory emphasizes sociocultural appropriateness in the enactment of facework strategies, Lim's (1994) IF theory emphasizes relational and individual intentions in facework strategy selection. IF theory assumes that no relationships are stable or constant enough to influence the use of specific facework strategy types. Rather, facework is the product of "internal purposes, its value should be measured in terms of effectiveness not appropriateness" (Lim, 1994, p. 227). Again, both theories (as in the case of AUM and EV theories) appear to complement one another. The FN theory deals with broader-level issues in linking cultural variability of individualism-collectivism and facework enactment. The IF theory concerns individual-level issues in the choice of facework strategy types. As the study of the linkages among culture, relational intentions, and facework is an intricate phenomenon, it is probably premature to opt for one approach to the neglect of another.

To summarize, past literature in *face* conceptualization has typically viewed face as (a) a claimed sense of favorable social self-worth that a person wants others to have of her or him; (b) a vulnerable resource in social interaction because this resource can be threatened, enhanced, maintained, and bargained over; and (c) a resource that is grounded in the webs of interpersonal and sociocultural variability. Face and facework can only be meaningfully interpreted within the values and belief system of the culture. While both FN and IF theories deal with cross-cultural interpersonal communication issues, the following theory addresses *intergroup* interaction issues.

Communication Accommodation Theory (CAT)

Francophones and Anglophones working in bilingual work settings in Montreal and Quebec often complained about each other's French/English language use. Korean shopkeepers and African American customers in South-Central Los Angeles often reported frustrations about each other's use of "English." Communication accommodation theory (CAT) (Gallois, Franklyn-Stokes, Giles, & Coupland, 1988; Gallois, Giles, Jones, Cargile, & Ota, 1995) emphasizes the importance of understanding speech *convergence* and speech *divergence* to increase or decrease communicative distance among members of different groups. The CAT approach is, essentially, an intergroup/interpersonal communication theory. The theory focuses on explaining the motivations, strategies, and contexts whereby group members (e.g., from different cultures, or ethnic, or age groups, etc.) use different communication strategies to converge with or diverge from their partners linguistically. CAT is based on an earlier body of work by Giles and associates (see Giles & Coupland, 1991; Giles & Johnson, 1987) on ethnolinguistic identity theory and ethnolinguistic vitality theory, and the related work by Tajfel and Turner (1986; Abrams & Hogg, 1990) on social identity theory.

According to Giles and associates, speakers move through their linguistic repertoire so as to converge or diverge linguistically, based on the following three motivations: to gain approval from their discourse partners vis-à-vis linguistic similarity, to show distinctiveness and thus accentuate their own group membership, and to achieve clearer and smoother communication. Gallois et al. (1988) extend this model and add the components of initial orientation (i.e., whether speakers are predisposed to view the encounter as solely intergroup, solely interpersonal, or both), intergroup discourse situation, and the positive/ negative evaluation that communicators take away with them concerning the encounter.

The most recent version of CAT (Gallois et al., 1995) incorporates the cultural variability dimension of individualism and collectivism in their theoretical propositions. Altogether, CAT contains 17 propositions that concern the socio-historical context, the immediate context, and the evaluation/future intentions concerning further intergroup encounters. Gallois and associates (1992) tested some of the propositions in a videotaped, scripted project (portrayed by actors) containing interactions between Chinese or Australian students and faculty members. The actors on the tapes engaged in accommodating or nonaccommo-dating scripted behavior, using interpersonal control strategies to treat the other person as an equal individual or as a subordinate. Judges were asked to evaluate the nonverbal behavior and the appropriateness of the behavior in general. Results indicated that nonaccommodating students and faculty members were rated less favorably than accommodating ones. In addition, the perception of nonverbal behavior (both vocal and nonvocal) outweighs other factors in induc-ing a favorable or unfavorable reaction. In another study, Jones, Gallois, Barker, and Callan (1994) tested the CAT model with videotaped naturalistic conver-sations between Australian and Chinese students and academic staff. The researchers found that the multiple roles (student vs. faculty member, gender, and ethnicity) of the speakers and the judges all exerted influences on perceived interaction accommodation.

Overall, CAT theory examines the perceived motivation and role dimensions of the intergroup speakers and how these dimensions affect interaction conver-gence/divergence issues. In addition, the theory probes how interaction conver-gence/divergence process fosters the evaluative reactions by observers. Finally, CAT research moves beyond survey data and actually taps into how members from different cultural or linguistic groups communicate with one another on the verbal/nonverbal interactional level.

Interpersonal Communication:
Research Directions

In this section, we discuss some of the salient research issues that are connected with previously reviewed theories. We conclude with some broader suggestions and ideas for the future theorizing of cross-cultural interpersonal communication.

Interpersonal Research Issues

Both the anxiety/uncertainty management (AUM) and expectancy violations (EV) theories are interested in people's social cognitions in thinking and processing information concerning the intergroup or interpersonal encounters. Both lines of research have generated rich sets of cross-cultural and interpersonal data. However, further refinement can be made concerning some of the focal concepts in the respective theories.

For example, two interesting research issues in AUM theory that wait to be explored include: the experience of anxiety/uncertainty in initial intergroup encounters, and the concept of "mindfulness." The first issue deals with the antecedent conditions of why some people experience high anxiety/uncertainty in encountering cultural strangers, whereas others may experience only moderate or low anxiety/uncertainty in encountering strangers. What past experiences or personal tendencies influence the development and the experience of anxiety/uncertainty? How are anxiety and uncertainty actually manifested in discourse (plus nonverbal) intergroup/interpersonal encounter process between strangers from different cultures?

The second issue concerns the concept of "mindfulness." Is mindfulness a trait issue, a situational issue, or a competence issue? What are the conceptual dimensions and the factor structures of mindfulness? In relating AUM theory with EV theory, how would "anxiety" and "uncertainty" be interpreted from the expectancy violations standpoint? How do people in different cultures "expect" anxiety and uncertainty to be tolerated and managed in different kinds of interpersonal relationship (e.g., extramarital affair relations, polygamous relations, gay relations, interethnic dating, etc.)? Moving beyond our discussion of AUM and EV theories, we turn to discuss some of the research issues in the face negotiation (FN) and interpersonal facework (IF) theories.

First, we need to learn in greater depth the various cultural indigenous approaches (such as Gao on Chinese face, Lim and Choi on Korean face, Garcia on *simpatico* and *respeto,* and Moemeka on African communal pride, Chapters 4, 6, 7, & 10, respectively, in this volume) in conceptualizing face and facework. Second, because collectivists tend to make a sharp distinction between ingroup and outgroup, future studies should pay mindful attention to the interpretation of ingroup/outgroup boundary and how it affects facework management process. Third, though some groundwork studies have been conducted in acquaintance facework interaction, we know little about how close friends or dating/marital partners deal with facework issues across different situations in different cultures. We need more research work to probe the relational parameters, affect, and facework-related concepts. Fourth, we need to utilize more rigorous, *comparative* case study and interview methods to ascertain insider accounts about facework meaning processes. Finally, more well-designed research studies are needed to probe the *dyadic* perception of facework and to examine how the conjoint perception of facework relates to the different turning points of an interpersonal relationship. Facework competence is a fascinating interpersonal construct. Appropriate and effective facework can transform a relationship into a satisfying one. Inappropriate and tactless facework can turn friends into enemies.

In terms of communication accommodation theory (CAT), concepts such as ethnocentrism and stereotype need to be integrated more systematically in the intergroup theoretical propositions. These two constructs typically permeate all initial intergroup contact processes. Most CAT research has also been conducted in stranger or acquaintance encounters in lab settings. More naturalistic discourse studies need to be employed to probe the meanings and the accommodation processes of a diverse range of intergroup-interpersonal encounters. Most CAT studies have also measured only short-term rather than long-term accommodation process. More longitudinal studies can help to shed light on the long-range patterns of interaction convergence and divergence between members of different groups.

Future Directions

There are many fascinating research questions remaining to be addressed by novice researchers. We believe that a meaningful first issue in the interpersonal theorizing cycle lies in the direction of multiple facets of a person's identity. Researchers should pay closer attention to such issues as how people in different cultures conceptualize their "cultural identities" or "relational identities," and in turn, how these identities influence the actual verbal/nonverbal communication process. For example, given the exponential rise of intergroup marriages in the United States, how do members from two contrastive groups negotiate their identity differences? How do the offspring of intergroup marriages conceptualize their cultural identities? How do these identities affect their interpersonal relationship development patterns? In addition, we recommend that interpersonal researchers should pay closer attention to ethnic and gender identity issues. Ethnicity does not equate race (which is a biological concept), and gender does not equate sex (which is also a biological concept). Both ethnicity and gender are socially constructed processes developed within the confines of the normative structure of society. Individuals construct their identities (e.g., identifying oneself as "a third-generation, 30-year old female Chinese American professor" vs. "an adventurous, outgoing female American professor") along different perceived salient dimensions in different situations (see Bem, 1993; Kashima et al., 1995; Ting-Toomey, 1993, 1994b). Situational parameters affect the conditions under which "ethnic" and "gender" identities are constructed. Specific relational factors (such as perceived solidarity, power, and intimacy), in turn, mediate between the identity construction process and the identity negotiation process between members of the two contrastive groups.

This leads to the second issue in the cross-cultural interpersonal theorizing cycle: the importance of studying different relational concepts along a full spectrum of interpersonal relationships (see Knapp & Miller, 1994; Wood, 1995). We need to probe deeper into the diverse types (such as sibling relations, blended friend-work relations, arranged marriage relations, elderly friendship, etc.) of interpersonal relationships across a diverse set of cultures. We also need to elicit the cultural ideologies, beliefs, expectations, and meanings that people hold concerning these different types of relationship. In addition, we need to investigate a fuller spectrum of interpersonal-related variables (such as relational commitment, comfort, support, trust, power, fate, loyalty, indebtedness, and reciprocity) concerning different stages and generations of relationship development.

The third direction concerns the study of the role of "communication process" in the various interpersonal relationship development phases. We should place more emphasis on the actual *communication* aspects of how people in different cultures negotiate and redefine their relationships via the use of actual verbal/ nonverbal accounts and stories. We should focus more attention on how people in different cultures use different communication strategies and skills in maintaining a social or personal relationship (see Montgomery, 1993). We should also probe deeper into how members of different cultures deal with different relational transgression issues (e.g., trust violation, abusive relations, etc.), in exiting a relationship, and in entering a new one. It is also critical to note that the study of autonomous, voluntary entry and exit of a personal relationship is, on the whole, an individualistic notion.

The fourth direction concerns how different contextual parameters influence different interpersonal interactions. Most of the existing theorizing effort in interpersonal communication has ignored "context" as a salient construct. We need to delineate how relevant contextual dimensions (such as public-private, formal-informal, scripted vs. nonscripted, direct vs. mediated channels, home-base vs. third-culture setting) influence interpersonal relationship development processes. We need to pay close attention to how "relational talk" or "silence" is conducted in different cross-cultural interpersonal contexts. We need to probe deeper into how nonnative speakers manage their personal relationship ties with native speakers and their respective family networks. With computer technologies rapidly changing societies, we also need to assess the impact of global technology as a communication tool in transforming intergroup relationship development boundaries.

In closing, we advocate the use of a constant, *comparative convergent method* (i.e., a combination of emic and etic levels of analysis or a funnel approach) on any interpersonal concepts of interest. *Emics,* generally speaking, are "ideas, behaviors, items, and concepts that are culture specific" and *etics,* generally speaking, are "ideas, behaviors, items, and concepts that are culture general, i.e., universal" (Triandis, 1994, p. 67). Emic concepts (e.g., Gao's notion of Chinese *bao* or "relational indebtedness," Chapter 4, this volume) are critical to our understanding of interpersonal formation process in a specific culture. Yet we cannot use emic concepts alone to develop *cross-cultural* interpersonal communication theories.

We basically need to discover culture-specific themes, sensitizing concepts, and meanings to arrive at the general level of cross-cultural theorizing of interpersonal communication. Concurrently, we need to establish a cross-cultural equivalence of concepts on the general level in order to arrive at a meaningful layer of cultural-specific interpersonal analysis. If we do not undertake this constant comparative step in our research design, we may run the danger of applying "imposed etic" concepts in our cross-cultural research effort. *Imposed etic* refers to the use of mismatched concepts and measurements that are developed in one culture (which is often Euro-American based) and are imposed upon another culture as if to assume universal meanings and significance. In contrast, *derived etic* refers to the use of comparative methods to integrate the knowledge gained from both the "imposed etic and emic approaches. They are etic because they are valid in more than one culture; they are derived because they have resulted in using the two approaches, rather than assumed in advance" (Berry & Kim, 1993, p. 278; Lonner, 1979).

Furthermore, we advocate the use of *a multimethod approach* in studying cultural variability and interpersonal relationship development. Intensive focus group interview method and ethnographic observation method can help us to generate derived etic concepts of interpersonal relationship development (see Spradley, 1979). Discourse analysis method, interaction analysis method, and experimental videotaped method can help us to observe verbal and nonverbal behavior on an interactional level (see, e.g., Montgomery & Duck, 1991). Social relations' analysis (Kenny, 1994, 1995), social network analysis (Allison, 1984), and event history analysis (Wassermann & Faust, 1993) methods can also yield a rich database in understanding interpersonal relationship development within the dyadic, social network, and longitudinal settings. More well-crafted meta-analysis studies are also needed to synthesize and compare the general strands of cross-cultural interpersonal research findings.

Finally, with the abundant research options that confront us in interpersonal communication research, more interdisciplinary and multigroup (such as multicultural, -ethnic, and -gender) research teams should be formed globally. The term *interdisciplinary team* means researchers from different disciplines (e.g., anthropology, psychology, sociology) who work collaboratively from the ground up by applying and integrating different perspectives to examine the same research problem (see Acitelli, 1995). We also believe that interactive, open dialogue among intercultural *and* interpersonal researchers *within* the speech communication discipline is urgently needed (see the "interpersonal" perspective in Sarason, Pierce, & Sarason, 1995) to share valuable insights in the study of cross-cultural interpersonal communication. Multigroup research teams may also want to be mindful of the ethical issues (such as individual researcher's accountability, differential subject risk factor, data fair use factor, and coauthorship factor, etc.) that confront cross-cultural interpersonal research. Such factors need to be clearly articulated and negotiated before the launching of any large-scale interpersonal study.

This chapter has scratched the surface of the theoretical trends and research directions in cross-cultural interpersonal communication. We believe that the study of cross-cultural interpersonal communication is a fruitful and challenging area of inquiry. We believe that with collaborative imagination and disciplinary rigor among multicultural researchers, a deeper understanding of universal interpersonal behavior can be achieved.

References

Abrams, D., & Hogg, M. (Eds.). (1990). *Social identity theory: Constructive and critical advances.* New York: Springer.

Acitelli, L. (1995). Disciplines at parallel play. *Journal of Social and Personal Relationships, 12,* 589-596.

Allison, P. (1984). *Event history analysis: Regression for longitudinal event data.* Beverly Hills, CA: Sage.

Bem, S. (1993). *The lenses of gender: Transforming the debate on sexual inequality.* New Haven, CT: Yale University Press.

Berry, J., & Kim, U. (1993). The way ahead: From indigenous psychologies to a universal psychology. In U. Kim & J. Berry (Eds.), *Indigenous psychologies: Research and experience in cultural context.* Newbury Park, CA: Sage.

Brown, P., & Levinson, S. (1987). *Politeness: Some universals in language usage.* Cambridge, UK: Cambridge University Press.

Burgoon, J. (1983). Nonverbal violation of expectations. In J. Wiemann & R. Harrison (Eds.), *Nonverbal interaction.* Beverly Hills, CA: Sage.

Burgoon, J. (1992). Applying a comparative approach to nonverbal expectancy violations theory. In J. Blumer, K. Rosengren, & J. McLeod (Eds.), *Comparatively speaking.* Newbury Park, CA: Sage.

Burgoon, J. (1995). Cross-cultural and intercultural applications of expectancy violations theory. In R. Wiseman (Ed.), *Intercultural communication theory.* Thousand Oaks, CA: Sage.

Chung L. C., & Ting-Toomey, S. (1994, July). *Ethnic identity and relational expectations among Asian Americans.* Paper presented at the annual conference of International Communication Association, Sydney, Australia.

Cocroft, B.-A., & Ting-Toomey, S. (1994). Facework in Japan and the United States. *International Journal of Intercultural Relations, 18,* 469-506.

Cupach, W., & Metts, S. (1994). *Facework.* Thousand Oaks, CA: Sage.

Dion, K. L., & Dion, K. K. (1988). Romantic love: Individual and cultural perspectives. In R. Sternberg & M. Barnes (Eds.), *The psychology of love.* New Haven, CT: Yale University Press.

Fiske, A. (1991). *Structures of social life: The four elementary forms of human relations.* New York: Free Press.

Fiske, A. (1992). The four elementary forms of sociality: Framework for a unified theory of social relations. *Psychological Review, 99,* 689-723.

Gallois, C., Barker, M., Jones, E., & Callan, J. (1992). Intercultural communication: Evaluations of lecturers and Australian and Chinese students. In S. Iwawaki, Y. Kashima, & K. Leung (Eds.), *Innovations in cross-cultural psychology.* Amsterdam: Swets & Zeitlinger.

Gallois, C., Franklyn-Stokes, A., Giles, H., & Coupland, N. (1988). Communication accommodation theory and intercultural encounters: Intergroup and interpersonal considerations. In Y. Y. Kim & W. B. Gudykunst (Eds.), *Theories in intercultural communication.* Newbury Park, CA: Sage.

Gallois, C., Giles, H., Jones, E., Cargile, A., & Ota, H. (1995). Accommodating intercultural encounters: Elaborations and extensions. In R. Wiseman (Ed.), *Intercultural communication theory.* Thousand Oaks, CA: Sage.

Gao, G. (1991). Stability in romantic relationships in China and the United States. In S. Ting-Toomey & F. Korzenny (Eds.), *Cross-cultural interpersonal communication.* Newbury Park, CA: Sage.

Gao, G. (1993, May). *An investigation of love and intimacy in romantic relationships in China and the United States.* Paper presented at the annual conference of the International Communication Association, Washington, D.C.

Giles, H., & Coupland, N. (1991). *Language, context, and consequences.* Pacific Grove, CA: Brooks/Cole.

Giles, H., & Johnson, P. (1987). Ethnolinguistic identity theory: A social psychological approach to language maintenance. *International Journal of the Sociology of Language, 68,* 66-99.

Gudykunst, W. B. (1988). Uncertainty and anxiety. In Y. Y. Kim & W. B. Gudykunst (Eds.), *Theories in intercultural communication.* Newbury Park, CA: Sage.

Gudykunst, W. B. (1993). Toward a theory of effective interpersonal and intergroup communication: An anxiety/uncertainty management (AUM) perspective. In R. Wiseman & J. Koester (Eds.), *Intercultural communication competence.* Newbury Park, CA: Sage.

Gudykunst, W. B. (1995). Anxiety/uncertainty management (AUM) theory: Current status. In R. Wiseman (Ed.), *Intercultural communication theory.* Thousand Oaks, CA: Sage.

Gudykunst, W. B., Matsumoto, Y., Ting-Toomey, S., Nishida, T., Kim, K., & Heyman, S. (1996). The influence of cultural individualism-collectivism, self construals, and individual values on communication styles across cultures. *Human Communication Research, 22,* 510-543.

Gudykunst, W. B., & Nishida, T. (1986). Attributional confidence in low- and high-context cultures. *Human Communication Research, 12,* 525-549.

Gudykunst, W. B., & Shapiro, R. (1996). Communication in everyday interpersonal and intergroup encounters. *International Journal of Intercultural Relations, 20,* 19-45.

Gudykunst, W. B., & Ting-Toomey, S. (1988). *Culture and interpersonal communication.* Newbury Park, CA: Sage.

Hall, E. T. (1976). *Beyond culture.* Garden City, NY: Doubleday.

Hall, E. T. (1983). *The dance of life.* Garden City, NY: Doubleday.

Hofstede, G. (1980). *Culture's consequences: International differences in work-related values.* Beverly Hills, CA: Sage.

Hofstede, G. (1991). *Cultures and organizations: Software of the mind.* London: McGraw-Hill.

Hubbert, K., Guerrero, S., & Gudykunst, W. B. (1995, May). *Intergroup communication over time.* Paper presented at the annual conference of the International Communication Association, Albuquerque, NM.

Imahori, T., & Cupach, W. (1994). Cross-cultural comparison of the interpretation and management of face: U.S. American and Japanese responses to embarrassing predicaments. *International Journal of Intercultural Relations, 18,* 193-220.

Jankowiak, W. (Ed.). (1995). *Romantic passion: A universal experience?* New York: Columbia University Press.

Jones, E., Gallois, C., Barker, M., & Callan, V. (1994). Communication between Australian and Chinese students and academic staff. In A. Bouvy, F. Van de Vijver, P. Boski, & P. Schmitz (Eds.), *Journeys into cross-cultural psychology.* Amsterdam: Swets & Zeitlinger.

Kashima, Y., Yamaguchi, S., Kim, U., Choi, S.-C., Gelfand, M., & Yuki, M. (1995). Culture, gender, and self: Perspectives from individualism-collectivism research. *Journal of Personality and Social Psychology, 5,* 925-937.

Kenny, D. (1994). *Interpersonal perception: A social relations analysis.* New York: Guilford.

Kenny, D. (1995). Relationship science in the 21st century. *Journal of Social and Personal Relationships, 12,* 597-600.

Kim, M. S., Sharkey, W., & Singelis, T. (1994). The relationship between individual's self construals and perceived importance of interactive constraints. *International Journal of Intercultural Relations, 18,* 1-24.

Kim, U., & Berry, J. (Eds.). (1993). *Indigenous psychologies: Research and experience in cultural context.* Newbury Park, CA: Sage.

Kim, U., Triandis, T., Kagitcibasi, C., Choi, S.-C., & Yoon, G. (Eds.). (1994). *Individualism and collectivism: Theory, method, and applications.* Thousand Oaks, CA: Sage.

Kluckhohn, F., & Strodtbeck, F. (1961). *Variations in value orientations.* New York: Row, Peterson.

Knapp, M., & Miller, G. (Eds.). (1994). *Handbook of interpersonal communication* (2nd ed.). Thousand Oaks, CA: Sage.

Langer, E. (1989). *Mindfulness.* Reading, MA: Addison-Wesley.

Lim, T.-S. (1994). Facework and interpersonal relationships. In S. Ting-Toomey (Ed.), *The challenge of facework: Cross-cultural and interpersonal issues.* Albany: State University of New York Press.

Lim, T.-S., & Bowers, J. (1991). Face-work: Solidarity, approbation, and tact. *Human Communication Research, 17,* 415-450.

Lobdell, C. (1990, June). *Expectations of family and friends of sojourners during the reentry adjustment process.* Paper presented at the annual meeting of the International Communication Association, Dublin, Ireland.

Lonner, W. (1979). Issues in cross-cultural psychology. In A. Marsella, A. Tharp, & T. Cobrowski (Eds.), *Perspectives in cross-cultural psychology.* New York: Academic Press.

Markus, H., & Kitayama, S. (1991). Culture and the self: Implications for cognition, emotion, and motivation. *Psychological Review, 2,* 224-253.

Montgomery, B. (1993). Relationship maintenance versus relationship change: A dialectical dilemma. *Journal of Social and Personal Relationships, 10,* 205-224.

Montgomery, B., & Duck, S. (Eds.). (1991). *Studying interpersonal interaction.* New York: Guilford.

Sarason, I., Pierce, G., & Sarason, B. (1995). Introduction: How should we study relationships? *Journal of Social and Personal Relationships, 12,* 521-522.

Schwartz, S., & Bilsky, W. (1990). Toward a theory of the universal content and structure of values. *Journal of Personality and Social Psychology, 58,* 879-891.

Spradley, J. P. (1979). *The ethnographic interview.* New York: Holt, Rinehart & Winston.

Tajfel, H., & Turner, J. (1986). The social identity theory of intergroup relations. In W. Austin & S. Worchel (Eds.), *The social psychology of intergroup relations.* Monterey, CA: Brooks/Cole.

Ting-Toomey, S. (1985). Toward a theory of conflict and culture. In W. B. Gudykunst, L. Stewart, & S. Ting-Toomey (Eds.), *Communication, culture, and organizational processes.* Beverly Hills, CA: Sage.

Ting-Toomey, S. (1988). Intercultural conflict styles: A face-negotiation theory. In Y. Y. Kim & W. B. Gudykunst (Eds.), *Theories in intercultural communication.* Newbury Park, CA: Sage.

Ting-Toomey, S. (1991a). Cross-cultural interpersonal communication: An introduction. In S. Ting-Toomey & F. Korzenny (Eds.), *Cross-cultural interpersonal communication.* Newbury Park, CA: Sage.

Ting-Toomey, S. (1991b). Intimacy expressions in three cultures: France, Japan, and the United States. *International Journal of Intercultural Relations, 15,* 29-46.

Ting-Toomey, S. (1993). Communicative resourcefulness: An identity negotiation perspective. In R. Wiseman & J. Koester (Eds.), *Intercultural communication competence.* Newbury Park, CA: Sage.

Ting-Toomey, S. (Ed.). (1994a). *The challenge of facework: Cross-cultural and interpersonal issues.* Albany: State University of New York Press.

Ting-Toomey, S. (1994b). Managing conflict in intimate intercultural relationships. In D. Cahn (Ed.), *Intimate conflict in personal relationships.* Hillsdale, NJ: Lawrence Erlbaum.

Ting-Toomey, S. (1994c). Managing intercultural conflicts effectively. In L. Samovar & R. Porter (Eds.), *Intercultural communication: A reader* (7th ed.). Belmont, CA: Wadsworth.

Ting-Toomey, S., Gao, G., Trubisky, P., Yang, Z., Kim, H. S., Lin, S.-L., & Nishida, T. (1991). Culture, face maintenance, and styles of handling interpersonal conflict: A study in five cultures. *The International Journal of Conflict Management, 2,* 275-296.

Triandis, H. C. (1972). *The analysis of subjective culture.* New York: John Wiley.

Triandis, H. C. (1989). Self and social behavior in differing cultural contexts. *Psychological Review, 96,* 269-289.

Triandis, H. C. (1990). Cross-cultural studies of individualism-collectivism. In J. Berman (Ed.), *Nebraska Symposium on Motivation 1989.* Lincoln: University of Nebraska Press.

Triandis, H. C. (1994). *Culture and social behavior.* New York: McGraw-Hill.

Triandis, H. C. (1995). *Individualism and collectivism.* Boulder, CO: Westview.

Trubisky, P., Ting-Toomey, S., & Lin, S.-L. (1991). The influence of individualism-collectivism and self-monitoring on conflict styles. *International Journal of Intercultural Relations, 15,* 65-84.

Wassermann, S., & Faust, K. (1993). *Social network analysis: Methods and applications.* Cambridge, UK: Cambridge University Press.

Wood, J. (1995). The part is not the whole: Weaving diversity into the study of relationships. *Journal of Social and Personal Relationships, 12,* 563-567.

Index

Cultural variability:
   dimensions of, 10-11
   See also Individualism-collectivism;
      Uncertainty avoidance; Masculinity-
      femininity; Power distance; Horizontal
      cultures; Vertical cultures
Culture:
   approaches to study of, 6-13
   definition, 4-6

Direct communication, 30, 32
Dissociation, 11
Dugri, 9

Egalitarianism, 47
Elementary structures of social life. *See*
      Authority ranking; Communial sharing;
      Market pricing; Equality matching
Emic, 6-7, 13-14, 256-257
Emotion expression, 46-47, 192-193
Enryo, 20
Equality matching, 13, 63-65, 70-71
Ethnic identity, 247-248, 255
Ethnography of speaking, 9
Etic, 6-7, 13-14, 256-257
Expectancy violations, 245, 247-248, 253

Face, 38-39, 82, 123-130, 152, 182, 188, 242-
      244, 248-251
Family, 86-87, 242-243
Farsi, 189
Folklore, 141-144
Formality, 11-12

Gan-quing, 90-91
Gestures, 115
Gong de, 87
Guan xi, 94

Hierarchy, 88-89
High-context communication, 8, 29-34, 105-
      106, 171, 181-184
Hong Kong, 36-37
Honne, 109
Horizontal cultures, 23-24

Ideology of intimacy, 218-219
Ilongot oratory, 8
Indirect communication 9, 31-32, 114, 188-
      189
Individualism, 10, 20, 25, 32-41, 67, 108-110,
      176-178, 186, 191, 225, 238-240, 249-
      250, 252
Ingroups, 22-23, 86, 237
Inshindenshin, 113
Insider, 85-88
Intentions, 30-31
Interpersonal relationships, attitudes toward,
      111-112
Intimacy, 11-12
Iran, 174-194
Israeli Sabra culture, 9
Italy, 37

Japan, 26, 36-39, 60, 63-64, 102-117
Japanese language, 113-114
Jung, 123, 132-134, 243

Korea, 38-39, 122-135
Kyodo-dantai-shugi, 109

Lian, 94-96, 244
Love, 132-134
Low-context communication, 8, 29-34, 105-
      106, 171, 181-184

Madre, 62
Manner maxim, 30-32, 131
Marital typology, 74-76
Market pricing, 13, 65-67
Masculinity-femininity, 10, 48-49, 67, 73-74,
      180-181
Mexico, 137-154
Mian zi, 94-96
Mineirice, 168
Models of communication, 184
Monochronic time, 184

Nagre, 181
Native Americans, 8
Nature, attitudes toward, 110-111

About the Contributors

Soo-Hyang Choi is a visiting scholar in the Department of Psychology at the University of British Columbia.

Leeva Chung is a doctoral candidate in Communication at the University of Oklahoma.

Beth-Ann Cocroft received her M.A. in Speech Communication from California State University, Fullerton.

Ge Gao is Associate Professor of Communication Studies at San Jose State University.

Wintilo Garcia is Lecturer in Speech Communication at California State University, Fullerton.

William B. Gudykunst is Professor of Speech Communication at California State University, Fullerton.

Angela K. Hoppe is Instructor in Communication at Cerritos College.

Tae-Seop Lim is Associate Professor in the Department of Journalism and Communication Studies at Kwangoon University, Seoul, Korea.

Catalin Mamali is a visiting scholar in Communication at the University of Iowa.

Yuko Matsumoto is a doctoral student in Communication at the University of California, Santa Barbara.

Andrew Moemeka is Professor of Communication at Central Connecticut State University.

Eduardo Neiva is Professor of Communication Studies at the University of Alabama, Birmingham.

Tsukasa Nishida is Professor of Communication and International Relations at Nihon University, Mishima, Japan.

Monica Rector is Professor of Romance Languages at the University of North Carolina, Chappel Hill.

Golnaz Sadri is Associate Professor of Management at California State University, Fullerton.

Lisa Snell received her M.A. in Speech Communication from California State University, Fullerton.

Stella Ting-Toomey is Professor of Speech Communication at California State University, Fullerton.

Fred Zandpour is Professor of Communications at California State University, Fullerton.